Summary of Mathematical Templates

Template	Synopsis	UML diagram	Use when
Hardcoded (seldom)	Specifies a type sequence, one for each level of the hierarchy.		The levels in a tree are known and ordered.
Simple (common)	Treats all nodes the same.		A tree has only data structure.
Structured (common)	Differentiates leaf nodes from branch nodes.		Branch nodes and leaf nodes differ.
Overlapping (occasional)	Permits a node to belong to multiple trees.		A node can have more than one tree.
Changing over time (occasional)	Stores variants of a tree over time.		There is history to record.
Degenerate node and edge (rare)	Groups a parent with its children.		The parent–child grouping has data.

Tree templates

Template	Synopsis	UML diagram	Use when
Simple (occasional)	Treats all nodes the same.		Edges are unimportant; nodes have similar data. The DG is acyclic.
Structured (occasional)	Differentiates leaf nodes from branch nodes.		Edges are unimportant; branch and leaf nodes differ. The DG is acyclic.
Node–edge (common)	Treats nodes and edges as peers.		Nodes and edges can have data; there can be multiple edges between nodes.
Connection (occasional)	Promotes a connection to an entity type.		Connections have data.
Simple changing over time (seldom)	Stores variants of a DG over time.		There is history; edges are unimportant. The DG is acyclic.

Directed graph templates

Summary of Mathematical Templates (continued)

Template	Synopsis	UML diagram	Use when
Node–edge DG changing over time (occasional)	Stores variants of a DG over time.		There is history; edges are important.

Directed graph templates (continued)

Template	Synopsis	UML diagram	Use when
Node–edge UDG (occasional)	Treats nodes and edges as peers.		No edge connects to the same node.
Connection UDG (occasional)	Promotes a node-edge connection to an entity type.		Connections have data, or an edge connects to the same node.
UDG changing over time (seldom)	Stores variants of a UDG over time.		There is history to record.

Undirected graph templates

Template	Synopsis	UML diagram	Use when
Item description (frequent)	Relates data and metadata in the same model.		The same model relates data and metadata.
Homomorphism (occasional)	Expresses an analogy between two item description templates.		Item description templates are involved in an analogy.

Item description templates

Template	Synopsis	UML diagram	Use when
Star schema (occasional except DW)	Represents data as facts that are bound to dimensions.		There must be a flexible structure for querying data.

Star schema template

PATTERNS OF DATA MODELING

EMERGING DIRECTIONS IN DATABASE SYSTEMS AND APPLICATIONS

Series Editor
Sham Navathe
Professor
Georgia Institute of Technology
College of Computing
Atlanta, Georgia, U.S.A.

Patterns of Data Modeling, Michael Blaha

Forthcoming Publications

Advanced Data Management, Edward Omiecinski

Bioinformatics Database Systems, Jason T.L. Wang and Katherine G. Herbert

Techniques for Automated Physical Database Design, Nicolas Bruno and Surajit Chaudhuri

PATTERNS OF DATA MODELING

MICHAEL BLAHA

CRC Press
Taylor & Francis Group
Boca Raton   London   New York

CRC Press is an imprint of the
Taylor & Francis Group, an **informa** business

CRC Press
Taylor & Francis Group
6000 Broken Sound Parkway NW, Suite 300
Boca Raton, FL 33487-2742

First issued in hardback 2017

ISBN 13: 978-1-138-40223-2 (hbk)
ISBN 13: 978-1-4398-1989-0 (pbk)

Library of Congress Cataloging-in-Publication Data

Blaha, Michael.
    Patterns of data modeling / Michael Blaha.
        p. cm.
    Includes bibliographical references and indexes.
    ISBN 978-1-4398-1989-0 (pbk. : alk. paper)
    1. Databases. 2. Software patterns. 3. Data structures (Computer science) I. Title.

QA76.9.D32B53 2010
005.7'3--dc22   2010000025

Visit the Taylor & Francis Web site at
http://www.taylorandfrancis.com

and the CRC Press Web site at
http://www.crcpress.com

To the memory of Brian.

Contents

Preface

I know there is a need for this book. I have been modeling application and enterprise data for 25 years now—the last 15 as a consultant to dozens of organizations. I'm often asked how I conceive software models, and why I construct them a certain way.

Methodology books (including my own prior books) give an answer for beginners. They present concepts, notation, and a simple process. This new book provides the next level of techniques for building models, for those who have mastered the basics. When I build models, my thought processes revolve around patterns. This book provides detailed patterns as a basis for more expertly building data models.

This book focuses on databases and not on programming, because most commercial software is built around a database. The database representation (the data model) sets the scope for the software, determines its flexibility, affects its quality, and influences whether the software succeeds or fails.

This book can help readers avoid mistakes. I know that with tried and tested patterns I could have avoided some of my past modeling mistakes.

This book can help readers build better models. I rifled through past consulting projects and noted the improvements in my recent models. If this book had been available earlier in my career, I could have had better models and built them more quickly.

Who Should Read This Book?

The new book has multiple audiences. It is targeted at practitioners but is also suitable for advanced courses.

- **Application architects**. Application architects help determine the focus of an application and drive that focus into the resulting software. They have to pin down the requirements, understand the requirements, determine what is in and out of scope, and set the key abstractions in the software. These tasks revolve around models and often data models. The skillful use of patterns is intrinsic to building quality models.

- **Enterprise architects**. These architects reach beyond a single application and address the needs of an entire enterprise. The suite of applications for an enterprise must provide the required business functionality and work well together. There is no better way to harmonize applications than by modeling them in-depth and aligning the models. With models, gaps become apparent and problems can be resolved.

- **Data modelers**. Experienced modelers will find the new book to be a helpful reference for its concise and in-depth advice. Beginning modelers can use the new book as a resource for learning.

- **Database administrators**. In many organizations DBAs do more than just attend to the day-to-day servicing of the database (backups, tuning, authorization, and so forth). Many DBAs create data models and maintain the models as applications evolve.

- **Programmers**. Databases pervade commercial applications. Nevertheless, many programmers have trouble with databases and are tentative about how to apply them. This book can help programmers represent their data, a mind-set that is essential for successful use of databases.

- **Courses**. Many universities offer advanced, special-topics courses as part of their graduate curriculum; this book could be used for such a course. The book is also suitable for commercial data modeling courses.

What You Will Find

My usage of the term *pattern* is different than the literature but consistent with the spirit of past work. I treat pattern as an overarching term encompassing mathematical templates, antipatterns, archetypes, identity, and canonical models.

Part I (Chapters 2–7) concerns ***mathematical templates***, abstract data structures that lie at the core of many application models. I use a deliberate style in presenting each template. First I present UML and IDEF1X diagrams. Then I show representative queries, followed by tables populated with sample data. Finally I present one or more examples using the template. I explain the trade-offs for alternative templates. The discussion of each template is mostly self contained; once you find an appropriate template you can understand it by reading only a few pages.

Part II (Chapters 8–9) provides another perspective with ***antipatterns***, characterizations of common software flaws. When developers find an antipattern, they should substitute the correction. The literature has antipatterns for programming code, but antipatterns also apply to data models.

Part III (Chapter 10) covers ***archetypes***, deep concepts that are prominent and cut across applications. Developers should keep these concepts in mind as they construct models. The use of an archetype can lead to a conceptual breakthrough. By necessity, my list is arbitrary and incomplete. The models and explanation are also incomplete, so readers will need to add detail as they include these concepts.

Part IV (Chapter 11) focuses on *identity*, that property of an entity that distinguishes each entity from all others. Identity is a prominent concern in databases because developers must have some way for finding and referring to things. This chapter emphasizes conceptual aspects of identity and minimizes discussion of implementation.

Part V (Chapters 12–15) discusses several *canonical models*, submodels that often arise during application modeling.

Part VI (Chapter 16) covers *relational database design*, how to take a UML model, prepare a corresponding IDEF1X model, and then finally create SQL code.

Appendices A and B explain the UML and IDEF1X notations. Appendix C collects major concepts from throughout the book and defines them.

Comparison with Other Books

Several existing books claim to cover data modeling patterns. They are informative books, but their emphasis is on seed models and not patterns. A *seed model* is a starter model that is specific to a particular application. In contrast, I define a *pattern* as a model fragment that transcends individual applications. Some of the books have latent patterns, but they are implicit and mingled with application content. All of the authors cited below use a different notation.

- Martin Fowler. *Analysis Patterns: Reusable Object Models*. Boston, Massachusetts: Addison-Wesley, 1997.

  Fowler's work is closest in spirit to this book. His is an excellent book but really does not discuss patterns. Instead it presents seed models with occasional commentary on the underlying patterns. Fowler presents models for various applications and evolves the models as he gradually complicates the requirements. Oddly, Fowler uses a database-oriented notation with object-oriented jargon.

- David C. Hay. *Data Model Patterns: Conventions of Thought*. New York: Dorset House, 1996.

  This is another excellent book, but it does not cover true patterns. Hay presents seed models for many applications. Hay uses a database notation that is less concise than the UML.

- Len Silverston. *The Data Model Resource Book, Volumes 1 and 2*. New York: Wiley, 2001.

  This book is similar in style to Hay's book, but covers a wider variety of applications. Silverston uses Richard Barker's notation.

- Len Silverston and Paul Agnew. *The Data Model Resource Book, Volume 3*. New York: Wiley, 2009.

Volume 3 is more abstract than Silverston's prior two volumes and has some deep insights about patterns. This book is most pertinent to Chapter 10 on archetypes. Volume 3 continues to use Richard Barker's notation.

- Jim Arlow and Ila Neustadt. *Enterprise Patterns and MDA: Building Better Software with Archetype Patterns and UML.* Boston, Massachusetts: Addison-Wesley, 2004.

Most of Arlow and Neustadt's book discusses seed models for several application domains. They use the UML notation, but include programming-oriented aspects that I omit.

Acknowledgments

I would like to thank the following reviewers of this book for their thoughtful and helpful comments: Paul Brown, Donna Burbank, Peter Chang, Alex Ebel, Chary Gottumukkala, Jack Hilty, Bill Huth, Steve Johnson, Patti Lee, Rod Sprattling, Joseph R. Stephen, Toby Teorey, Sam Wegner, Rui Xu, and Roberto Zicari.

In particular I would like to thank Paul Brown for his deep insights. He caught several errors, had many suggestions, and caused me to redouble my efforts to explain the patterns clearly.

Of course, a book like this is not written in a vacuum. I also thank the many colleagues and companies with whom I've worked and interacted over the years.

I used several tools in the writing of this book. Specifically, I used Enterprise Architect to create the UML models and then rekeyed them with the Framemaker desktop publishing software for a precise layout. I used ERwin CE to create IDEF1X models and also typeset them with Framemaker. I tested the SQL code with Microsoft's SQL Server.

Michael Blaha
Chesterfield, Missouri, USA
blaha@computer.org

1

Introduction

Models provide the means for building quality software in a predictable manner. Models let developers think deeply about software and cope with large size and complexity. Developers can think abstractly before becoming enmeshed in the details of writing code. Although models are beneficial, they can be difficult to construct. That is where patterns come in. Patterns provide building blocks that help developers construct models faster and better.

This chapter starts with a discussion of models and then introduces the topic of patterns.

1.1 What Is a Model?

A *model* is an abstraction of some aspect of a problem. Most software models are expressed as graphical diagrams and by their form appeal to human intuition. Developers must understand a problem before attempting a solution. Models let developers express their understanding of a problem and communicate it to others — technologists, business experts, users, managers, and other project stakeholders. Developers can focus on the essence of an application and defer implementation details. Chapter 8 of [Blaha-2001] lists additional reasons for building models.

There are various kinds of models (such as data models, state-transition models, and data-flow models) that are used for databases, programming, and other purposes. This book concerns data models and the focus is on databases.

1.2 Modeling Notation

Data modeling has no widely-accepted, dominant notation. To appeal to a broad audience, this book uses two notations—UML (Unified Modeling Language) and IDEF1X—and presents most patterns and models with both notations. These notations largely express the same content, so you can readily understand this book as long as you are fluent with either one. The Appendix summarizes both notations and gives references for further details.

1.2.1 UML

The UML's data structure notation specifies entities and their relationships. This sets the scope and level of abstraction for subsequent development. The UML encompasses about a dozen notations of which one (the *class model*) concerns data structure.

The UML data structure notation derives from the original Chen notation [Chen-1976]. The Chen notation and its derivatives have been influential in the database community, but there are many dialects and a lack of consensus. This UML data structure model is just another Chen dialect, but one that has the backing of a standard. The Object Management Group has been actively working towards standardizing all of the UML notations.

The UML is normally used in conjunction with object-oriented jargon which I avoid. Object-oriented jargon connotes programming which I do not intend. This book's focus is on data modeling.

1.2.2 IDEF1X

The IDEF1X notation [Bruce-1992] specifies tables, keys, and indexes. IDEF1X also is a standard language and has been in use for many years. IDEF1X is closer to database design than the UML and more clearly shows the details of patterns.

1.2.3 Using Both Notations

In my consulting practice, I use both notations. I start with the UML to conceive the abstractions of an application. Then I translate the ideas into IDEF1X and add database details. From IDEF1X I generate database code. The UML is good for abstract modeling and not for database design. IDEF1X is good for database design and not for abstract modeling. Both notations are useful, but each has its place.

1.3 What Is a Pattern?

This book defines a *pattern* as a model fragment that is profound and recurring. A pattern is a proven solution to a specified problem that has stood the test of time. Here are some other definitions from the literature.

- A pattern solves a problem in a context. [Alexander-1979]
- "A pattern for software architecture describes a particular recurring design problem that arises in specific design contexts, and presents a well-proven generic scheme for its solution." [Buschmann-1996]
- "A pattern is a template. It's a template that is an example worthy of emulation, and something observed from things in actuality. It's a template to a solution, not a solution. It's a template that has supporting guidelines (not so much that it keeps one from seeing how it might be used in novel ways)." [Coad-1994]

- "A pattern is a template of interacting objects, one that may be used again and again by analogy." [Coad-1995]

- "A pattern ... provides a proven solution to a common problem individually documented in a consistent format and usually as part of a larger collection." [Erl-2009]

- "A pattern is an idea that has been useful in one practical context and will probably be useful in others." [Fowler-1997]

- "A design pattern systematically names, motivates, and explains a general design that addresses a recurring design problem... It describes the problem, the solution, when to apply the solution, and its consequences." [Gamma-1995]

- "A pattern describes a problem to be solved, a solution, and the context in which that solution works. It names a technique and describes its costs and benefits. Developers who share a set of patterns have a common vocabulary for describing their designs, and also a way of making design trade-offs explicit. Patterns are supposed to describe recurring solutions that have stood the test of time." [Johnson-1997]

- "A pattern is a recurring solution to a standard problem... Patterns have a context in which they apply." [Schmidt-1996]

- A pattern is "a form or model proposed for imitation." [Webster's dictionary]

- "In general, a pattern is a problem-solution pair in a given context. A pattern does not only document 'how' a solution solves a problem but also 'why' it is solved, i.e. the rationale behind this particular solution." [Zdun-2005]

Since this book is about data modeling, the patterns focus on data structure (entities and relationships). I de-emphasize attributes as they provide fine details that can vary for applications.

1.4 Why Are Patterns Important?

Patterns have many benefits.

- **Enriched modeling language**. Patterns extend a modeling language—you need not think only in terms of primitives; you can also think in terms of frequent combinations. Patterns provide a higher level of building blocks than modeling primitives. Patterns are prototypical model fragments that distill the knowledge of experts.

- **Improved documentation**. Patterns offer standard forms that improve modeling uniformity. When you use patterns, you tap into a language that is familiar to other developers. Patterns pull concepts out of the heads of experts and explicitly represent them. Development decisions and rationale are made apparent.

- **Reduce modeling difficulty**. Many developers find modeling difficult because of the intrinsic abstraction. Patterns are all about abstraction and give developers a better place to start. Patterns identify common problems and present alternative solutions along with their trade-offs.

- **Faster modeling**. With patterns developers do not have to create everything from scratch. Developers can build on the accomplishments of others.

- **Better models**. Patterns reduce mistakes and rework. Each pattern has been carefully considered and has already been applied to problems. Consequently, a pattern is more likely to be correct and robust than an untested, custom solution.

- **Reuse**. You can achieve reuse by using existing patterns, rather than reinventing solutions. Patterns provide a means for capturing and transmitting development insights so that they can be improved on and used again.

1.5 Drawbacks of Patterns

Even though patterns have much to offer, they are not a panacea for the difficulties of software development.

- **Sporadic coverage**. You cannot build a model by merely combining patterns. Typically you will use only a few patterns, but they often embody core insights.

- **Pattern discovery**. It can be difficult to find a pertinent pattern, especially if the idea in your mind is ill-formed. Nevertheless, this difficulty does not detract from the benefits when you find a suitable pattern.

- **Complexity**. Patterns are an advanced topic and can be difficult to fully understand.

- **Inconsistencies**. There has been a real effort in the literature to cross reference other work and build on it. However, inconsistencies still happen.

- **Immature technology**. The patterns literature is active but the field is still evolving.

1.6 Pattern vs. Seed Model

It is important to differentiate between patterns and seed models. The programming pattern books, such as [Gamma-1995], have true patterns that are abstract and stand apart from any particular application. In contrast most of the database literature ([Arlow-2004], [Fowler-1997], [Hay-1996], [Silverston-2001a,b]) confuses patterns with seed models.

A *seed model* is a model that is specific to a problem domain. A seed model provides a starting point for applications from its problem domain. Seed models are valuable in that they can save work, reduce errors, contribute deep insights, and accelerate development.

Thus seed models are truly useful. But if you are working in a different problem domain, you must first find the relevant seed models, understand the seed models, extract the implicit patterns, and then apply the patterns to your own application. In contrast, this book makes patterns explicit so that they are ready to go for any problem domain. Table 1.1 contrasts patterns with seed models.

Table 1.1   Pattern vs. Seed Model

Characteristic	Data modeling pattern	Seed model
Applicability	Application independent	Application dependent
Scope	An excerpt of an application	Intended to be the starting point for an application
Model size	Typically few concepts and relationships (< 10)	Typically 10-50 concepts and relationships
Abstraction	More abstract	Less abstract
Model type	Can be described with a data model	Can be described with a data model

Note: A pattern is abstract and stands apart from any particular application, unlike a seed model.

1.7 Aspects of Pattern Technology

My usage of the term pattern is different than the literature but consistent with the spirit of past work. I treat pattern as an overarching term encompassing mathematical templates, antipatterns, archetypes, identity, and canonical models.

- *Mathematical template*: an abstract model fragment that is useful for a variety of applications. A mathematical template is devoid of application content. Mathematical templates are driven by deep data structures that often arise in database models. Most templates have a basis in topology and graph theory, both of which are branches of mathematics.

  Mathematical templates have parameters that are placeholders. The parameters must be instantiated for each use. I use the notation of angle brackets to denote template parameters. You incorporate a mathematical template into a model by substituting application concepts for the parameters.

- *Antipattern*: a characterization of a common software flaw. An antipattern shows what not to do and how to fix it. The literature emphasizes antipatterns for programming but they also apply to databases.

- *Archetype*: a deep concept that is prominent and cuts across problem domains. This book's archetype models are small and focus on core concepts. [Arlow-2004] nicely articulates the idea of an archetype, but their models are so large that they are really more like seed models. A small model is more likely to be application independent and widely reusable than a large model.

- *Identity*: the means for denoting individual entities, so that they can be found. There are different aspects of identity that deeply affect application models.

- *Canonical model*: a submodel that provides a useful service for many applications. A canonical model is an abstract service that is not bound to a particular problem domain in contrast to a seed model.

1.8 Chapter Summary

Models are the key to successful software development. Models help you think deeply, focus on the important issues, reconcile your thoughts with others, and ultimately build the software. Models enable you to achieve the conceptual integrity that is essential to quality development.

A pattern is a model fragment that is profound and recurring. A pattern is a proven solution to a specified problem that has stood the test of time. Patterns are important in that they help developers build models better and faster, which leads to building software better and faster. The fundamental treatment of patterns in this book contrasts with the application-specific seed models that dominate the database literature. In this book pattern is an overarching term that encompasses mathematical templates, antipatterns, archetypes, identity, and canonical models.

Bibliographic Notes

[Hoberman-2009] has an especially lucid explanation of modeling. [Blaha-1998], [Elmasri-2006], [Hernandez-2003], and [Teorey-2006] present processes for data modeling and database design.

[Alexander-1979] discusses patterns for the architecture of buildings. Alexander's book has been highly influential in the software patterns community and helped to initiate the field.

Most of the software patterns literature concerns design and implementation patterns. [Gamma-1995] is a classic book that focuses on patterns for programming design. [Buschmann-1996] discusses architectural patterns, design patterns, and idioms.

[Arlow-2004], [Coad-1992], [Fowler-1997], [Hay-1996], and [Silverston-2001a,b] address data modeling patterns. I regard many of their "patterns"—with no criticism intended—to be seeds for applications rather than true patterns. Ironically, each of the authors use a different notation. [Silverston-2009] is more abstract and closer in spirit to this new book.

[Coad-1992] has an excellent discussion of patterns in other disciplines. [Coad-1995] is really an object-oriented methodology book. It does not discuss deep data modeling patterns.

[Appleton] is a helpful Web site about patterns. [Backlund-2001] has a nice overview of the pattern technology available at that time. [Brown-1998] and [Laplante-2006] are good references for antipatterns.

References

[Alexander-1979] Christopher Alexander. *The Timeless Way of Building*. New York: Oxford University Press, 1979.

[Appleton] http://www.cmcrossroads.com/bradapp/docs/patterns-nutshell.html#Patterns_What

[Arlow-2004] Jim Arlow and Ila Neustadt. *Enterprise Patterns and MDA: Building Better Software with Archetype Patterns and UML*. Boston, Massachusetts: Addison-Wesley, 2004.

[Backlund-2001] Per Backlund. *The Use of Patterns in Information System Engineering*. M.Sc. dissertation, University of Skövde, Sweden, 2001.

[Blaha-1998] Michael Blaha and William Premerlani. *Object-Oriented Modeling and Design for Database Applications*. Upper Saddle River, New Jersey: Prentice-Hall, 1998.

[Blaha-2001] Michael Blaha. *A Manager's Guide to Database Technology*. Upper Saddle River, New Jersey: Prentice-Hall, 2001.

[Brown-1998] William J. Brown, Raphael C. Malveau, Hays W. "Skip" McCormick, and Thomas J. Mowbray. *AntiPatterns: Refactoring Software, Architectures, and Projects in Crisis*. John Wiley & Sons, Ltd, 1998.

[Bruce-1992] Thomas A. Bruce. *Designing Quality Databases with IDEF1X Information Models*. New York: Dorset House, 1992.

[Buschmann-1996] Frank Buschmann, Regine Meunier, Hans Rohnert, Peter Sommerlad, and Michael Stal. *Pattern-Oriented Software Architecture: A System of Patterns*. Chichester, United Kingdom: Wiley, 1996.

[Chen-1976] PPS Chen. The entity-relationship model—toward a unified view of data. *ACM Transactions on Database Systems 1*, 1 (March 1976).

[Coad-1992] Peter Coad. Object-oriented patterns. *Communications ACM 35*, 9 (September 1992), 152–159.

[Coad-1994] Peter Coad and Mark Mayfield. Object Model Patterns Workshop Report. *ACM OOPSLA Conference*, October 23–27, 1994, Portland, Oregon, 102–104.

[Coad-1995] Peter Coad, David North, and Mark Mayfield. *Object Models: Strategies, Patterns, and Applications*. Upper Saddle River, New Jersey: Yourdon Press, 1995.

[Elmasri-2006] Ramez Elmasri and Shamkant B. Navathe. *Fundamentals of Database Systems (5th Edition)*. Boston: Addison-Wesley, 2006.

[Erl-2009] Thomas Erl. *SOA Design Patterns*. Upper Saddle River, New Jersey: Prentice-Hall, 2009.

[Fowler-1997] Martin Fowler. *Analysis Patterns: Reusable Object Models*. Boston, Massachusetts: Addison-Wesley, 1997.

[Gamma-1995] Erich Gamma, Richard Helm, Ralph Johnson, and John Vlissides. *Design Patterns: Elements of Reusable Object-Oriented Software*. Boston, Massachusetts: Addison-Wesley, 1995.

[Hay-1996] David C. Hay. *Data Model Patterns: Conventions of Thought*. New York, New York: Dorset House, 1996.

[Hernandez-2003] Michael J. Hernandez. *Database Design for Mere Mortals: A Hands-On Guide to Relational Database Design (2nd Edition)*. Boston: Addison-Wesley, 2003.

[Hoberman-2009] Steve Hoberman. *Data Modeling Made Simple, 2nd edition*. Bradley Beach, New Jersey: Technics Publications, 2009.

[Johnson-1997] Ralph E. Johnson. Frameworks = (components+patterns). *Communications ACM 40*, 10 (October 1997), 39–42.

[Laplante-2006] Phillip A. Laplante and Colin J. Neill. *Antipatterns: Identification, Refactoring, and Management*. Boca Raton, FL: Auerbach Publications, 2006.

[Schmidt-1996] Douglas C. Schmidt, Mohamed Fayad, and Ralph E. Johnson. Software patterns. *Communications ACM 39*, 10 (October 1996), 36–39.

[Silverston-2001a] Len Silverston. The *Data Model Resource Book, Volume 1*. New York, New York: Wiley, 2001.

[Silverston-2001b] Len Silverston. The *Data Model Resource Book, Volume 2*. New York, New York: Wiley, 2001.

[Silverston-2009] Len Silverston and Paul Agnew. *The Data Model Resource Book, Volume 3*. New York, New York: Wiley, 2009.

[Teorey-2006] Toby Teorey, Sam Lightstone, and Tom Nadeau. *Database Modeling and Design (4th Edition)*. New York: Morgan Kaufmann, 2006.

[Zdun-2005] Uwe Zdun and Paris Avgeriou. Modeling Architectural Patterns Using Architectural Primitives. *ACM OOPSLA Conference*, October 16–20, 2005, San Diego, California, 133–146.

Part I

Mathematical Templates

Part I concerns mathematical templates, abstract model fragments that are devoid of application content. Mathematical templates are driven by deep data structures that often arise in database models.

Chapters 2, 3, and 4 cover terms from graph theory: trees, directed graphs, and undirected graphs.

Chapter 2 presents six templates for trees. A tree is a set of nodes that connect from child to parent. A node can have many child nodes; all nodes have one parent node except for the node at the tree's top. There are no cycles—that means at most one path connects any two nodes.

Chapter 3 presents six templates for directed graphs. A directed graph is a set of nodes and a set of directed edges. Each directed edge originates at a source node and terminates at a target node (which may be the same as the source node). The nodes of a directed graph can have any number of edges.

Chapter 4 presents three templates for undirected graphs. An undirected graph is a set of nodes and a set of edges. Each edge connects two nodes (which may be the same). The nodes of an undirected graph can have any number of edges.

Chapter 5 explains the item description template that relates an item to its description. The item description template arises when the same model relates data and metadata. There is one template for item description and another template (the homomorphism) for analogies between two item descriptions.

Chapter 6 discusses the star schema template that represents data as facts that are bound to dimensions. A fact measures the performance of a business. A dimension specifies one of the bases for facts. There is one template for the star schema.

Chapter 7 concludes with a summary of the mathematical templates. A table provides an overview to help you choose the appropriate template.

I use a uniform style in explaining the templates. First I present each template with both the UML and IDEF1X notations. Then I present some representative SQL queries—the queries clarify how to use the template and help you compare alternative templates. Next, synthetic data shows the mechanics of populating data. And finally I illustrate each template with one or more realistic examples.

The chapters mostly explain each template independently — then you can understand a particular template by reading only a few pages. However there is some comparison and contrast of templates, so you can more readily see the similarities and differences.

2

Tree Template

The tree is a term from graph theory. A *tree* is a set of nodes that connect from child to parent. A node can have many child nodes; each node in a tree has one parent node except for the node at the tree's top. There are no cycles — that means at most one path connects any two nodes.

Figure 2.1 shows an example of a tree. *A* is at the top of the tree and has no parent node. *A* is the parent for *B*, *C*, and *D*. *B* is the parent for *E* and *C* is the parent for *F*.

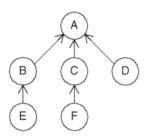

Figure 2.1 Sample tree. A tree organizes data into a hierarchy.

There are six templates for trees. The first hardcodes an entity type for each level of the tree. The others are more abstract and use the same entity types for all levels.

- **Hardcoded tree**. Hardcodes entity types, one for each level of the tree. Use when the structure of a tree is well known and it is important to enforce the sequence of types in the levels of the hierarchy.
- **Simple tree**. Restricts nodes to a single tree. Treats nodes the same. Use when tree decomposition is merely a matter of data structure.
- **Structured tree**. Restricts nodes to a single tree. Differentiates leaf nodes from branch nodes. Use when branch nodes and leaf nodes have different attributes, relationships, and/or semantics.

- **Overlapping trees**. Permits a node to belong to multiple trees. Treats nodes the same. Use when a node can belong to multiple trees.

- **Tree changing over time**. Stores multiple variants of a tree. A particular tree can be extracted by specifying a time. Restricts nodes to a single tree. Treats nodes the same. Use when the history of a tree must be recorded.

- **Degenerate node and edge**. Groups a parent with its children. The grouping itself can be described with attributes and relationships. Restricts nodes to a single tree. Treats nodes the same. Use when the grouping of a parent and its children must be described.

2.1 Hardcoded Tree Template

2.1.1 UML Template

Figure 2.2 shows the UML template for hardcoded trees. (The Appendix explains UML notation.) The diagram has three levels, but in practice there can be any number of levels. The angle brackets denote parameters that require substitution. A **Tree** is a hierarchy of entities with the entities of each level having the same entity type. You need not show *Tree* in a use of the template.

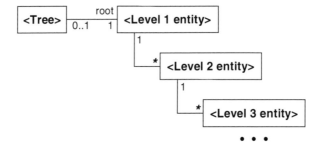

Figure 2.2 Hardcoded tree: UML template. Use when the structure is well known and
            it is important to enforce the sequence of types in the levels of the hierarchy.

The hardcoded representation is easy to understand, but it is fragile. The hardcoded template is only appropriate when the data structure is well known and unlikely to change. Otherwise a change to the hierarchy of types breaks the model and database structure necessitating rework of application code.

In practice I seldom build applications with the hardcoded tree template. Nevertheless, this is a good template to keep in mind. It is often helpful to model data using a hardcoded template — so that business persons and other stakeholders can understand the model. Then you can build the application with an abstract representation (Section 2.2 – Section 2.6) and populate it with the content of the hardcoded model.

2.1.2 IDEF1X Template

Figure 2.3 restates Figure 2.2 with the IDEF1X notation. (The Appendix explains IDEF1X notation.) The following are foreign keys: *rootID* references *Level1entity*, *level1ID* references *Level1entity*, and *level2ID* references *Level2entity*. Although it is not shown, the levels would have fields for application data.

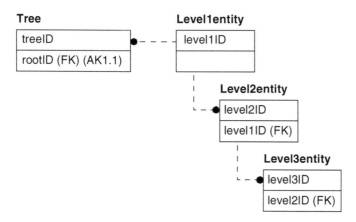

Figure 2.3 Hardcoded tree: IDEF1X template.

2.1.3 SQL Queries

Figure 2.4 and Figure 2.5 show representative SQL queries for the template. These queries are very simple which is an attraction of the hardcoded approach. The colon prefix denotes variable values that must be provided. The subsequent levels of the hierarchy (level 3, level 4, and so forth) have similar queries.

```
SELECT level1ID
FROM Level2entity AS L2
WHERE level2ID = :aLevel2ID;
```

Figure 2.4 Hardcoded tree: SQL query. Find the parent for a child.

```
SELECT level2ID
FROM Level2entity
WHERE level1ID = :aLevel1ID
ORDER BY level2ID;
```

Figure 2.5 Hardcoded tree: SQL query. Find the children for a parent.

2.1.4 Sample Populated Tables

Figure 2.6 shows hardcoded tables populated with data. A is at level 1; B, C, and D are at level 2; E and F are at level 3. The ID values are arbitrary but internally consistent.

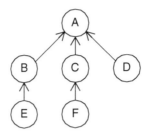

Level_1 table

level1ID	name	treeID
1	A	1

Level_2 table

level2ID	name	level1ID
1	B	1
2	C	1
3	D	1

Level_3 table

level3ID	name	level2ID
1	E	1
2	F	2

Figure 2.6 Hardcoded tree: Populated tables.

2.1.5 Examples

Figure 2.7 shows a fixed organization chart. Of course, more levels could be added. This simple model could be appropriate for a small company but is risky for a large company as it is rigid and does not accommodate change.

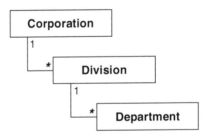

Figure 2.7 Hardcoded tree: Organizational chart model.

Figure 2.8 has another example, the division of a book into chapters, sections, and subsections.

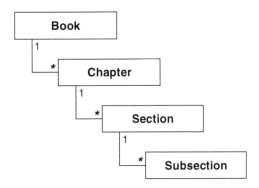

Figure 2.8 Hardcoded tree: Book structure model.

2.2 Simple Tree Template

2.2.1 UML Template

In the simple tree template (Figure 2.9) all nodes are the same and decomposition is merely a matter of data structure. A *Tree* is a hierarchy of nodes and has one node as the root. A *Node* is an entity type whose records are organized as a *Tree*. An individual node may, or may not, be the root. You need not show *Tree* in a use of the template.

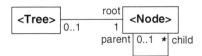

{All nodes have a parent except the root node. There cannot be any cycles.}

Figure 2.9 Simple tree: UML template. Use when tree decomposition
is merely a matter of data structure.

Figure 2.9 adds the constraint that the tree cannot have any cycles. (Consider Figure 2.1. *A* cannot have *F* as a parent even though the template in Figure 2.9 does not prevent it. Traversing parent relationships, this would cause a cycle from *F* to *C* to *A* back to *F*.) Similarly each node must have a parent, except for the root node — the template alone is more lax.

Each node may have a name. As Figure 2.10 shows, node names can be globally unique (left template) or unique within the context of a parent node (right template). The box under *Node* in Figure 2.10b is a UML qualifier (see the Appendix for an explanation).

In Figure 2.1 node names are globally unique. In contrast, a node name can be unique within a context. Figure 2.11 shows an excerpt of this book's file structure where I have kept old copies of files from reviews. File names are unique within the context of their directory.

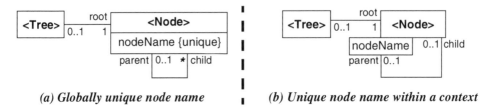

(a) Globally unique node name   *(b) Unique node name within a context*

Figure 2.10 Simple tree: UML template, with node names. There are two variations of the template—globally unique names and names within a context.

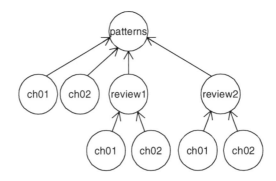

Figure 2.11 Sample tree with node names that are unique within a context.

2.2.2 *IDEF1X Template*

Figure 2.12 restates Figure 2.10 with the IDEF1X notation. The following are foreign keys: *rootID* references *Node* and *parentID* references *Node*.

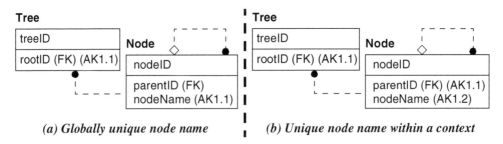

(a) Globally unique node name   *(b) Unique node name within a context*

Figure 2.12 Simple tree: IDEF1X template.

Figure 2.12 uses existence-based identity which is my preferred approach for database design. (See Chapter 16.) ***Existence-based identity*** means that each entity has its own artificial identifier (such as an Oracle sequence or a SQL Server identity field) as a primary key. Thus the primary key of *Node* is *nodeID* and not, for example, *nodeName* (Figure 2.12a) or *parentID + nodeName* (Figure 2.12b). Although I favor existence-based identity, the templates in this book do not require it.

In Figure 2.12 the *AK* notation denotes a candidate key, that is a combination of attributes that is unique for each record in a table. No attribute in a candidate key can be null. All candidate key attributes are required for uniqueness.

Figure 2.12b defines *parentID + nodeName* as a candidate key, but one record is an exception. The root node for a tree has a null *parentID* and a candidate key cannot involve a null. Most relational DBMSs treat NULL as just another value and do not strictly enforce candidate keys, so the definition of a unique key for *parentID + nodeName* does work. (I verified this for SQL Server and expect that it would work for most relational DBMSs.) Alternatively, you can forego the unique key and check the constraint with application code.

2.2.3 SQL Queries

Figure 2.13 and Figure 2.14 show SQL queries for common traversals of the template. The colon prefix denotes variable values that must be provided.

```
SELECT Parent.nodeID AS parentNodeID,
    Parent.nodeName AS parentNodeName
FROM Node AS Child
    INNER JOIN Node AS Parent ON Child.parentID = Parent.nodeID
WHERE Child.nodeID = :aChildNodeID;
```

Figure 2.13 Simple tree: SQL query. Find the parent for a child node.

```
SELECT Child.nodeID AS childNodeID,
    Child.nodeName AS childNodeName
FROM Node AS Child
WHERE Child.parentID = :aParentNodeID
ORDER BY Child.nodeName;
```

Figure 2.14 Simple tree: SQL query. Find the children for a parent node.

2.2.4 Sample Populated Tables

Figure 2.15 shows sample simple tree tables populated with data. The ID values are arbitrary, but internally consistent.

2.2.5 Examples

Simple trees also arise in many applications.

In Figure 2.16 a *manager* has many *subordinates*. Each *subordinate* reports to at most one *manager*: The CEO reports to no *manager*, and all others report to one *manager*. The management hierarchy can be arbitrarily deep.

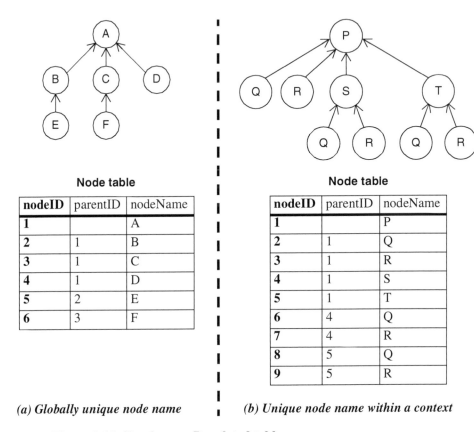

Node table

nodeID	parentID	nodeName
1		A
2	1	B
3	1	C
4	1	D
5	2	E
6	3	F

Node table

nodeID	parentID	nodeName
1		P
2	1	Q
3	1	R
4	1	S
5	1	T
6	4	Q
7	4	R
8	5	Q
9	5	R

(a) Globally unique node name   *(b) Unique node name within a context*

Figure 2.15 Simple tree: Populated tables.

{Every person has a manager, except the CEO.}
{The management hierarchy must be acyclic.}

Figure 2.16 Simple tree: Management hierarchy model.

In Figure 2.17 formal requests for proposals (RFPs), such as government projects, often involve extensive requirements that are captured with an indented list. Level 0 is the requirement for the RFP as a whole that elaborates into levels 1, 2, 3, and so forth. A level 1 requirement can have sub requirements such as 1.1 and 1.2. These sub requirements can have further detail such as 1.1.1, 1.1.2, and 1.2.1. The nesting can be arbitrarily deep depending on the desired level of detail. The RFP yields a tree of requirements.

{Every requirement has a parent, except for level 0.}
{The requirement hierarchy must be acyclic.}

Figure 2.17 Simple tree: Nested requirements for RFPs model.

2.3 Structured Tree Template

2.3.1 UML Template

Figure 2.18 shows the UML template for structured trees when there is a need to differentiate leaf nodes from branch nodes. A *Tree* is a hierarchy of nodes and has one node as the root. A particular node may, or may not, be the root. You need not show *Tree* in a use of the template.

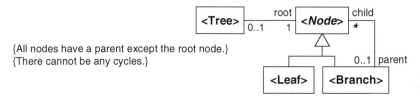

{All nodes have a parent except the root node.}
{There cannot be any cycles.}

Figure 2.18 Structured tree: UML template. Use when branch nodes and leaf nodes have different attributes, relationships, and/or semantics.

A *Node* is either a leaf node or a branch node. A *Leaf* node (such as *D*, *E*, and *F* in Figure 2.1) terminates the tree recursion. A *Branch* node (such as *A*, *B*, and *C* in Figure 2.1) can have child nodes each of which, in turn, can be a leaf node or a further branch node.

Figure 2.18 adds the constraint that a tree cannot have any cycles. (See Section 2.2.1 for an explanation of cycles.) Similarly each node must have a parent, except for the root node — the template alone is more lax.

As with simple trees, the node names in Figure 2.19 can be globally unique (left template) or unique within a context (right template).

2.3.2 IDEF1X Template

Figure 2.20 restates Figure 2.19 with the IDEF1X notation. The following are foreign keys: *rootID* references *Node*, *parentID* references *Branch*, *leafID* references *Node*, and *branchID* references *Node*. The generalization is exhaustive—every *Node* record must have a corresponding *Leaf* record or *Branch* record. The *nodeDiscriminator* field is an enumeration with values "Leaf" and "Branch" indicating the appropriate subtype record.

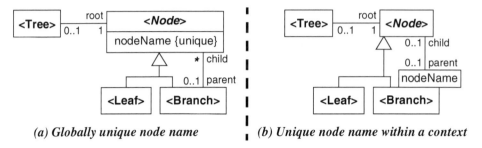

(a) Globally unique node name | *(b) Unique node name within a context*

Figure 2.19 Structured tree: UML template, with node names. There are two variations of the template—globally unique names and names within a context.

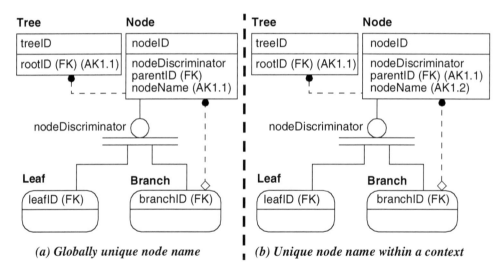

(a) Globally unique node name | *(b) Unique node name within a context*

Figure 2.20 Structured tree: IDEF1X template.

As with Figure 2.12b, Figure 2.20b defines *parentID* + *nodeName* as a candidate key, but one record is an exception. The root node for a tree has a null *parentID* and a candidate key cannot involve a null. Since most relational DBMSs are lax and treat NULL as just another value, the definition of a unique key for *parentID* + *nodeName* does work. Although it is not shown, the *Leaf* and *Branch* tables would have additional fields for application data.

2.3.3 SQL Queries

Figure 2.21 and Figure 2.22 show SQL queries for common traversals of the template. The queries could omit the *Branch* table, but I wrote them according to template traversal—then it is easy to retrieve any data that is added to the template. The colon prefix denotes variable values that must be provided.

```
SELECT Parent.nodeID AS parentNodeID,
    Parent.nodeName AS parentNodeName
FROM Node AS Child
    INNER JOIN Branch AS B ON Child.parentID = B.branchID
    INNER JOIN Node AS Parent ON B.branchID = Parent.nodeID
WHERE Child.nodeID = :aChildNodeID;
```

Figure 2.21 Structured tree: SQL query. Find the parent for a child node.

```
SELECT Child.nodeID AS childNodeID,
    Child.nodeName AS childNodeName
FROM Node AS Child
    INNER JOIN Branch AS B ON Child.parentID = B.branchID
    INNER JOIN Node AS Parent ON B.branchID = Parent.nodeID
WHERE Parent.nodeID = :aParentNodeID
ORDER BY Child.nodeName;
```

Figure 2.22 Structured tree: SQL query. Find the children for a parent node.

2.3.4 Sample Populated Tables

Figure 2.23 shows sample structured tree tables populated with data. The ID values are arbitrary, but internally consistent.

2.3.5 Examples

Trees often arise in applications and sometimes the structured tree template is the best choice.

Many drawing applications and user interfaces have the notion of a group. In Figure 2.24 a *DrawingObject* is *Text*, a *GeometricObject*, or a *Group*. A *Group* has two or more lesser *DrawingObjects*; the resulting recursion yields trees of *DrawingObjects*. Note the further refinement from Figure 2.18—a group must include at least two *DrawingObjects*.

Figure 2.25 is the analog to Figure 2.16. Figure 2.16 suffices if you merely need to record the reporting structure. In Figure 2.25 a *Person* can be a *Manager* or an *IndividualContributor*. Except for the CEO, each *Person* reports to a *Manager*. The management hierarchy can be arbitrarily deep. There are material differences between *Managers* and *Individual-Contributors* necessitating the use of subtypes. For example, only *Managers* can be in charge of *Departments*.

Many years ago, the original Microsoft PC-DOS file structure was a hierarchy. Each file belonged to at most one directory. (Modern operating systems permit files to belong to multiple directories as the next chapter explains.) In Figure 2.26 a *File* may be a *DataFile* or a *DirectoryFile*. Directories contain multiple files, some or all of which may be subdirectories. The combination of a *DirectoryFile* and a *fileName* yields a specific *File*—file names are unique within the context of their directory. All *Files* belong to a single directory except for

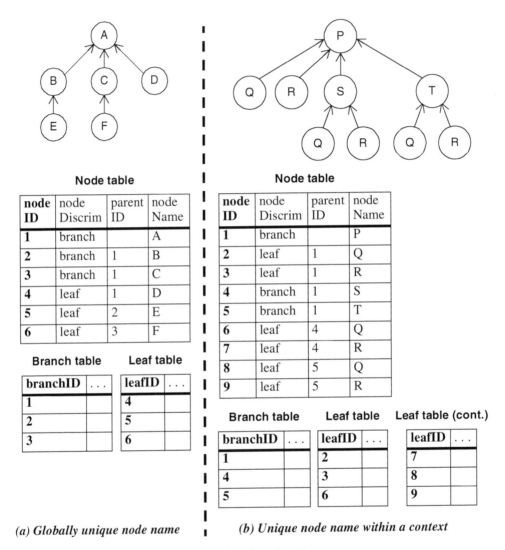

Node table

node ID	node Discrim	parent ID	node Name
1	branch		A
2	branch	1	B
3	branch	1	C
4	leaf	1	D
5	leaf	2	E
6	leaf	3	F

Branch table

branchID	...
1	
2	
3	

Leaf table

leafID	...
4	
5	
6	

(a) Globally unique node name

Node table

node ID	node Discrim	parent ID	node Name
1	branch		P
2	leaf	1	Q
3	leaf	1	R
4	branch	1	S
5	branch	1	T
6	leaf	4	Q
7	leaf	4	R
8	leaf	5	Q
9	leaf	5	R

Branch table

branchID	...
1	
4	
5	

Leaf table

leafID	...
2	
3	
6	

Leaf table (cont.)

leafID	...
7	
8	
9	

(b) Unique node name within a context

Figure 2.23 Structured tree: Populated tables.

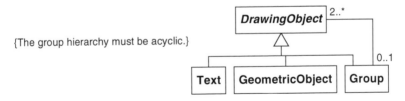

{The group hierarchy must be acyclic.}

Figure 2.24 Structured tree: Graphical editor model.

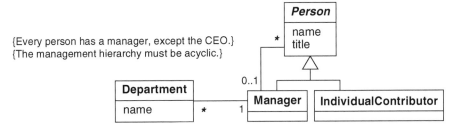

Figure 2.25 Structured tree: Management hierarchy model.

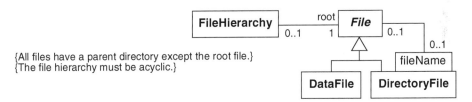

Figure 2.26 Structured tree: File hierarchy directory model.

the *root File*, which belongs to none. Directories can be nested to an arbitrary depth, with *DataFiles* and empty *DirectoryFiles* terminating the recursion.

2.4 Overlapping Trees Template

2.4.1 UML Template

Figure 2.27 permits a node to belong to multiple trees. A *Tree* is a hierarchy of nodes and has one node as the root. A *Node* is an entity type whose records are organized as a *Tree*. A node may be the root of multiple trees. You should include *Tree* when using this template, so that you can distinguish the multiple trees. The dotted line and attached box is UML notation for an entity type that is also a relationship (see the Appendix for an explanation.)

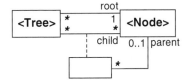

{All nodes have a parent in a tree except for the root node. There may not be any cycles of nodes.}
{A parent must only have children for trees to which the parent belongs.}

Figure 2.27 Overlapping tree: UML template. Use when a node can
belong to more than one tree.

You can retrieve a tree by starting with a tree record and retrieving the node that is the root of the tree. Traverse the parent relationship to retrieve the collection of children for the root node. You can recursively expand the tree, level by level, traversing parent relationships to get the next lower level of children. As you traverse nodes, filter records and only consider children of the tree under consideration.

Figure 2.27 treats nodes uniformly like the simple tree template. It would be confusing to distinguish between branches and leaves as with the structured tree template because the distinction could vary across the different trees for a node. All the overlapping–tree examples I have seen to date treat nodes uniformly.

As with the other tree templates, Figure 2.27 adds a constraint that forbids cycles, as the template alone cannot prevent them. Each node in a tree must have a parent except for the root node. Another constraint is that a parent must only have children for trees to which the parent belongs.

This template is already complex, so it is best to handle node names in a simple manner. Each node has a globally unique name and there is no provision to vary node name by context.

2.4.2 IDEF1X Template

Figure 2.28 restates Figure 2.27 with the IDEF1X notation. The following are foreign keys: *rootID*, *treeID*, *childID,* and *parentID*.

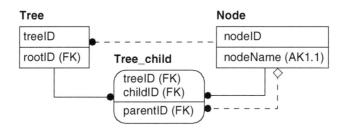

Figure 2.28 Overlapping tree: IDEF1X template.

2.4.3 SQL Queries

Figure 2.29 and Figure 2.30 show SQL queries for common traversals of the template. The colon prefix denotes variable values that must be provided for each query.

```
SELECT N.nodeID AS parentNodeID, N.nodeName AS parentNodeName
FROM Tree_child Tc
   INNER JOIN Node AS N ON Tc.parentID = N.nodeID
WHERE Tc.treeID = :aTreeID AND Tc.childID = :aChildNodeID;
```

Figure 2.29 Overlapping tree: SQL query. Find the parent for a child node.

```
SELECT N.nodeID AS childNodeID, N.nodeName AS childNodeName
FROM Tree_child Tc
    INNER JOIN Node AS N ON Tc.childID = N.nodeID
WHERE Tc.treeID = :aTreeID AND Tc.parentID = :aParentNodeID
ORDER BY N.nodeName;
```

Figure 2.30 Overlapping tree: SQL query. Find the children for a parent node.

2.4.4 Sample Populated Tables

Figure 2.31 shows sample overlapping tree tables populated with data using globally unique node names. The ID values are arbitrary, but internally consistent.

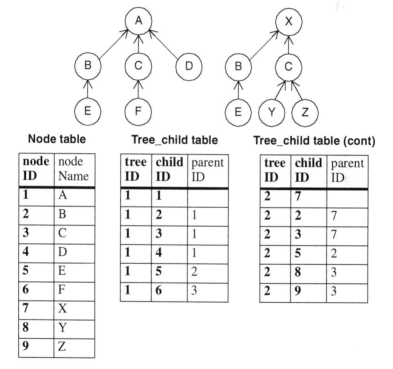

node ID	node Name
1	A
2	B
3	C
4	D
5	E
6	F
7	X
8	Y
9	Z

Node table

tree ID	child ID	parent ID
1	1	
1	2	1
1	3	1
1	4	1
1	5	2
1	6	3

Tree_child table

tree ID	child ID	parent ID
2	7	
2	2	7
2	3	7
2	5	2
2	8	3
2	9	3

Tree_child table (cont)

Figure 2.31 Overlapping tree: Populated tables.

2.4.5 Example

Overlapping trees occur less often than structured and simple trees.

Mechanical parts provide a compelling example. In Figure 2.32 a *PartRole* can be the *root* of a *BOM* (bill-of-material) and have multiple children, successively forming a tree. A

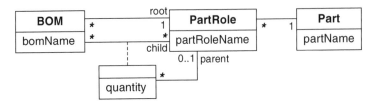

{Each BOM must be acyclic.}

Figure 2.32 Overlapping tree: Mechanical parts model.

PartRole is the usage of a *Part*. The same part may have different usages within the same *BOM* and across *BOMs*. There are overlapping trees because a *PartRole* can belong to multiple *BOMs*, such as one for a product's design (engineering BOM), another for how it is built (manufacturing BOM), and another for how it is maintained (service BOM).

Figure 2.33 shows engineering and manufacturing BOMs for a lamp.

Engineering BOM for a Lamp				Manufacturing BOM for a Lamp			
Level	PartName	PartRoleName	Qty	Level	PartName	PartRoleName	Qty
01	L101	Lamp	1	01	L101	Lamp	1
02	SA1	Socket asm	1	02	SA1	Socket asm	1
03	WA1	Wiring assembly	1	03	WA1	Wiring assembly	1
04	Plg2	Plug	1	04	WAC1	Wiring asm core	1
04	C2	Cord	1	05	Plg2	Plug	1
04	PS1	Power switch	1	05	C2	Cord	1
04	Scr1	Switch screw	2	05	PS1	Power switch	1
03	Skt1	Socket	3	04	Scr1	Switch screw	2
02	SS1	Shade support	1	03	Skt1	Socket	3
02	Shd5	Shade	1	02	SS1	Shade support	1
02	BA1	Base assembly	1	02	Shd5	Shade	1
03	M2	Mat	1	02	BA1	Base assembly	1
03	B1	Base	1	03	BAC1	Base asm core	1
03	Sft1	Shaft	1	04	B1	Base	1
03	Scr25	Shaft-base screw	1	04	Sft1	Shaft	1
02	Scr25	Sft-shd supp scr	1	04	Scr25	Shaft-base screw	1
				03	M2	Mat	1
				02	Scr25	Sft-shd supp scr	1

Figure 2.33 Overlapping tree: Sample data for mechanical parts model.

2.5 Tree Changing over Time Template

2.5.1 UML Template

For some applications, there is a need not only to store trees, but also to store the history of trees as they evolve over time. Figure 2.34 shows such a template. To represent change over time, the template separates an entity from its position in a tree (node). The timeline for an entity can differ from that of its various positions.

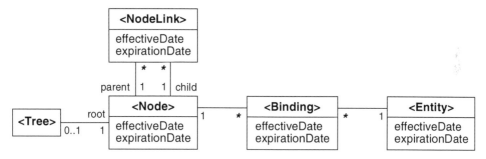

{All nodes have a parent except the root node. There may not be any cycles of nodes.}
{A child has at most one parent at a time.}

Figure 2.34 Tree changing over time: UML template. Use when you must store the history of a tree as it changes over time.

A *Tree* is a hierarchy of nodes and has one node as the root. A *Node* is a position within a *Tree*. An *Entity* is something with identity and data. A *Binding* is the coupling of an *Entity* to a *Node*. A *NodeLink* is the parent–child relationship between the *Nodes* of a *Tree*.

Strictly speaking, the template does not enforce a tree. The intent is that a child may have multiple parents over time, but only one parent at any time. The template implies that if an application changes the node at the root of a tree, it must start a new tree.

You can access a *Tree* by retrieving its *root* node and then retrieving the descendants for the desired time. Start with the *root Node* and then traverse from *Node* to *NodeLink* to *child Nodes* for the desired time. Repeat this traversal for each level to obtain the full tree. Each *Node* can be dereferenced to an *Entity* via *Binding*. (Even though the template does not enforce the constraint, each *Node* should bind to one *Entity* at a time.) Applications must carefully check to ensure that a tree is returned and catch any illegal data. The template itself permits nonsensical combinations of dates that do not yield a proper tree.

This template is already complex, so it is best to handle node names in a simple manner. Each node has a globally unique name and there is no provision to vary node name by context. The effective and expiration dates permit *Node* data and *Entity* data to vary over time.

2.5.2 IDEF1X Template

Figure 2.35 shows the template for trees that change over time using the IDEF1X notation. The following are foreign keys: *rootID* references *Node*, *nodeID* references *Node*, *entityID*

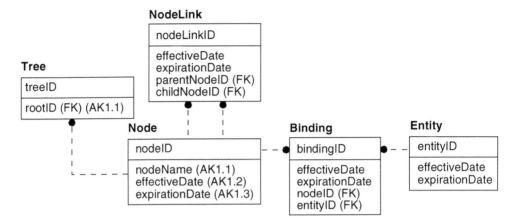

Figure 2.35 Tree changing over time: IDEF1X template.

references *Entity, parentNodeID* references *Node*, and *childNodeID* references *Node*. In Figure 2.35 the node name can change over time (three part candidate key—*nodeName* + *effectiveDate* + *expirationDate*), but the node name could also be invariant over time (candidate key of *nodeName* alone). Note that the handling of time reflects a limitation of relational DBMSs. It would be better to use time intervals but most relational DBMSs only support points in time.

2.5.3 SQL Queries
Figure 2.36 and Figure 2.37 show SQL queries for common traversals of the template. The colon prefix denotes variable values that must be provided for each query. A null *effectiveDate* means that a *Node* applies indefinitely from the past. A null *expirationDate* means that a *Node* applies indefinitely into the future.

2.5.4 Sample Populated Tables
Figure 2.38 shows sample tables for trees that change over time populated with data. For brevity Figure 2.38 only shows the *Node* and *NodeLink* tables. The ID values are arbitrary, but internally consistent. A null *effectiveDate* means that a *Node* applies indefinitely from the past. A null *expirationDate* means that a *Node* applies indefinitely into the future.

2.5.5 Example
This template can be difficult to follow, but it is powerful and has a compelling example.

Figure 2.16 shows a model of a management hierarchy where there is no change in structure over time. Figure 2.39 extends the model to track the evolution over time. The model can store the current reporting hierarchy, reporting hierarchies of the past, and planned hierarchies of the future. The hierarchy changes as persons join and leave a company. The hierarchy also changes due to promotions and demotions and management restructuring.

```
SELECT Parent.nodeID AS parentNodeID,
   Parent.nodeName AS parentNodeName
FROM Node AS Child
   INNER JOIN NodeLink AS NL ON Child.nodeID = NL.childNodeID
   INNER JOIN Node AS Parent ON NL.parentNodeID = Parent.nodeID
WHERE Child.nodeID = :aChildNodeID AND
   (Child.effectiveDate IS NULL OR
      :aDate >= Child.effectiveDate) AND
   (Child.expirationDate IS NULL OR
      :aDate <= Child.expirationDate) AND
   (NL.effectiveDate IS NULL OR
      :aDate >= NL.effectiveDate) AND
   (NL.expirationDate IS NULL OR
      :aDate <= NL.expirationDate) AND
   (Parent.effectiveDate IS NULL OR
      :aDate >= Parent.effectiveDate) AND
   (Parent.expirationDate IS NULL OR
      :aDate <= Parent.expirationDate);
```

Figure 2.36 Tree changing over time: SQL query. Find the parent for a child node.

```
SELECT Child.nodeID AS childNodeID,
   Child.nodeName AS childNodeName
FROM Node AS Child
   INNER JOIN NodeLink AS NL ON Child.nodeID = NL.childNodeID
   INNER JOIN Node AS Parent ON NL.parentNodeID = Parent.nodeID
WHERE Parent.nodeID = :aParentNodeID AND
   (Child.effectiveDate IS NULL OR
      :aDate >= Child.effectiveDate) AND
   (Child.expirationDate IS NULL OR
      :aDate <= Child.expirationDate) AND
   (NL.effectiveDate IS NULL OR
      :aDate >= NL.effectiveDate) AND
   (NL.expirationDate IS NULL OR
      :aDate <= NL.expirationDate) AND
   (Parent.effectiveDate IS NULL OR
      :aDate >= Parent.effectiveDate) AND
   (Parent.expirationDate IS NULL OR
      :aDate <= Parent.expirationDate)
ORDER BY Child.nodeName;
```

Figure 2.37 Tree changing over time: SQL query. Find the children for a parent node.

A person may hold multiple positions over time and even two positions at the same time. Thus a person can be manager of one group and an acting manager of another group. The same person may be an individual contributor and a manager during different portions of a

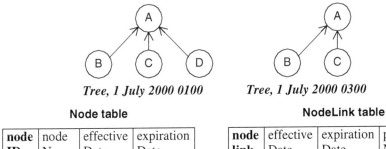

Tree, 1 July 2000 0100   *Tree, 1 July 2000 0300*

Node table

node ID	node Name	effective Date	expiration Date
1	A		
2	B		
3	C		
4	D		1 July 2000 0100

NodeLink table

node link ID	effective Date	expiration Date	parent Node ID	child Node ID
1			1	2
2			1	3
3		1 July 2000 0100	1	4

Figure 2.38 Tree changing over time: Populated tables.

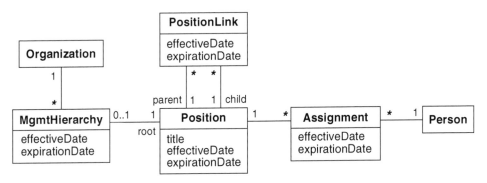

Figure 2.39 Tree changing over time: Evolving management hierarchy model.

career. The actual positions that are available also evolve. *Assignment* is an entity type because a person may hold the same position several times in a career.

The model provides matrix management (whether or not it is desired). This is because the model does not enforce a tree—that a child can only have a single parent at a time. Application code would need to provide such a constraint if it was desired.

2.6 Degenerate Node and Edge Template

2.6.1 UML Template

The degenerate node and edge template (Figure 2.40) is useful when there is a need to store data about the parent–child grouping. I call it *degenerate node and edge* because it is based on the *node and edge* directed graph template presented in the next chapter. This template rarely occurs.

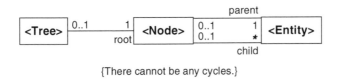

{There cannot be any cycles.}

Figure 2.40 Degenerate node and edge: UML template. Use when you need to store data about the parent–child coupling.

A ***Tree*** is a hierarchy of entities and has one entity as the root. A ***Node*** is a position within a *Tree* and groups one parent *Entity* with all of its child *Entities*. An ***Entity*** is something with identity and data. The sequencing of the *Nodes* of a *Tree* occurs via the couplings to *Entities*. You need not show *Tree* in a use of the template.

In this template, *Nodes* have globally unique names as there is no context for defining the scope of uniqueness.

2.6.2 IDEF1X Template

Figure 2.41 restates Figure 2.40 with the IDEF1X notation. The following are foreign keys: *rootID* references *Node*, *nodeID* references *Node*, and *parentID* references *Entity*.

Figure 2.41 Degenerate node and edge: IDEF1X template.

2.6.3 SQL Queries

Figure 2.42 and Figure 2.43 show SQL queries for common traversals of the template. The colon prefix denotes variable values that must be provided for each query.

```
SELECT Parent.entityID AS parentEntityID,
   Parent.entityName AS parentEntityName
FROM Entity AS Child
   INNER JOIN Node AS N ON Child.nodeID = N.nodeID
   INNER JOIN Entity AS Parent ON N.parentID = Parent.entityID
WHERE Child.entityID = :aChildEntityID;
```

Figure 2.42 Degenerate node and edge: SQL query. Find the parent for a child node.

```
SELECT Child.entityID AS childEntityID,
   Child.entityName AS childEntityName
FROM Entity AS Child
   INNER JOIN Node AS N ON Child.nodeID = N.nodeID
   INNER JOIN Entity AS Parent ON N.parentID = Parent.entityID
WHERE Parent.entityID = :aParentEntityID
ORDER BY Child.entityName;
```

Figure 2.43 Degenerate node and edge: SQL query. Find the children for a parent node.

2.6.4 Sample Populated Tables

Figure 2.44 shows sample tables for the degenerate node and edge template populated with data. The ID values are arbitrary, but internally consistent.

2.6.5 Example

Figure 2.45 uses the degenerate node and edge template in a metamodel of a generalization tree for single inheritance. Each *Generalization* involves one *supertype* and one or more *subtypes*. An *EntityType* may participate in *Generalization* at most once as a *supertype* and at most once as a *subtype*. A *Generalization* may or may not be exhaustive—indicating whether or not every *supertype* record has a corresponding *subtype* record. The *discriminator* is a special *Attribute* that indicates the appropriate *subtype* record for each *supertype* record and may be implicit or explicitly noted in an application model.

In Figure 2.45 there is a need to store data about the parent–child grouping. The diagram notes whether each generalization level is exhaustive and its optional discriminator.

Figure 2.46 shows an excerpt of an application model with one level of generalization illustrating the metamodel. In Figure 2.46 a *ScheduleEntry* can be a *Meeting*, *Appointment*, *Task*, or *Holiday*. The generalization is exhaustive—each *ScheduleEntry* must be exactly one of these four possibilities. *ScheduleEntry* is the supertype and *Meeting*, *Appointment*, *Task*, and *Holiday* are subtypes.

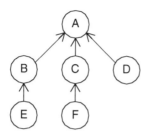

Entity table			Node table	
entityID	entityName	nodeID	**nodeID**	parentID
1	A		**11**	1
2	B	11	**12**	2
3	C	11	**13**	3
4	D	11		
5	E	12		
6	F	13		

Figure 2.44 Degenerate node and edge: Populated tables.

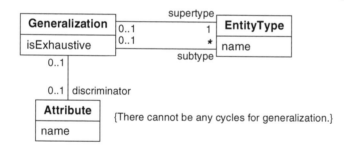

Figure 2.45 Degenerate node and edge: Metamodel for single inheritance.

2.7 Chapter Summary

Trees occur in many application models and are often a critical issue for representation. There are six templates for trees with different trade-offs.

- **Hardcoded tree**. Use when each level of a tree has a different entity type and the sequence of entity types is well known and unlikely to change.
- **Simple tree**. Suffices when tree decomposition is merely a matter of data structure and all nodes are the same.

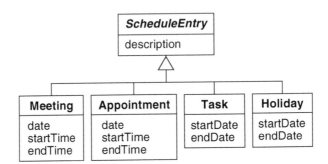

Figure 2.46 Excerpt of data model for calendar application.

- **Structured tree**. Use when branch nodes differ from leaf nodes. For example, the command *dir directoryFileName* elicits a different response from *dir dataFileName*. The structured tree is preferred when branch nodes and leaf nodes have different attributes, relationships, and/or semantics.
- **Overlapping trees**. Use when there are multiple trees and a node can belong to more than one tree.
- **Tree changing over time**. Records the history of a tree. This template permits storing of the past, present, and future content of trees.
- **Degenerate node and edge**. Use when there is data for the parent–child grouping.

Table 2.1 summarizes the tree templates.

Bibliographic Notes

Figure 2.27 was partially motivated by [Fowler-1997], pages 21–22 but is a more powerful template capturing the constraint that a child has one parent for a tree.

References

[Fowler-1997] Martin Fowler. *Analysis Patterns: Reusable Object Models*. Boston, Massachusetts: Addison-Wesley, 1997.

Table 2.1   Summary of the Tree Templates

Template name	Synopsis	UML template	Use when	Frequency
Hardcoded tree	Specifies a sequence of entity types, one for each level of the hierarchy.		A tree's structure is known and the types in the hierarchy are ordered.	Seldom
Simple tree	Restricts nodes to a single tree. Treats all nodes the same.		Tree decomposition is merely a matter of data structure.	Common
Structured tree	Restricts nodes to a single tree. Differentiates leaf nodes from branch nodes.		Branches and leaves have different attributes, relationships, and/or semantics.	Common
Overlapping trees	Permits a node to belong to multiple trees. Treats all nodes the same.		A node can belong to more than one tree.	Occasional
Tree changing over time	Stores multiple variants of a tree. Extract a particular tree by specifying a time.		A tree changes over time and you must store the history.	Occasional
Degenerate node and edge	Groups a parent with its children. The grouping itself can be described.		There is data for the parent–child grouping.	Rare

Note: This table can help you choose among the tree templates.

3

Directed Graph Template

The directed graph is another term from graph theory. A ***directed graph*** is a set of nodes and a set of directed edges. Each directed edge originates at a source node and terminates at a target node (which may be the same as the source node). The nodes of a directed graph can have any number of edges. Directed graphs arise for applications with important topology or connectivity. For example, a directed graph is a natural representation for airline flights between airports.

Figure 3.1 shows two examples of directed graphs.

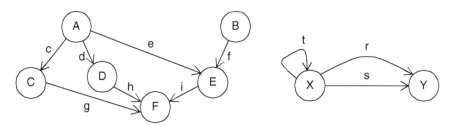

Figure 3.1 Sample directed graphs. A directed graph is a set of nodes and a set of directed edges that connect the nodes.

There are six templates for directed graphs.

- **Simple directed graph**. Similar to the simple tree (Section 2.2) but relaxes multiplicity constraints. Use when edges are unimportant and nodes have the same kind of data.
- **Structured directed graph**. Similar to the structured tree (Section 2.3) but relaxes multiplicity constraints. Use when edges are unimportant.
- **Node and edge directed graph**. Regards nodes and edges as peers. Treats nodes the same. Use when edges are important and have data of their own.

- **Connection directed graph**. Promotes the connection between a node and an edge to an entity type. Treats nodes the same. Use when there is data for the connection itself as well as for nodes and edges.

- **Simple directed graph changing over time**. Stores variants of a directed graph. A particular directed graph can be extracted by specifying a time. Expresses nodes and implies edges. Use when the history of a directed graph must be recorded and edges are unimportant.

- **Node and edge directed graph changing over time**. Stores variants of a directed graph. A particular directed graph can be extracted by specifying a time. Expresses both nodes and edges. Use when the history of a directed graph must be recorded and edges are important.

There appears to be no directed graph counterpart to the *overlapping trees* template.

3.1 Simple Directed Graph Template

3.1.1 UML Template

In the simple directed graph template (Figure 3.2) all nodes have the same kind of data. Figure 3.2 corresponds to the simple tree template and relaxes the multiplicity constraints for the parent and root nodes. A directed graph may have multiple roots and each node may have multiple parents.

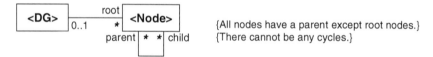

Figure 3.2 Simple directed graph: UML template. Use when edges are
unimportant and nodes have the same kind of data.

    A **DG** (directed graph) is a set of nodes and a set of directed edges that connect nodes. (Note: in a directed graph all the nodes do not have to be connected.) You need not include *DG* in a use of the template. A **Node** is an entity type whose records are organized as a directed graph. The distinction between *parent* and *child* causes the sense of direction that effects directed edges. There can be at most one coupling between a pair of nodes.

    Figure 3.2 adds the constraint that each node has a parent except for root nodes. (The template itself is more permissive and lacks this constraint.) In general, a directed graph may have cycles but this template disallows them. (A cycle starts at a node and after traversing a series of edges reaches the starting node.) Since this template is based on a tree template, it doesn't make sense to permit cycles.

    Each node may have a name. As Figure 3.3 shows, node names can be globally unique (left template) or unique within a context (right template).

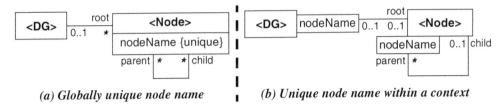

Figure 3.3 Simple directed graph: UML template, with node names. The template has
two variations—globally unique names and unique names within a context.

3.1.2 IDEF1X Template

Figure 3.4 restates Figure 3.3 with the IDEF1X notation. The following are foreign keys:
dgID references *DG*, *childID* references *Node*, *parentID* references *Node*, and *rootID* references *Node*. For brevity, Figure 3.4 omits *DG* data.

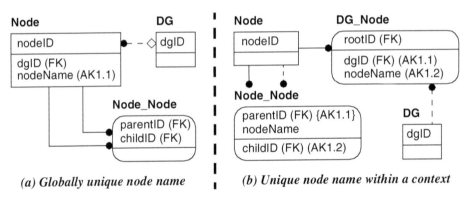

Figure 3.4 Simple directed graph: IDEF1X template.

Figure 3.4b defines *parentID* + *nodeName* as the *Node_Node* primary key. (This is an
arbitrary choice and *parentID* + *childID* could be the primary key instead.) *Node_Node* defines node names for all nodes except for the roots. The root nodes obtain their name from
the combination of *dgID* + *nodeName*. Once again the choice of primary key is arbitrary for
DG_Node and could have been the alternate key instead.

3.1.3 SQL Queries

Figure 3.5 and Figure 3.6 show SQL queries for common traversals of the template. The colon prefix denotes variable values that must be provided for each query.

3.1.4 Sample Populated Tables

Figure 3.7 shows simple directed graph tables populated with data. The ID values are arbitrary, but internally consistent. In accordance with the template, there are no explicit edges;

```
SELECT P.nodeID AS parentNodeID, P.nodeName AS parentNodeName
FROM Node AS Child
    INNER JOIN Node_Node AS NN ON Child.nodeID = NN.childID
    INNER JOIN Node AS P ON NN.parentID = P.nodeID
WHERE Child.nodeID = :aChildNodeID
ORDER BY P.nodeName;
```

Figure 3.5 Simple directed graph: SQL query. Find the parents for a child node.

```
SELECT Child.nodeID AS childNodeID,
    Child.nodeName AS childNodeName
FROM Node AS Child
    INNER JOIN Node_Node AS NN ON Child.nodeID = NN.childID
    INNER JOIN Node AS Parent ON NN.parentID = Parent.nodeID
WHERE Parent.nodeID = :aParentNodeID
ORDER BY Child.nodeName;
```

Figure 3.6 Simple directed graph: SQL query. Find the children for a parent node.

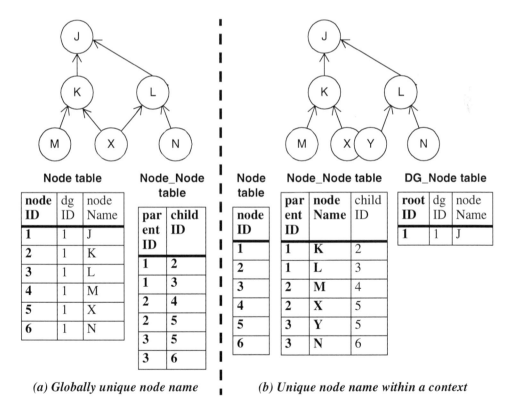

(a) Globally unique node name   *(b) Unique node name within a context*

Figure 3.7 Simple directed graph: Populated tables.

edges are represented via the coupling between nodes. The populated tables use different data than Figure 3.1 because the premise of the template is a tree that is generalized to having multiple parents.

3.1.5 Example

Simple directed graphs occasionally arise.

Figure 3.8 revisits the management hierarchy model of Figure 2.16. Some organizations do not limit their reporting structure to a strict hierarchy and can have subordinates reporting to more than one manager.

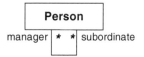

{Every person has a manager except the CEO. The management graph must be acyclic.}

Figure 3.8 Simple directed graph: Matrix management model.

3.2 Structured Directed Graph Template

3.2.1 UML Template

Figure 3.9 shows the UML template for structured directed graphs when there is a need to differentiate leaf nodes from branch nodes. This template is based on the structured tree and relaxes the multiplicity constraints for the parent and root nodes. A directed graph may have multiple roots and each node may have multiple parents.

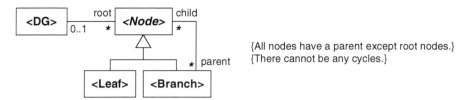

Figure 3.9 Structured directed graph: UML template. Use when edges are unimportant; branch nodes and leaf nodes have different attributes, relationships, and/or semantics.

A **DG** (directed graph) is a set of nodes and a set of directed edges that connect nodes. (Note: in a directed graph all the nodes do not have to be connected.) You need not include *DG* in a use of the template. A **Node** is either a leaf node or a branch node. A **Leaf** node (such as *M*, *X*, and *N* in Figure 3.7a) terminates the recursion. A **Branch** node (such as *J*, *K*, and *L* in Figure 3.7a) can have child nodes each of which in turn can be a leaf node or a further branch node. The distinction between *parent* and *child* causes the sense of direction that effects directed edges. Note that with this template there can be at most one coupling between a pair of nodes.

Figure 3.9 adds the constraint that each node has a parent except for root nodes. (The template itself is more permissive and lacks this constraint.) In general, a directed graph may have cycles but this template disallows them. (A cycle starts at a node and after traversing a series of edges reaches the starting node.) Since this template is based on a tree template, it doesn't make sense to permit cycles.

Each node may have a name. As Figure 3.10 shows, node names can be globally unique (left template) or unique within a context (right template).

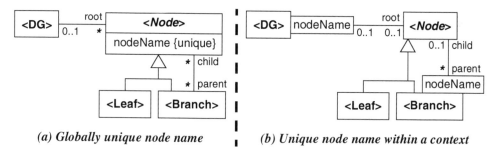

(a) Globally unique node name   (b) Unique node name within a context

Figure 3.10 Structured directed graph: UML template, with node names.
There are two variations of the template—globally unique names and unique names within a context.

3.2.2 IDEF1X Template

Figure 3.11 restates Figure 3.10 with the IDEF1X notation. The following are foreign keys: *dgID* references *DG*, *rootID* references *Node*, *parentID* references *Branch*, *childID* references *Node*, *leafID* references *Node*, and *branchID* references *Node*. The generalization is exhaustive—every *Node* record must have a corresponding *Leaf* record or *Branch* record. The *nodeDiscrim* field is an enumeration with values "Leaf" and "Branch" indicating the subtype record.

Figure 3.11b defines *parentID* + *nodeName* as the *Node_Branch* primary key, but *parentID* + *childID* could be the primary key instead. *Node_Branch* defines node names for all nodes except for the roots. The root nodes obtain their name from the combination of *dgID* + *nodeName*. Once again the choice of primary key is arbitrary for *DG_Node* and could have been the alternate key instead.

3.2.3 SQL Queries

Figure 3.12 and Figure 3.13 show SQL queries for common traversals of the template. The colon prefix denotes variable values that must be provided for each query.

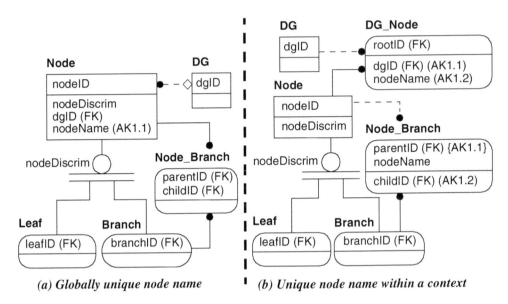

(a) Globally unique node name | *(b) Unique node name within a context*

Figure 3.11 Structured directed graph: IDEF1X template.

```
SELECT Parent.nodeID AS parentNodeID,
    Parent.nodeName AS parentNodeName
FROM Node AS Child
    INNER JOIN Node_Branch AS NB ON Child.nodeID = NB.childID
    INNER JOIN Branch AS B ON NB.parentID = B.branchID
    INNER JOIN Node AS Parent ON B.branchID = Parent.nodeID
WHERE Child.nodeID = :aChildNodeID
ORDER BY Parent.nodeName;
```

Figure 3.12 Structured directed graph: SQL query. Find the parents for a child node.

```
SELECT Child.nodeID AS childNodeID,
    Child.nodeName AS childNodeName
FROM Node AS Child
    INNER JOIN Node_Branch AS NB ON Child.nodeID = NB.childID
    INNER JOIN Branch AS B ON NB.parentID = B.branchID
    INNER JOIN Node AS Parent ON B.branchID = Parent.nodeID
WHERE Parent.nodeID = :aParentNodeID
ORDER BY Child.nodeName;
```

Figure 3.13 Structured directed graph: SQL query. Find the children for a parent node.

3.2.4 Sample Populated Tables

Figure 3.14 shows structured directed graph tables populated with data. The ID values are arbitrary, but internally consistent. In accordance with the template, there are no explicit edges; edges are represented via the coupling between nodes. The populated tables use different data than Figure 3.1 because the premise of the template is a tree that is generalized to having multiple parents.

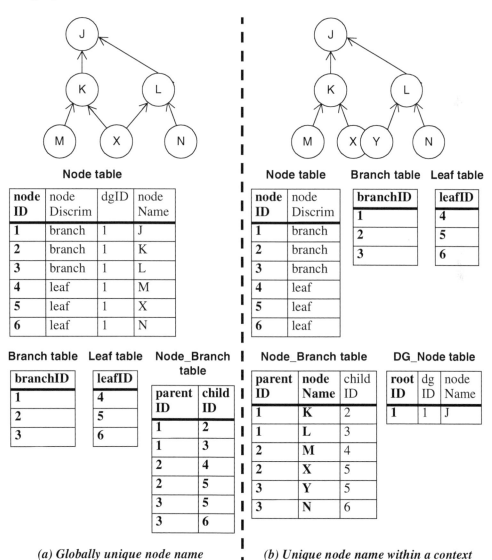

(a) Globally unique node name

Node table

node ID	node Discrim	dgID	node Name
1	branch	1	J
2	branch	1	K
3	branch	1	L
4	leaf	1	M
5	leaf	1	X
6	leaf	1	N

Branch table

branchID
1
2
3

Leaf table

leafID
4
5
6

Node_Branch table

parent ID	child ID
1	2
1	3
2	4
2	5
3	5
3	6

(b) Unique node name within a context

Node table

node ID	node Discrim
1	branch
2	branch
3	branch
4	leaf
5	leaf
6	leaf

Branch table

branchID
1
2
3

Leaf table

leafID
4
5
6

Node_Branch table

parent ID	node Name	child ID
1	K	2
1	L	3
2	M	4
2	X	5
3	Y	5
3	N	6

DG_Node table

root ID	dg ID	node Name
1	1	J

Figure 3.14 Structured directed graph: Populated tables.

3.2.5 Examples

Directed graphs often arise in applications and sometimes the structured directed graph is a good choice.

Figure 3.15 revisits the file directory model of Figure 2.26. With a UNIX^{TM} file directory a hierarchy no longer suffices because a file can belong to multiple directories via symbolic links. A file may have a different name in each directory where it is referenced.

Figure 3.15 Structured directed graph: File system directory model.

In Figure 3.15 a *File* may be a *DataFile* or a *DirectoryFile*. Directories contain multiple files, some or all of which may be subdirectories. The combination of a *DirectoryFile* and a *fileName* yields a specific *File*—file names are unique within the context of a directory. All *Files* belong to one or more directories except for the *root File*. Directories can be nested to an arbitrary depth, with *DataFiles* and empty *DirectoryFiles* terminating the recursion. Files require an acyclic graph, so the model has an added constraint. (The term "acyclic" means that you cannot start with a file and traverse some sequence of files and reach the starting file.)

Web email services (such as Yahoo, Google, and Hotmail) let users define lists that group together email addresses. Although most services don't support it, there is no reason why a list could not contain lesser lists. In Figure 3.16 the *friends* list contains the *family* list, the *colleagues* list, and additional email addresses. Bill P and Paul B belong to both the *friends* and *colleagues* lists. Figure 3.17 models nested email address lists. For this example, names are globally unique and do not vary by context.

friends list	family list	colleagues list
family list	Jim B	Bill P
colleagues list	Barb B	Paul B
Mike E	Ron B	Serge T
Ed S	Karen B	Neil C
Mark L	Jean B	
Bill P		
Paul B		

Figure 3.16 Sample data for email address lists.

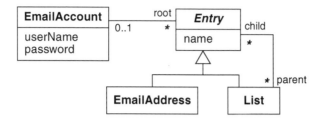

Figure 3.17 Structured directed graph: Nested email address list model.

3.3 Node and Edge Directed Graph Template

3.3.1 UML Template

A third template for directed graphs has explicit edges (Figure 3.18). Nodes and the edges that connect them can both bear information.

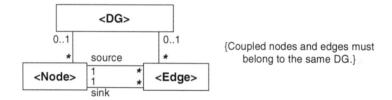

Figure 3.18 Node– and edge–directed graph: UML template. Use when there is data for edges as well as nodes.

Figure 3.2 and Figure 3.9 describe directed graphs with at most one edge between nodes; edges are implicitly represented by *parent–child* relationships. Figure 3.18 is more powerful and can describe any directed graph.

A *DG* (directed graph) is a set of nodes and a set of directed edges that connect nodes. (Note: in a directed graph all nodes do not have to be connected.) You need not show *DG* in a use of the template. A *Node* is an entity type whose records are organized as a directed graph. An *Edge* is a coupling from a *source Node* to a *sink Node*. Coupled nodes and edges must belong to the same directed graph.

Note that this template permits cycles. In practice, some applications of the template permit cycles and others do not.

With this template the names of nodes and edges are globally unique. There is no context to provide an alternative approach to naming.

3.3.2 IDEF1X Template

Figure 3.19 restates Figure 3.18 with the IDEF1X notation. The following are foreign keys: *dgID* references *DG, sourceNodeID* references *Node,* and *sinkNodeID* references *Node*.

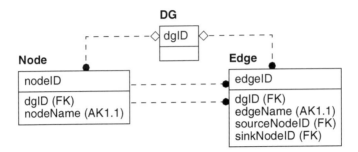

Figure 3.19 Node and edge directed graph: IDEF1X template.

3.3.3 SQL Queries

Figure 3.20, Figure 3.21, and Figure 3.22 show SQL queries for common traversals of the template. The colon prefix denotes variable values that must be provided for each query.

```
SELECT E.edgeID, E.edgeName
FROM Edge AS E
    INNER JOIN Node AS Source ON E.sourceNodeID = Source.nodeID
WHERE Source.nodeID = :aSourceNodeID
ORDER BY E.edgeName;
```

Figure 3.20 Node and edge directed graph: SQL query. Find the edges
that originate from a node.

```
SELECT E.edgeID, E.edgeName
FROM Edge AS E
    INNER JOIN Node AS Sink ON E.sinkNodeID = Sink.nodeID
WHERE Sink.nodeID = :aSinkNodeID
ORDER BY E.edgeName;
```

Figure 3.21 Node and edge directed graph: SQL query. Find the edges
that terminate at a node.

```
SELECT Src.nodeID AS srcNodeID, Src.nodeName AS srcNodeName,
    Sink.nodeID AS sinkNodeID, Sink.nodeName AS sinkNodeName
FROM Edge AS E
    INNER JOIN Node AS Src ON E.sourceNodeID = Src.nodeID
    INNER JOIN Node AS Sink ON E.sinkNodeID = Sink.nodeID
WHERE E.edgeID = :anEdgeID;
```

Figure 3.22 Node and edge directed graph: SQL query. Find the
source and sink nodes for an edge.

3.3.4 Sample Populated Tables

Figure 3.23 and Figure 3.24 show node and edge directed graph tables populated with data. The values of the IDs are arbitrary, but internally consistent.

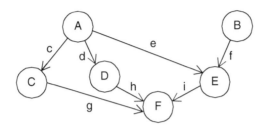

Node table

node ID	dgID	node Name
1	1	A
2	1	B
3	1	C
4	1	D
5	1	E
6	1	F

Edge table

edgeID	dgID	edgeName	sourceNodeID	sinkNodeID
51	1	c	1	3
52	1	d	1	4
53	1	e	1	5
54	1	f	2	5
55	1	g	3	6
56	1	h	4	6
57	1	i	5	6

Figure 3.23 Node and edge directed graph: Populated tables.

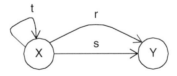

Node table

node ID	dgID	node Name
11	2	X
12	2	Y

Edge table

edgeID	dgID	edgeName	sourceNodeID	sinkNodeID
61	2	r	11	12
62	2	s	11	12
63	2	t	11	11

Figure 3.24 Node and edge directed graph: Populated tables.

3.3.5 Examples

The node and edge directed graph is the most common representation. Figure 3.25 shows an example for published flights.

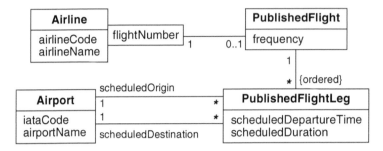

Figure 3.25 Node and edge directed graph: Airline flight model.

Airlines operate flights between airports. A *PublishedFlight* refers to the published description of air travel between two airports. The *frequency* indicates the days of the week for which the *PublishedFlight* applies. A *PublishedFlight* consists of a sequence of *PublishedFlightLegs* that describe the travel from airport to airport.

Figure 3.26 shows an excerpt of a model for supply chain tracing for food manufacture. The application traces foodstuffs (*MaterialLots*) as they proceed from the farm to manufacturers, distributors, and eventually the marketplace (various *SupplyChainStages*). Using the node and edge template, intervening *MaterialLots* connect a network of *SupplyChainStages*.

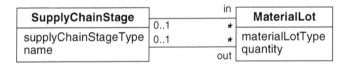

Figure 3.26 Node and edge directed graph: Supply chain tracing model.

A *SupplyChainStage* may have any number of *MaterialLots* as input and any number as output. A *MaterialLot* may enter and exit at most one *SupplyChainStage*. Although the model does not enforce it (application code must enforce it), the entering and exiting *MaterialLot* for a *SupplyChainStage* must be different.

3.4 Connection Directed Graph Template

3.4.1 UML Template

Figure 3.27 elaborates the node and edge template, promoting the connection between nodes and edges to an entity type. Figure 3.27, as stated, does not permit unconnected *Nodes*. You could add a relationship between *DG* and *Node* if unconnected *Nodes* were important.

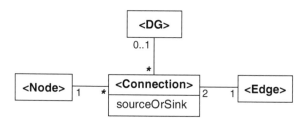

Figure 3.27 Connection directed graph: UML template. Use when it is important to store data about the connection itself.

A **DG** (directed graph) is a set of nodes and a set of directed edges that connect nodes. You need not show *DG* in a use of the template. A **Node** is an entity type whose records are organized as a directed graph. An **Edge** is a coupling from a *source Node* to a *sink Node*. A **Connection** is the linking between a *Node* and an *Edge*. Each *Connection* may be a source or a sink.

With this template the names of nodes and edges are globally unique. There is no context to provide an alternative approach to naming.

Figure 3.27 lacks the constraint that nodes and edges may only have connections for one directed graph. The template also lacks the constraint that an edge must have one source node and one sink node.

3.4.2 IDEF1X Template

Figure 3.28 restates Figure 3.27 with the IDEF1X notation. The following are foreign keys: *dgID* references *DG*, *nodeID* references *Node*, and *edgeID* references *Edge*.

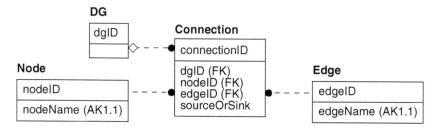

Figure 3.28 Connection directed graph: IDEF1X template.

3.4.3 SQL Queries

Figure 3.29, Figure 3.30, and Figure 3.31 show SQL queries for common traversals of the template. The colon prefix denotes variable values that must be provided for each query.

```
SELECT E.edgeID, E.edgeName
FROM Edge AS E
    INNER JOIN Connection AS C ON E.edgeID = C.edgeID AND
        C.sourceOrSink = 'source'
    INNER JOIN Node AS Source ON C.nodeID = Source.nodeID
WHERE Source.nodeID = :aSourceNodeID
ORDER BY E.edgeName;
```

Figure 3.29 Connection directed graph: SQL query. Find the edges
that originate from a node.

```
SELECT E.edgeID, E.edgeName
FROM Edge AS E
    INNER JOIN Connection AS C ON E.edgeID = C.edgeID AND
        C.sourceOrSink = 'sink'
    INNER JOIN Node AS Sink ON C.nodeID = Sink.nodeID
WHERE Sink.nodeID = :aSinkNodeID
ORDER BY E.edgeName;
```

Figure 3.30 Connection directed graph: SQL query. Find the edges
that terminate at a node.

```
SELECT Source.nodeID AS sourceNodeID,
    Source.nodeName AS sourceNodeName,
    Sink.nodeID AS sinkNodeID,
    Sink.nodeName AS sinkNodeName
FROM Edge AS E
    INNER JOIN Connection AS C1 ON E.edgeID = C1.edgeID AND
        C1.sourceOrSink = 'source'
    INNER JOIN Node AS Source ON C1.nodeID = Source.nodeID
    INNER JOIN Connection AS C2 ON E.edgeID = C2.edgeID AND
        C2.sourceOrSink = 'sink'
    INNER JOIN Node AS Sink ON C2.nodeID = Sink.nodeID
WHERE E.edgeID = :anEdgeID
```

Figure 3.31 Connection directed graph: SQL query. Find the source
and sink nodes for an edge.

3.4.4 Sample Populated Tables

Figure 3.32 and Figure 3.33 show connection directed graph tables populated with data. The
values of the IDs are arbitrary, but internally consistent. For brevity, the *Connection* tables
omit the *dgID* column.

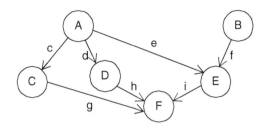

Node table		Edge table		Connection table				Connection table (cont)			
node ID	node Name	**edge ID**	edge Name	**connec tionID**	node ID	edge ID	source OrSink	**connec tionID**	node ID	edge ID	source OrSink
1	A	**51**	c	**1**	1	51	source	**8**	5	54	sink
2	B	**52**	d	**2**	3	51	sink	**9**	3	55	source
3	C	**53**	e	**3**	1	52	source	**10**	6	55	sink
4	D	**54**	f	**4**	4	52	sink	**11**	4	56	source
5	E	**55**	g	**5**	1	53	source	**12**	6	56	sink
6	F	**56**	h	**6**	5	53	sink	**13**	5	57	source
		57	i	**7**	2	54	source	**14**	6	57	sink

Figure 3.32 Connection directed graph: Populated tables.

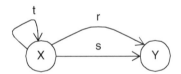

Node table		Edge table		Connection table				Connection table (cont)			
node ID	node Name	**edge ID**	edge Name	**connec tionID**	node ID	edge ID	source OrSink	**connec tionID**	node ID	edge ID	source OrSink
11	X	**61**	r	**21**	11	61	source	**24**	12	62	sink
12	Y	**62**	s	**22**	12	61	sink	**25**	11	63	source
		63	t	**23**	11	62	source	**26**	11	63	sink

Figure 3.33 Connection directed graph: Populated tables.

3.4.5 Example

The connection template is sometimes helpful for representing directed graphs as Figure 3.34 illustrates. A manufacturing plant can have a variety of equipment that is connected by piping. Nozzles connect piping to equipment and have a direction of normal fluid flow.

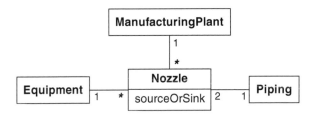

Figure 3.34 Connection directed graph: Equipment and piping model.

3.5 Simple DG Changing over Time Template

There are two templates for directed graphs that can change over time. The first (this section) is based on the simple directed graph. The second (next section) is based on the node and edge directed graph. It is also possible to extend the connection template for variations over time, but I have never seen it used in practice.

3.5.1 UML Template

The template for simple directed graphs that change over time (Figure 3.35) is similar to the tree template in Section 2.5. Figure 3.35 separates an entity from its directed graph position (node) because the timeline for an entity can differ from that of its involvement in a graph.

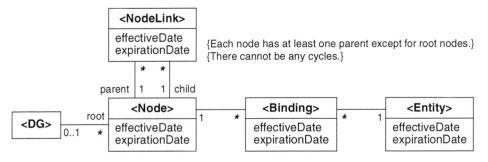

Figure 3.35 Simple directed graph changing over time: UML template.
Use when edges are unimportant and history must be recorded.

A **DG** (directed graph) is a set of nodes and a set of directed edges that connect nodes. (Note: in a directed graph all the nodes do not have to be connected.) You need not show *DG* in a use of the template. A **Node** is a position within a directed graph. The distinction between *parent* and *child* causes the sense of direction that effects directed edges.

Figure 3.35 adds the constraint that each node has at least one parent except for root nodes. (The template itself is more permissive and lacks this constraint.) In general, a directed graph may have cycles but this template disallows them. (A cycle starts at a node and after traversing a series of edges reaches the starting node.) Since this template is based on a tree template, it doesn't make sense to permit cycles.

This template is already complex, so it is best to handle node names in a simple manner. Each node has a globally unique name and there is no provision to vary node name by context. The effective and expiration dates permit *Node* and *Entity* data to vary over time.

3.5.2 IDEF1X Template

Figure 3.36 restates Figure 3.35 with the IDEF1X notation. The following are foreign keys: *dgID* references *DG*, *nodeID* references *Node*, *entityID* references *Entity*, *parentNodeID* references *Node*, and *childNodeID* references *Node*.

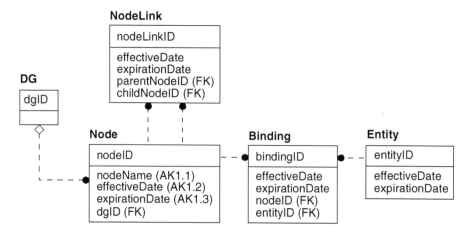

Figure 3.36 Simple directed graph changing over time: IDEF1X template.

In Figure 3.36 the node name can change over time (three part candidate key—*nodeName* + *effectiveDate* + *expirationDate*), but the node name could also be invariant over time (candidate key of *nodeName* alone). Note that the handling of time reflects a limitation of relational DBMSs. It would be better to use time intervals but most relational DBMSs only support points in time.

3.5.3 SQL Queries

Figure 3.37 and Figure 3.38 show SQL queries for common traversals of the template. The colon prefix denotes variable values that must be provided for each query.

```
SELECT Parent.nodeID AS parentNodeID,
    Parent.nodeName AS parentNodeName
FROM Node AS Child
    INNER JOIN NodeLink AS NL ON Child.nodeID = NL.childNodeID
    INNER JOIN Node AS Parent ON NL.parentNodeID = Parent.nodeID
WHERE Child.nodeID = :aChildNodeID AND
    (Child.effectiveDate IS NULL OR
        :aDate >= Child.effectiveDate) AND
    (Child.expirationDate IS NULL OR
        :aDate <= Child.expirationDate) AND
    (NL.effectiveDate IS NULL OR
        :aDate >= NL.effectiveDate) AND
    (NL.expirationDate IS NULL OR
        :aDate <= NL.expirationDate) AND
    (Parent.effectiveDate IS NULL OR
        :aDate >= Parent.effectiveDate) AND
    (Parent.expirationDate IS NULL OR
        :aDate <= Parent.expirationDate)
ORDER BY Parent.nodeName;
```

Figure 3.37 Simple directed graph changing over time: SQL query.
Find the parents for a child node.

```
SELECT Child.nodeID AS childNodeID,
    Child.nodeName AS childNodeName
FROM Node AS Child
    INNER JOIN NodeLink AS NL ON Child.nodeID = NL.childNodeID
    INNER JOIN Node AS Parent ON NL.parentNodeID = Parent.nodeID
WHERE Parent.nodeID = :aParentNodeID AND
    (Child.effectiveDate IS NULL OR
        :aDate >= Child.effectiveDate) AND
    (Child.expirationDate IS NULL OR
        :aDate <= Child.expirationDate) AND
    (NL.effectiveDate IS NULL OR
        :aDate >= NL.effectiveDate) AND
    (NL.expirationDate IS NULL OR
        :aDate <= NL.expirationDate) AND
    (Parent.effectiveDate IS NULL OR
        :aDate >= Parent.effectiveDate) AND
    (Parent.expirationDate IS NULL OR
        :aDate <= Parent.expirationDate)
ORDER BY Child.nodeName;
```

Figure 3.38 Simple directed graph changing over time: SQL query.
Find the children for a parent node.

3.5.4 Sample Populated Tables

Figure 3.39 shows tables populated with data for the simple directed graph changing over time. The values of the IDs are arbitrary, but internally consistent. A null *effectiveDate* means that a *Node* applies indefinitely from the past. A null *expirationDate* means that a *Node* applies indefinitely into the future. In accordance with the template, there are no explicit edges and edges are represented via the coupling between nodes.

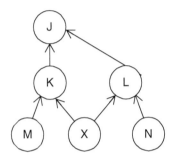

Directed graph, 1 July 2000 0100

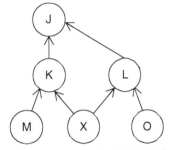

Directed graph, 1 July 2000 0300

Node table

node ID	node Name	effective Date	expiration Date
1	J		
2	K		
3	L		
4	M		
5	X		
6	N		1 July 2000 0100
7	O	1 July 2000 0300	

NodeLink table

node link ID	effective Date	expiration Date	parent Node ID	child Node ID
1			1	2
2			1	3
3			2	4
4			2	5
5			3	5
6		1 July 2000 0100	3	6
7	1 July 2000 0300		3	7

Figure 3.39 Simple directed graph changing over time: Populated tables.

As in Section 3.1, the template cannot express directed graphs with multiple edges between a pair of nodes. For brevity, the *Node* table omits the *dgID* column. This simple example does not populate *Binding* and *Entity*.

3.5.5 Example

Figure 3.40 revisits the example from Section 2.5. The management structure can be a matrix, instead of a simple hierarchy; then a person can report to more than one manager at the same time. For example, a chief information officer may report to both the chief operating officer and chief financial officer. The model can store the current reporting structure, reporting structures of the past, and planned structures of the future. The structure changes as persons join and leave a company. The structure also changes due to promotions and demotions and management changes.

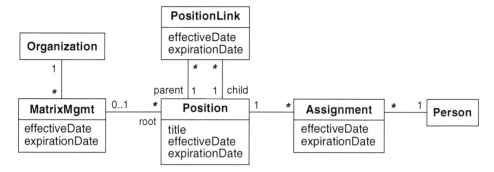

Figure 3.40 Simple DG changing over time: Evolving matrix management model.

3.6 Node and Edge DG Changing over Time Template

This template adds time intervals to the *Node* and *Edge* entity types from Section 3.3.

3.6.1 UML Template

Figure 3.41 shows the template for node and edge directed graphs that change over time. Unlike the simple directed graph changing over time, Figure 3.41 does not separate an entity from its position in a directed graph. It is not clear how to make such a distinction with nodes and edges as peer concepts; I have not needed such a distinction in practice.

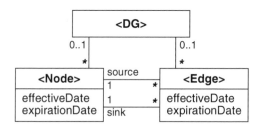

Figure 3.41 Node and edge directed graph changing over time: UML template.
Use when there is data for edges and history must be recorded.

A **DG** (directed graph) is a set of nodes and a set of directed edges that connect nodes. (Note: in a directed graph all the nodes need not be connected.) You need not show *DG* in a use of the template. A **Node** is an entity type whose records are organized as a directed graph. An **Edge** is a coupling from a *source Node* to a *sink Node*.

With this template the names of nodes and edges are globally unique. There is no context to provide an alternative approach to naming.

3.6.2 IDEF1X Template

Figure 3.42 restates Figure 3.41 with the IDEF1X notation. The following are foreign keys: *dgID* references *DG*, *sourceNodeID* references *Node,* and *sinkNodeID* references *Node*. Similar to Section 3.5, we allow node and edge names to change over time.

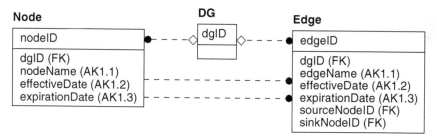

Figure 3.42 Node and edge directed graph changing over time: IDEF1X template.

3.6.3 SQL Queries

Figure 3.43, Figure 3.44, and Figure 3.45 show SQL queries for common traversals of the template. The colon prefix denotes variable values that must be provided for each query.

```
SELECT E.edgeID, E.edgeName
FROM Edge AS E
    INNER JOIN Node AS Source ON E.sourceNodeID = Source.nodeID
WHERE Source.nodeID = :aSourceNodeID AND
    (E.effectiveDate IS NULL OR
        :aDate >= E.effectiveDate) AND
    (E.expirationDate IS NULL OR
        :aDate <= E.expirationDate) AND
    (Source.effectiveDate IS NULL OR
        :aDate >= Source.effectiveDate) AND
    (Source.expirationDate IS NULL OR
        :aDate <= Source.expirationDate)
ORDER BY E.edgeName;
```

Figure 3.43 Node and edge directed graph changing over time: SQL query.
Find the edges that originate from a node.

```
SELECT E.edgeID, E.edgeName
FROM Edge AS E
    INNER JOIN Node AS Sink ON E.sinkNodeID = Sink.nodeID
WHERE Sink.nodeID = :aSinkNodeID AND
    (E.effectiveDate IS NULL OR
        :aDate >= E.effectiveDate) AND
    (E.expirationDate IS NULL OR
        :aDate <= E.expirationDate) AND
    (Sink.effectiveDate IS NULL OR
        :aDate >= Sink.effectiveDate) AND
    (Sink.expirationDate IS NULL OR
        :aDate <= Sink.expirationDate)
ORDER BY E.edgeName;
```

Figure 3.44 Node and edge directed graph changing over time: SQL query.
Find the edges that terminate at a node.

```
SELECT Source.nodeID AS sourceNodeID,
    Source.nodeName AS sourceNodeName,
    Sink.nodeID AS sinkNodeID,
    Sink.nodeName AS sinkNodeName
FROM Edge AS E
    INNER JOIN Node AS Source ON E.sourceNodeID = Source.nodeID
    INNER JOIN Node AS Sink ON E.sinkNodeID = Sink.nodeID
WHERE E.edgeID = :anEdgeID AND
    (E.effectiveDate IS NULL OR
        :aDate >= E.effectiveDate) AND
    (E.expirationDate IS NULL OR
        :aDate <= E.expirationDate) AND
    (Source.effectiveDate IS NULL OR
        :aDate >= Source.effectiveDate) AND
    (Source.expirationDate IS NULL OR
        :aDate <= Source.expirationDate) AND
    (Sink.effectiveDate IS NULL OR
        :aDate >= Sink.effectiveDate) AND
    (Sink.expirationDate IS NULL OR
        :aDate <= Sink.expirationDate);
```

Figure 3.45 Node and edge directed graph changing over time: SQL query.
Find the source and sink nodes for an edge.

3.6.4 Sample Populated Tables

Figure 3.46 shows tables populated with data for the node and edge directed graph changing
over time. The values of the IDs are arbitrary, but internally consistent. A null *effectiveDate*

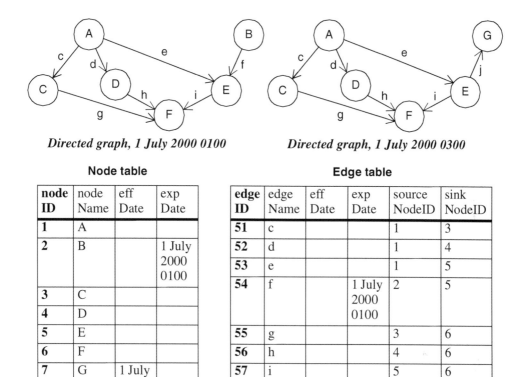

Directed graph, 1 July 2000 0100   Directed graph, 1 July 2000 0300

Node table

node ID	node Name	eff Date	exp Date
1	A		
2	B		1 July 2000 0100
3	C		
4	D		
5	E		
6	F		
7	G	1 July 2000 0300	

Edge table

edge ID	edge Name	eff Date	exp Date	source NodeID	sink NodeID
51	c			1	3
52	d			1	4
53	e			1	5
54	f		1 July 2000 0100	2	5
55	g			3	6
56	h			4	6
57	i			5	6
58	j	1 July 2000 0300		5	7

Figure 3.46 Node and edge directed graph changing over time: Populated tables.

means that a *Node* applies indefinitely from the past. A null *expirationDate* means that a *Node* applies indefinitely into the future. For brevity, the *Node* and *Edge* tables omit the *dgID* column.

3.6.5 *Examples*

This template is often the best way to handle a directed graph that changes over time. Figure 3.47 takes the airline flight model from Figure 3.25 and extends it for time. The revised model can store the scheduled flights of the past as well as those planned for the future. The example adds time variance to the edges (*PublishedFlight* + *PublishedFlightLeg*) but the nodes (*Airports*) can also vary by time if that is desirable.

Figure 3.48 shows a simple model for *CurrencyConversion*. Examples of *Currency* include U.S. dollars, Euros, and Japanese Yen. There is an *exchangeRate* for a *source Currency* to a *target Currency* in effect for some time interval.

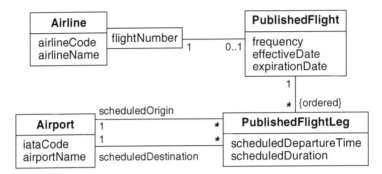

Figure 3.47 Node and edge directed graph changing over time: Airline flight model.

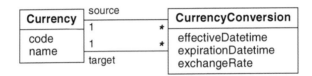

Figure 3.48 Node and edge directed graph: Currency conversion model.

3.7 Chapter Summary

Directed graphs occur in many application models and are often a critical issue for representation. There are six templates for directed graphs with different trade-offs.

- **Simple directed graph.** Suffices when edges are unimportant and nodes have the same kind of data.
- **Structured directed graph.** Use when edges are unimportant and branch nodes differ from leaf nodes. For example, the command *dir directoryFileName* elicits a different response from *dir dataFileName*. The structured directed graph is also preferred when branch nodes and leaf nodes have different attributes, relationships, and/or semantics.
- **Node and edge directed graph.** Use when there is data for edges as well as nodes.
- **Connection directed graph.** Use when there is data for the connection itself as well as nodes and edges.
- **Simple directed graph changing over time.** Use when edges are unimportant and the history of a directed graph must be recorded.
- **Node and edge directed graph changing over time.** Use when there is data for edges and the history of a directed graph must be recorded.

Table 3.1 summarizes the directed graph templates.

Table 3.1   Summary of the Directed Graph Templates

Template name	Synopsis	UML template	Use when	Frequency
Simple DG	Treats all nodes the same.		Edges are unimportant; nodes have the same kind of data. The DG is acyclic.	Occasional
Structured DG	Differentiates leaf nodes from branch nodes.		Edges are unimportant; branch nodes and leaf nodes have different data. The DG is acyclic.	Occasional
Node and edge DG	Treats nodes and edges as peers.		Nodes and edges can both have data; there can be multiple edges between a pair of nodes.	Common
Connection DG	Promotes the connection between a node and an edge to an entity type.		There is data for the connection itself as well as for nodes and edges.	Occasional
Simple DG changing over time	Stores multiple variants of a DG. Extract a particular DG by specifying a time.		A DG changes over time; edges are unimportant. The DG is acyclic.	Seldom
Node and edge DG changing over time	Stores multiple variants of a DG. Extract a particular DG by specifying a time.		A DG changes over time; edges are important.	Occasional

Note: This table can help you choose among the directed graph templates.

Bibliographic Notes

Page 89 of [Hay-1996] has an example of projects that involve the node and edge directed graph.

References

[Hay-1996] David C. Hay. *Data Model Patterns: Conventions of Thought*. New York, New York: Dorsett House, 1996.

4

Undirected Graph Template

The undirected graph is also a term from graph theory. An ***undirected graph*** is a set of nodes and a set of edges. Each edge connects two nodes (which may be the same). The nodes of an undirected graph can have any number of edges. Undirected graphs arise for applications with important topology or connectivity. For example, the network of members on the LinkedIn Web site is an undirected graph.

Figure 4.1 shows two examples of undirected graphs.

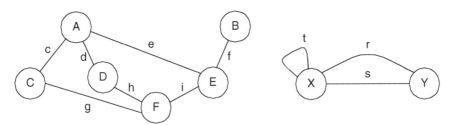

Figure 4.1 Sample undirected graphs. An undirected graph is a set of nodes and a set of edges that connect the nodes.

There are three templates for undirected graphs.

- **Node and edge undirected graph**. Regards nodes and edges as peers. Use as the default template when there are no edges that connect to the same node.
- **Connection undirected graph**. Promotes the connection between a node and an edge to an entity type. Use when there is data for the connection itself.
- **Undirected graph changing over time**. Stores variants of a node and edge undirected graph. A particular undirected graph can be extracted by specifying a time. Use when the history of an undirected graph must be recorded.

There is no undirected graph counterpart to the *simple* and *structured* templates of directed graphs. The simple counterpart violates the symmetry antipattern (see Chapter 8). The structured counterpart shares a similar flaw as it is not clear which end of an edge should be the parent and which should be the child. In principle, it would be possible to add time intervals to the connection template, but we have never seen a need for this in practice.

4.1 Node and Edge Undirected Graph Template

4.1.1 UML Template

Figure 4.2 shows the UML template for node and edge undirected graphs.

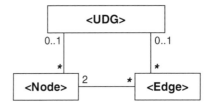

Figure 4.2 Node and edge undirected graph: UML template. Use as the default template when no edges connect to the same node.

A *UDG* (undirected graph) is a set of nodes and a set of edges that connect nodes. (Note: in an undirected graph all nodes do not have to be connected.) You need not show *UDG* in a use of the template. A *Node* is an entity type whose records are organized as an undirected graph. An *Edge* is a coupling between *Nodes*.

With this template the names of nodes and edges are globally unique. There is no context to provide an alternative approach to naming.

Figure 4.2 lacks the constraint that related nodes and edges must all belong to the same undirected graph. The template also cannot handle edges that connect twice to the same node (the "2" in Figure 4.2 refers to two different nodes); use the connection undirected graph if an edge connects twice to the same node.

4.1.2 IDEF1X Template

Figure 4.3 restates Figure 4.2 with the IDEF1X notation. The following are foreign keys: *udgID* references *UDG*, *edgeID* references *Edge*, and *nodeID* references *Node*. The "2" multiplicity in Figure 4.2 becomes "many" multiplicity in a database design.

4.1.3 SQL Queries

Figure 4.4 and Figure 4.5 show SQL queries for common traversals of the template. The colon prefix denotes variable values that must be provided for each query.

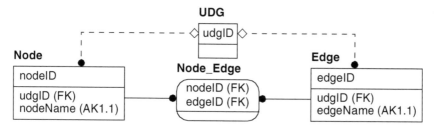

Figure 4.3 **Node and edge undirected graph: IDEF1X template**.

```
SELECT E.edgeID, E.edgeName
FROM Node as N
    INNER JOIN Node_Edge AS NE ON N.nodeID = NE.nodeID
    INNER JOIN Edge AS E ON NE.edgeID = E.edgeID
WHERE N.nodeID = :aNodeID
ORDER BY E.edgeName;
```

Figure 4.4 Node and edge undirected graph: SQL query. Find the edges for a node.

```
SELECT N.nodeID, N.nodeName
FROM Edge AS E
    INNER JOIN Node_Edge AS NE ON E.edgeID = NE.edgeID
    INNER JOIN Node AS N ON NE.nodeID = N.nodeID
WHERE E.edgeID = :anEdgeID
ORDER BY N.nodeName;
```

Figure 4.5 Node and edge undirected graph: SQL query. Find the nodes for an edge.

4.1.4 Sample Populated Tables

Figure 4.6 shows node and edge undirected graph tables populated with data. The values of the IDs are arbitrary, but internally consistent.

4.1.5 Examples

Undirected graphs occur only occasionally and when they occur, the node and edge template is often appropriate.

The LinkedIn Web site is popular for professional networking. Members can connect to other members and find those who are closely connected via intermediate colleagues. Such contacts can be useful for seeking employers, seeking employees, and sharing information. An undirected graph is the proper representation because there is a lack of direction in connections between members. It does not matter who initiated the contact; all that matters is that pairs of members are connected. Furthermore, it makes no sense for a member to connect to himself or herself. Thus the limitation of the node and edge template is not a problem.

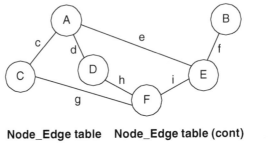

Node table				Node_Edge table			Node_Edge table (cont)			Edge table		

node ID	node Name	udg ID
1	A	1
2	B	1
3	C	1
4	D	1
5	E	1
6	F	1

node ID	edge ID
1	51
3	51
1	52
4	52
1	53
5	53
2	54

node ID	edge ID
5	54
3	55
6	55
4	56
6	56
5	57
6	57

edge ID	edge Name	udg ID
51	c	1
52	d	1
53	e	1
54	f	1
55	g	1
56	h	1
57	i	1

Figure 4.6 Node and edge undirected graph: Populated tables.

Figure 4.7 shows a model for the LinkedIn network using the node and edge undirected graph template. The LinkedIn Web site manages extensive data about members that Figure 4.7 does not show as the emphasis is on the template.

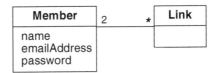

Figure 4.7 Node and edge undirected graph: Personal networking model.

4.2 Connection Undirected Graph Template

4.2.1 UML Template

Figure 4.8 elaborates the node and edge template, promoting the connection between nodes and edges to an entity type. Figure 4.8, as stated, does not permit unconnected *Nodes*. You could add a relationship between *UDG* and *Node* if unconnected *Nodes* were important.

A *UDG* (undirected graph) is a set of nodes and a set of edges that connect nodes. You need not show *UDG* in a use of the template. A *Node* is an entity type whose records are

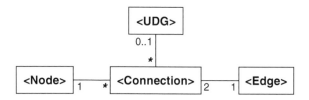

Figure 4.8   Connection undirected graph: UML template. Use when there is
data for the connection itself or edges connect to the same node.

organized as an undirected graph. An **Edge** is a coupling between *Nodes*. A **Connection** is
the linking between a *Node* and an *Edge*.

With this template the names of nodes and edges are globally unique. There is no context
to provide an alternative approach to naming.

Figure 4.8 lacks the constraint that related nodes and edges must all belong to the same
undirected graph.

4.2.2 IDEF1X Template

Figure 4.9 restates Figure 4.8 with the IDEF1X notation. The following are foreign keys:
udgID references *UDG*, *nodeID* references *Node*, and *edgeID* references *Edge*. The combination of *nodeID* + *edgeID* need not be unique for a *Connection* as a *Node* and *Edge* can connect twice.

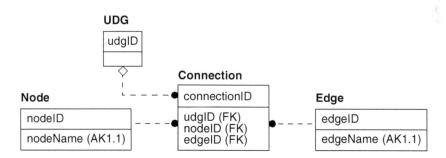

Figure 4.9   Connection undirected graph: IDEF1X template.

4.2.3 SQL Queries

Figure 4.10 and Figure 4.11 show SQL queries for common traversals of the template. The
colon prefix denotes variable values that must be provided for each query.

4.2.4 Sample Populated Tables

Figure 4.12 and Figure 4.13 show connection undirected graph tables populated with data.
The values of the IDs are arbitrary, but internally consistent.

```
SELECT E.edgeID, E.edgeName, COUNT(*) AS edgeCount
FROM Node as N
    INNER JOIN Connection AS C ON N.nodeID = C.nodeID
    INNER JOIN Edge AS E ON C.edgeID = E.edgeID
WHERE N.nodeID = :aNodeID
GROUP BY E.edgeID, E.edgeName
ORDER BY E.edgeName;
```

Figure 4.10 Connection undirected graph: SQL query. Find the edges
that connect to a node and how often they connect.

```
SELECT DISTINCT N.nodeID, N.nodeName, COUNT(*) AS nodeCount
FROM Edge AS E
    INNER JOIN Connection AS C ON E.edgeID = C.edgeID
    INNER JOIN Node AS N ON C.nodeID = N.nodeID
WHERE E.edgeID = :anEdgeID
GROUP BY N.nodeID, N.nodeName
ORDER BY N.nodeName;
```

Figure 4.11 Connection undirected graph: SQL query. Find the nodes
for an edge and how often they connect.

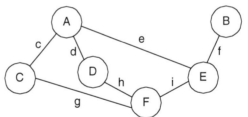

Node table

node ID	node Name
1	A
2	B
3	C
4	D
5	E
6	F

Edge table

edge ID	edge Name
51	c
52	d
53	e
54	f
55	g
56	h
57	i

Connection table

connec tionID	node ID	edge ID	udg ID
1	1	51	1
2	3	51	1
3	1	52	1
4	4	52	1
5	1	53	1
6	5	53	1
7	2	54	1

Connection table (cont)

connec tionID	node ID	edge ID	udg ID
8	5	54	1
9	3	55	1
10	6	55	1
11	4	56	1
12	6	56	1
13	5	57	1
14	6	57	1

Figure 4.12 Connection undirected graph: Populated tables.

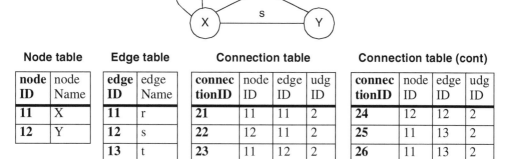

Node table		Edge table		Connection table				Connection table (cont)			
node ID	node Name	**edge ID**	edge Name	**connec tionID**	node ID	edge ID	udg ID	**connec tionID**	node ID	edge ID	udg ID
11	X	**11**	r	**21**	11	11	2	**24**	12	12	2
12	Y	**12**	s	**22**	12	11	2	**25**	11	13	2
		13	t	**23**	11	12	2	**26**	11	13	2

Figure 4.13 Connection undirected graph: Populated tables.

4.2.5 Examples

Figure 4.14 illustrates the template. A manufacturing plant can have a variety of equipment that is connected by piping. For stress calculations, all that matters is that the equipment is connected. Stress calculations ensure that piping does not break under the load of forces such as wind and temperature changes.

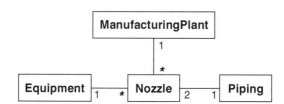

Figure 4.14 Connection undirected graph: Equipment and piping model.

4.3 Undirected Graph Changing over Time Template

This template adds time intervals to the *Node* and *Edge* entity types from Section 4.1.

4.3.1 UML Template

Figure 4.15 shows the template for the node and edge undirected graphs that change over time, extending the template in Figure 4.2. The template in Figure 4.15 cannot handle edges that connect twice to the same node.

A **UDG** (undirected graph) is a set of nodes and a set of edges that connect nodes. (Note: in an undirected graph all the nodes need not be connected.) You need not show *UDG* in a

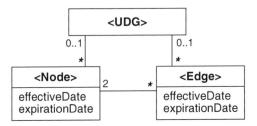

Figure 4.15 Undirected graph changing over time: UML template. Use when
history must be recorded and no edges connect to the same node.

use of the template. A **Node** is an entity type whose records are organized as an undirected
graph. An **Edge** is a coupling between *Nodes*.

With this template the names of nodes and edges are globally unique. There is no context
to provide an alternative approach to naming.

4.3.2 IDEF1X Template

Figure 4.16 restates Figure 4.15 with the IDEF1X notation. The following are foreign keys:
udgID references *UDG*, *nodeID* references *Node,* and *edgeID* references *Edge*. In Figure
4.16 the node name can change over time (three part candidate key—*nodeName* + *effective-
Date* + *expirationDate*), but the node name could also be invariant over time (candidate key
of *nodeName* alone). Similarly the edge name could be invariant over time.

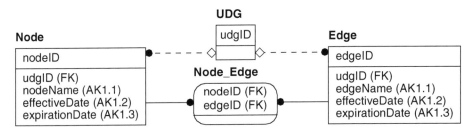

Figure 4.16 Undirected graph changing over time: IDEF1X template.

4.3.3 SQL Queries

Figure 4.17 and Figure 4.18 show SQL queries for common traversals of the template. The
colon prefix denotes variable values that must be provided for each query. With this template
an edge cannot connect twice to the same node, so there is no need to group nodes in Figure
4.18.

4.3.4 Sample Populated Tables

Figure 4.19 shows tables populated with data for the node and edge undirected graph changing over time. The values of the IDs are arbitrary, but internally consistent. A null *effective-*

```
SELECT E.edgeID, E.edgeName
FROM Node as N
    INNER JOIN Node_Edge AS NE ON N.nodeID = NE.nodeID
    INNER JOIN Edge AS E ON NE.edgeID = E.edgeID
WHERE N.nodeID = :aNodeID AND
    (E.effectiveDate IS NULL OR
        :aDate >= E.effectiveDate) AND
    (E.expirationDate IS NULL OR
        :aDate <= E.expirationDate) AND
    (N.effectiveDate IS NULL OR
        :aDate >= N.effectiveDate) AND
    (N.expirationDate IS NULL OR
        :aDate <= N.expirationDate)
ORDER BY E.edgeName;
```

Figure 4.17 Undirected graph changing over time: SQL query. Find
the edges that connect to a node.

```
SELECT N.nodeID, N.nodeName
FROM Edge AS E
    INNER JOIN Node_Edge AS NE ON E.edgeID = NE.edgeID
    INNER JOIN Node AS N ON NE.nodeID = N.nodeID
WHERE E.edgeID = :anEdgeID AND
    (E.effectiveDate IS NULL OR
        :aDate >= E.effectiveDate) AND
    (E.expirationDate IS NULL OR
        :aDate <= E.expirationDate) AND
    (N.effectiveDate IS NULL OR
        :aDate >= N.effectiveDate) AND
    (N.expirationDate IS NULL OR
        :aDate <= N.expirationDate)
ORDER BY N.nodeName;
```

Figure 4.18 Undirected graph changing over time: SQL query. Find
the nodes for an edge.

Date means that a *Node* applies from the past. A null *expirationDate* means that a *Node*
applies into the future.

4.3.5 Example

An extended model (Figure 4.20) could add the aspect of time to the LinkedIn example. Such
a model could track the history of members and connections. From firsthand experience with
LinkedIn, I know this is a realistic example. Member data (not shown in the model) changes
over time. Also links can come and go as users join and leave the Web site.

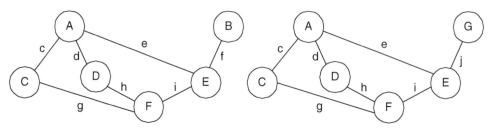

Undirected graph, 1 July 2000 0100   *Undirected graph, 1 July 2000 0300*

Node table   **Edge table**

node ID	node Name	effective Date	expiration Date	udg ID
1	A			1
2	B		1 July 2000 0100	1
3	C			1
4	D			1
5	E			1
6	F			1
7	G	1 July 2000 0300		1

edge ID	edge Name	effective Date	expiration Date	udg ID
51	c			1
52	d			1
53	e			1
54	f		1 July 2000 0100	1
55	g			1
56	h			1
57	i			1
58	j	1 July 2000 0300		1

Node_Edge table   **Node_Edge table (cont)**

nodeID	edgeID
1	51
3	51
1	52
4	52
1	53
5	53
2	54
5	54

nodeID	edgeID
3	55
6	55
4	56
6	56
5	57
6	57
5	58
7	58

Figure 4.19 Undirected graph changing over time: Populated tables.

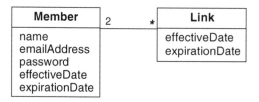

Figure 4.20 Undirected graph changing over time: Personal networking model.

4.4 Chapter Summary

Undirected graphs occasionally occur and can be a critical issue for representation. There are three templates for undirected graphs that have different trade-offs.

- **Node and edge undirected graph**. Use as the default template when there are no edges that connect to the same node.
- **Connection undirected graph**. Use when it is important to store data about the connection itself or there are edges that connect to the same node.
- **Undirected graph changing over time**. Use when history must be recorded.

Table 4.1 summarizes the undirected graph templates.

Table 4.1   Summary of the Undirected Graph Templates

Template name	Synopsis	UML template	Use when	Frequency
Node and edge undirected graph	Treats nodes and edges as peers.		No edge connects to the same node.	Occasional
Connection undirected graph	Promotes the connection between a node and an edge to an entity type.		There is data for the connection itself or there is an edge that connects to the same node.	Occasional
Undirected graph changing over time	Stores multiple variants of a UDG. Extract a particular UDG by specifying a time.		History must be recorded. No edge connects to the same node.	Seldom

Note: This table can help you choose among the undirected graph templates.

5

Item Description Template

There are two templates that involve items and their description.

- **Item description**. Arises when the same model relates data and metadata. The item description template frequently occurs, but is visually less striking than other templates in this book—the template involves only two entity types and one relationship. You must exercise judgment in deciding when one entity type is metadata with regard to another.

- **Homomorphism.** Maps between two *Item Description* templates and expresses an analogy. The description of item 1 is to item 1 as the description of item 2 is to item 2. The relationship between items connects occurrences. The relationship between descriptions constrains occurrences.

5.1 Item Description Template

5.1.1 UML Template

Figure 5.1 shows the UML template for item description. The template involves data (***Item***) and metadata (***ItemDescription***) and typically appears when a model concerns both an item and its description. It is important to keep the two planes (data and metadata) separate or the model will be deeply flawed. A color coding or shading convention can be helpful; Figure 5.1 uses a white background for data and a light gray for metadata.

The item description template is useful if you cannot fully describe data as software is being developed. The template lets you enter data and its description at run time, as opposed to the more typical approach of defining data structure at compile time. Table 5.1 compares *Item* and *ItemDescription*.

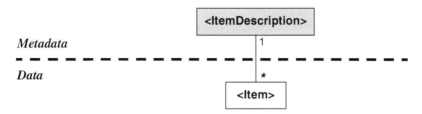

Figure 5.1 Item description: UML template. Use when the same model relates data and metadata.

Table 5.1   Comparison of Item (data) and ItemDescription (metadata)

	ItemDescription	**Item**
Characterization	Metadata	Data
Flexibility	General purpose	Specific
Volatility	Changes slowly	Can change quickly
Authorization	Requires high authorization level to modify	Depends on the application
Number of records	Few records	Many records

5.1.2 IDEF1X Template

Figure 5.2 restates Figure 5.1 with the IDEF1X notation. The following is a foreign key: *itemDescriptionID* references *ItemDescription*.

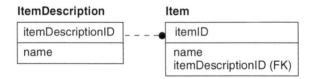

Figure 5.2 Item description: IDEF1X template.

5.1.3 SQL Queries

Figure 5.3 and Figure 5.4 show representative SQL queries for the template. The colon prefix denotes variable values that must be provided.

5.1.4 Sample Populated Tables

Figure 5.5 shows item description tables populated with data. The values of the IDs are arbitrary, but internally consistent.

```
SELECT ID.itemDescriptionID, ID.name
FROM Item AS I
   INNER JOIN ItemDescription AS ID
       ON I.itemDescriptionID = ID.itemDescriptionID
WHERE I.itemID = :anItemID;
```

Figure 5.3 Item description: SQL query. Find the description given an item.

```
SELECT I.itemID, I.name
FROM Item AS I
   INNER JOIN ItemDescription AS ID
       ON I.itemDescriptionID = ID.itemDescriptionID
WHERE ID.itemDescriptionID = :anItemDescriptionID
ORDER BY I.name;
```

Figure 5.4 Item description: SQL query. Find the items for a description.

ItemDescription table

item DescriptionID	name
11	1986 Ford Escort
12	1989 Mazda 323

Item table

item ID	name	item DescriptionID
1	VIN 1032547698	11
2	VIN 5724916835	11
3	VIN 3761952953	11
4	VIN 1123581321	12

Figure 5.5 Item description: Populated tables.

5.1.5 Examples

The item description template occurs frequently. Of all the templates, it is the one you will find most often.

Figure 5.6 shows the nucleus of a model for motor vehicles. *VehicleModel* corresponds to *ItemDescription* and *PhysicalVehicle* corresponds to *Item*. Physical vehicles are items with individual identification numbers. In contrast, vehicle models refer to the year and make, such as 1986 Ford Escort and 1989 Mazda 626. Customer repair records refer to physical vehicles, while design documents describe vehicle models.

The library loan model in Figure 5.7 further demonstrates the template. A ***LibraryItem*** is something that a library offers for borrowing. A ***LibraryItemCopy*** is a physical copy of a *LibraryItem*. For example, a library may list *The Grapes of Wrath* in its card catalog (a *LibraryItem*) and have five copies of the book available (*LibraryItemCopies*).

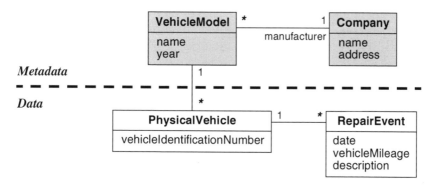

Figure 5.6 Item description: Vehicle model.

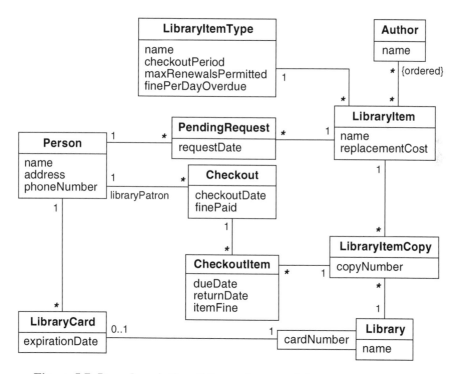

Figure 5.7 Item description: Library loan model.

Each category of *LibraryItem* (***LibraryItemType***) has a standard checkout period and number of renewals. For example, children's books may be checked out for a month, while adult books may be checked out for only two weeks.

A *LibraryItem* may have multiple ***PendingRequests*** to borrow the next available copy. In contrast, a *LibraryItemCopy* can have at most one ***Checkout*** at a time.

Figure 5.7 illustrates that there can be multiple levels of item description. *LibraryItem-Type* is metadata with regard to *LibraryItem*. And *LibraryItem* is metadata with regard to *LibraryItemCopy*. Thus Figure 5.7 applies the template twice. I omitted color coding from this diagram since there are three levels instead of two.

In addition, some types cannot be classified as data or metadata. For example, *Person* relates both to *Checkout* and *PendingRequest*. It is not entirely clear if *Person* should be treated as data or metadata.

Figure 5.8 shows another example, relating report definition to report execution.

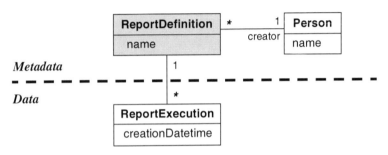

Figure 5.8 Item description: Report model.

5.2 Homomorphism Template

5.2.1 UML Template

Figure 5.9 shows the UML template for homomorphism. An analogy relates the item description template on the left to the item description template on the right. As with the previous section, a shading convention differentiates metadata from data. Light gray indicates metadata and white indicates data.

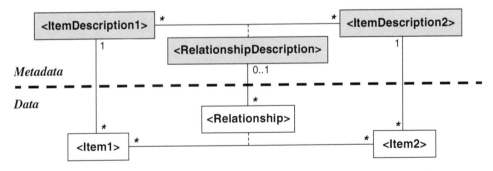

Figure 5.9 Homomorphism: UML template. Use when there is an analogy between item description templates.

5.2.2 IDEF1X Template

Figure 5.10 restates Figure 5.9 with the IDEF1X notation. The following are foreign keys:
itemDescription1ID, *itemDescription2ID*, *item1ID*, and *item2ID*.

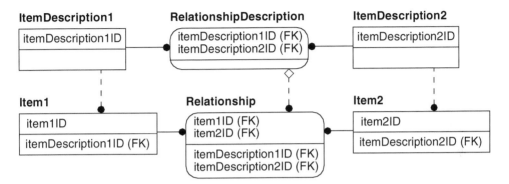

Figure 5.10 Homomorphism: IDEF1X template.

5.2.3 SQL Queries

The homomorphism template has the same queries as the item description template — find
the description given an item and find the items for a description. In addition a homomorphism is important for constraining data as Figure 5.11 illustrates.

```
SELECT R.item1ID, R.item2ID
FROM Relationship R
WHERE NOT EXISTS (
    SELECT I1.item1ID, I2.item2ID
    FROM Item1 AS I1
        INNER JOIN ItemDescription1 AS ID1
            ON I1.itemDescription1ID = ID1.itemDescription1ID
        INNER JOIN RelationshipDescription AS RD
            ON ID1.itemDescription1ID = RD.itemDescription1ID
        INNER JOIN ItemDescription2 AS ID2
            ON RD.itemDescription2ID = ID2.itemDescription2ID
        INNER JOIN Item2 AS I2
            ON ID2.itemDescription2ID = I2.itemDescription2ID
    WHERE   R.item1ID = I1.item1ID AND
            R.item2ID = I2.item2ID );
```

Figure 5.11 Homomorphism: SQL query. Find data that violates the
homomorphism constraint.

Note that Figure 5.11 finds any data that violates the homomorphism constraint and
could execute slowly due to the nested SQL inside the EXISTS clause. In practice data would

probably be checked as it is entered, either with SQL or programming code, and the checking would be more efficient.

5.2.4 Sample Populated Tables

Figure 5.12 shows homomorphism tables populated with data. The example is entirely contrived and abstract, but it does indicate the mechanics of populating homomorphism tables. The values of the IDs are arbitrary, but internally consistent.

ItemDescription1 table

itemDescription1ID	name
101	letter

ItemDescription2 table

itemDescription2ID	name
201	number

Item1 table

item1ID	name	itemDescription1ID
11	a	101
12	c	101
13	e	101

Item2 table

item2ID	name	itemDescription2ID
21	1	201
22	3	201
23	5	201

RelationshipDescription table

item Description1ID	item Description2ID
101	201

Relationship table

item 1ID	item 2ID	item Description1ID	item Description2ID
11	21	101	201
12	22	101	201
13	23	101	201

Figure 5.12 Homomorphism: Populated tables.

5.2.5 Examples

The homomorphism template is not as esoteric as it might seem. Analogies between item description templates do occasionally occur in practice. You will construct better data models if you recognize homomorphisms and show their symmetry in your model layout. The flight model in Figure 5.13 has one homomorphism.

An *Airline* offers *PublishedFlights* on a recurring basis. The *flightNumber* uniquely identifies each *PublishedFlight* for an *Airline*. Each *PublishedFlight* has one or more *PublishedFlightLegs*, each from some origin *Airport* to a destination *Airport*.

An *Airport* has an IATA code and a name. For example, some *Airport* names would be Chicago O'Hare and Houston Hobby with IATA codes of ORD and HOU.

An *ActualFlightLeg* is the flying of an *Aircraft* on a particular date corresponding to a *PublishedFlightLeg*. A *PublishedFlightLeg* denotes the intent to provide service on a regular basis. In contrast, an *ActualFlightLeg* is the actual provision of service on a particular date.

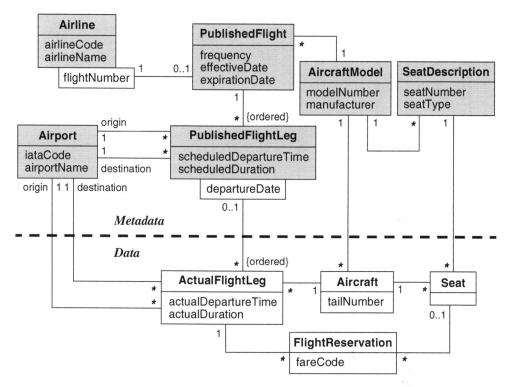

Figure 5.13 Homomorphism: Flight model.

Normally there is one *ActualFlightLeg* for a *PublishedFlightLeg* and *departureDate*, but flight problems can lead to multiple *ActualFlightLegs*.

An *AircraftModel* is a standard kind of aircraft, such as a Boeing 727. An *Aircraft* is a physical specimen of an *AircraftModel* and is uniquely identified with its tail number.

Figure 5.13 has three occurrences of the item description template.

- *PublishedFlightLeg* to *ActualFlightLeg*
- *AircraftModel* to *Aircraft*
- *SeatDescription* to *Seat*

The example has one homomorphism.

- *AircraftModel* to *Aircraft* corresponds to *SeatDescription* to *Seat*.

Figure 5.14 extends the model of Figure 5.8 and shows another homomorphism. *ReportDefinition* relates to *ReportExecution*. *ReportDefinitions* have *Variables*; each *Variable* is assigned a *Value* for a *ReportExecution*.

Figure 5.15 extends the model of Figure 5.6 resulting in two homomorphisms, one with vehicle and event and the other with event and task. A tune-up is an example of a *RepairEventType*. The replacement of spark plugs, replacing points, and setting the timing are examples of *RepairTaskType*.

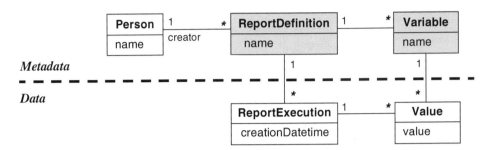

Figure 5.14 Homomorphism: Report model.

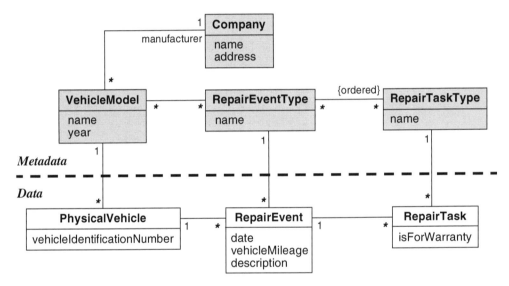

Figure 5.15 Homomorphism: Vehicle model.

5.3 Chapter Summary

The *item description* template arises when a model relates data and metadata. There is one template for item description and the template frequently occurs.

The *homomorphism* template maps between two *Item Description* templates and expresses an analogy. The description of item 1 is to item 1 as the description of item 2 is to item 2. The relationship between items connects occurrences. The relationship between descriptions constrains occurrences. There is one template for homomorphism that occasionally occurs.

Table 5.2 summarizes the item description and homomorphism templates.

Table 5.2 Summary of the item description and homomorphism templates

Template name	Synopsis	UML template	Use when	Frequency
Item description	Relates data and metadata in the same model.		The same model relates data and metadata.	Frequent
Homomor-phism	Expresses an analogy between two item descrip-tion templates.		Item description templates are involved in an analogy.	Occasional

Note: Consider these templates when a model has both data and metadata.

Bibliographic Notes

[Coad-1992] also associates an item with its description.

[Rumbaugh-1991] discusses homomorphisms as part of advanced modeling. Section 2.5 of [Fowler-1997] does not mention the term homomorphism, but Fowler also distinguishes between metadata and data layers. He structures his model in a manner that shows the symmetry.

References

[Coad-1992] Peter Coad. Object-oriented patterns. *Communications ACM 35*, 9 (September 1992), 152–159.

[Fowler-1997] Martin Fowler. *Analysis Patterns: Reusable Object Models*. Boston, Massachusetts: Addison-Wesley, 1997.

[Rumbaugh-1991] J. Rumbaugh, M. Blaha, W. Premerlani, F. Eddy, and W. Lorensen. *Object-Oriented Modeling and Design*. Englewood Cliffs, New Jersey: Prentice Hall, 1991.

6

Star Schema Template

The *star schema* represents data as facts that are bound to dimensions. A *fact* measures the performance of a business or some aspect of a business; examples include sales, budget, revenue, profit, and inventory. A *dimension* specifies one of the bases for facts; examples include date, location, product, customer, and salesperson.

The star schema is the usual approach to data warehouse applications. A data warehouse takes the disjointed, functional applications of a business and integrates them, putting their data in one database and storing data in a common format for reporting purposes. The simple structure of the star schema makes it easier to write ad-hoc queries that mine data and gain insight into an enterprise. However, the simple structure cannot enforce constraints about data—that is the purpose of the functional applications that handle the day-to-day operations of a business.

The star schema is not limited to data warehouses and can also be used for functional applications with much reading and little writing.

There is one template for the star schema.

6.1 Star Schema Template

6.1.1 UML Template

Figure 6.1 shows the UML template for the star schema. A fact is surrounded by dimensions. The diagram happens to show eight dimensions, but there can be any number of dimensions. [Kimball-1998] suggests that a fact should have between five and fifteen dimensions for a well-designed star schema. Most dimensions are mandatory but some can be optional.

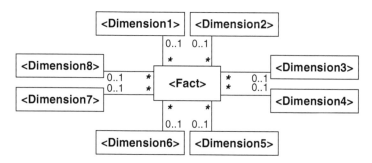

Figure 6.1 Star schema: UML template. Use when there must be a flexible structure for querying data and constraints on data are unimportant.

6.1.2 IDEF1X Template

Figure 6.2 restates Figure 6.1 with the IDEF1X notation. All the dimension IDs in *Fact* are foreign keys. The dimension foreign keys are specified to be mandatory to simplify database joins. There is no conflict between the UML and IDEF1X templates, as a conceptual NULL can be indicated with a special "NONE" record. The combination of dimensions identifies each fact and is used as the primary key to reduce fact table size.

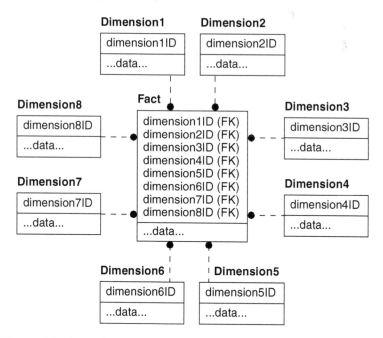

Figure 6.2 Star schema: IDEF1X template.

6.1.3 SQL Queries

Typically there are two kinds of queries for this template—querying facts and querying dimensions.

Figure 6.3 illustrates the first category of queries— selecting groups of facts and summarizing them for various combinations of dimensions. (Section 6.1.5 discusses the store sales example.) Such queries can involve massive amounts of data, so performance is always a concern. Data warehouses use special techniques to speed performance [Inmon-1993] [Kimball-1998]. The colon prefix denotes variable values that must be provided.

```
SELECT storeID, SUM(saleQuantity)
FROM Sale
    INNER JOIN Product AS P ON Sale.productID = P.productID
    INNER JOIN Date AS D ON Sale.dateID = D.dateID
    INNER JOIN Store AS S ON Sale.storeID = S.storeID
WHERE  P.productID = :aProductID AND
        D.fullDate = 'July 1, 2000'
GROUP BY storeID
ORDER BY storeID;
```

Figure 6.3 Star schema: SQL query. Summarize facts for a combination of dimensions.

The second kind of query searches dimension data to retrieve descriptive details (Figure 6.4). Such queries involve a straightforward search through a table or a few related tables.

```
SELECT storeName, streetAddress, cityName, stateName,
        postalCode
FROM Store
WHERE storeID = :aStoreID
```

Figure 6.4 Star schema: SQL query. Retrieve dimension data.

6.1.4 Sample Populated Tables

Figure 6.5 shows star schema tables populated with data. The values of the IDs are arbitrary, but internally consistent. Also for a real problem the dimension tables would have more descriptive attributes than the ones shown. The data is a subset of data for store sales and is covered further in the next section. In practice there are a modest number of dimension records (tens or hundreds per table) and a large number of facts (thousands or millions).

6.1.5 Examples

Figure 6.6 illustrates the star schema template with a store sales model. Sale is a fact that is surrounded by the dimensions of product, payment type, cashier, store, date, and customer.

In data warehouse terminology Figure 6.6 is called a snowflake schema—the dimensions are not shown as a single entity type, but rather as several associated entity types. For

Fact table

dimen-sion1ID	dimen-sion2ID	dimen-sion3ID	dimen-sion4ID	dimen-sion5ID	dimen-sion6ID	quantity	price	saletime
1	2	1	1	1	2	3	0.50	13:20
2	2	1	1	1	2	1	3.25	13:20
3	2	1	1	1	2	1.35	4.05	13:20
1	1	1	1	1	1	2	0.50	13:30
1	1	2	1	1	0	6	0.50	13:30
3	1	2	1	1	0	1.15	3.45	13:30

Dimension1 table

dimension1ID	name
1	16 oz can generic green beans
2	fresh pineapple
3	lean ground beef

Dimension2 table

dimension2ID	name
1	cash
2	credit card
3	debit card

Dimension3 table

dimension3ID	name
1	John Doe
2	Sally Smith

Dimension4 table

dimension4ID	name
1	primary store
2	secondary store

Dimension5 table

dimension5ID	date
1	January 1, 2010
2	January 2, 2010

Dimension6 table

dimension6ID	name
0	NONE
1	John Jones
2	Mary James

Figure 6.5 Star schema: Populated tables.

example, the *Product* dimension is associated with *Category* and *Industry*. When designing data warehouse tables, it is a common practice to denormalize dimensions and collapse their details. For example, *Industry* and *Category* could be folded into a *Product* table to reduce the number of tables and simplify the database.

The example shows six store dimensions. There could be additional dimensions including:

- promotional data (such as coupons)
- customer visit (enabling the grouping of products purchased by the customer in a visit)
- product placement (end of aisle, next to checkout, location on Web site)
- price range

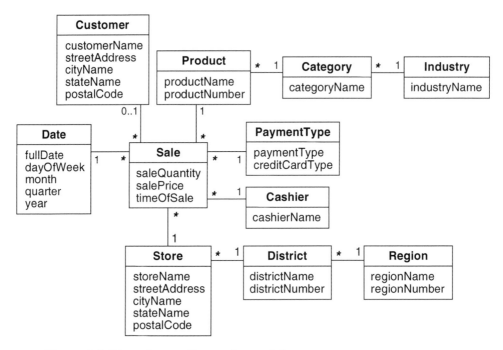

Figure 6.6 Star schema: Store sales model.

Note that *Customer* is optional in the store sales example; a person paying with cash may not be identifiable to the store. All other dimensions are mandatory.

Figure 6.7 shows another example for processing an insurance application on a property. Various events occur as an application is processed and they must all be tracked. The star schema can store the events but does not enforce constraints such as the order of the processing. (That is the purpose of the functional applications.) The star schema can answer questions regarding:

- the status of each application (the latest event type that has been processed)
- the average time for processing between each event as an application progresses
- the fastest employees
- the fastest offices

A property may have more than one owner and hence there can be multiple applicants. For example, a husband and wife may own a property. Thus there is a many-to-many relationship between *ApplicationEvent* and *Applicant*. Many-to-many relationships are troublesome for a star schema and the *Applicants* dimension groups together the multiple owners of a property to finesse the issue. The owners of a property may have unequal ownership.

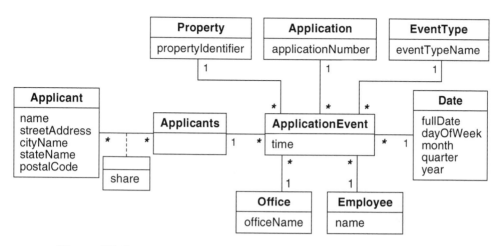

Figure 6.7 Star schema: Application processing model.

6.2 Chapter Summary

The star schema template is pervasive for data warehouse applications and sometimes occurs for functional applications. Table 6.1 summarizes the star schema template.

Table 6.1   Summary of the Star Schema Template

Template	Synopsis	UML diagram	Use when	Frequency
Star schema	Represents data as facts that are bound to dimensions.		There must be a flexible structure for querying data.	Occasional (frequent for data warehouse)

Note: Consider when there must be a flexible structure for querying data and constraints on data are unimportant.

Bibliographic Notes

[Blaha-2001] has a further explanation about data warehouses. Chapter 4 of [Fowler-1997] also discusses the star schema. Inmon and Kimball are prominent authors in the data warehouse community and have written excellent books.

References

[Blaha-2001] Michael Blaha. *A Manager's Guide to Database Technology: Building and Purchasing Better Applications*. Upper Saddle River, NJ: Prentice Hall, 2001.

[Fowler-1997] Martin Fowler. *Analysis Patterns: Reusable Object Models*. Boston, Massachusetts: Addison-Wesley, 1997.

[Inmon-1993] W. H. Inmon. *Building the Data Warehouse*. New York, New York: Wiley-QED, 1993.

[Kimball-1998] Ralph Kimball, Laura Reeves, Margy Ross, and Warren Thornthwaite. *The Data Warehouse Lifecycle Toolkit*. New York, New York: Wiley, 1998.

7

Summary of Templates

Table 7.1 through Table 7.5 summarize the mathematical templates.

Table 7.1 Tree Templates

Template	Synopsis	UML diagram	Use when	Frequency
Hardcoded tree	Specifies a type sequence, one for each level of the hierarchy.		The levels in a tree are known and ordered.	Seldom
Simple tree	Treats all nodes the same.		A tree concerns only data structure.	Common
Structured tree	Differentiates leaf nodes from branch nodes.		Branch nodes and leaf nodes differ.	Common
Overlapping tree	Permits a node to belong to multiple trees.		A node can belong to more than one tree.	Occasional
Tree changing over time	Stores variants of a tree over time.		There is history to record.	Occasional
Degenerate node and edge	Groups a parent with its children.		There is data for the parent–child grouping.	Rare

Table 7.2   Directed Graph Templates

Template	Synopsis	UML diagram	Use when	Frequency
Simple DG	Treats all nodes the same.		Edges are unimportant; nodes have the same kind of data. The DG is acyclic.	Occasional
Structured DG	Differentiates leaf nodes from branch nodes.		Edges are unimportant; branch nodes and leaf nodes have different data. The DG is acyclic.	Occasional
Node–edge DG	Treats nodes and edges as peers.		Nodes and edges can both have data; there can be multiple edges between a pair of nodes.	Common
Connection DG	Promotes a node–edge connection to an entity type.		Connections have data.	Occasional
Simple DG changing over time	Stores variants of a DG over time.		There is history to record; edges are unimportant. The DG is acyclic.	Seldom
Node–edge DG changing over time	Stores variants of a DG over time.		There is history to record; edges are important.	Occasional

Table 7.3   Undirected Graph Templates

Template	Synopsis	UML diagram	Use when	Frequency
Node–edge UDG	Treats nodes and edges as peers.		No edge connects to the same node.	Occasional
Connection UDG	Promotes a node–edge connection to an entity type.		Connections have data or an edge connects to the same node.	Occasional
UDG changing over time	Stores variants of a UDG over time.		There is history to record.	Seldom

Table 7.4   Item Description Templates

Template	Synopsis	UML diagram	Use when	Frequency
Item description	Relates data and metadata in the same model.		The same model relates data and metadata.	Frequent
Homomorphism	Expresses an analogy between two item description templates.		Item description templates are involved in an analogy.	Occasional

Table 7.5   Star Schema Template

Template	Synopsis	UML diagram	Use when	Frequency
Star schema	Represents data as facts that are bound to dimensions.		There must be a flexible structure for querying data.	Occasional (frequent for data warehouse)

Part II

Antipatterns

Part I covers templates — mathematical constructs that often occur and that you should re-use.

Part II provides the opposite advice with antipatterns. An antipattern is a characterization of a common software flaw. When you find an antipattern, substitute the correction. Most patterns are good ideas that can be reapplied to new situations. In contrast, antipatterns look at what can go wrong and offer fixes for the problems. The literature focuses on anti-patterns for programming code, but antipatterns also apply to data models.

Many of the examples in these chapters are from my consulting experiences with data modeling and reverse engineering (inspecting the databases of others). Reverse engineering is the process of starting with implementation artifacts and deducing the intent. Reverse engineering complements data modeling as legacy applications often pertain to a new application. A legacy application might be a source of ideas, a source of data for a new database, or something with which to integrate.

Chapter 8 presents antipatterns that you should always avoid.

Chapter 9 presents antipatterns to avoid for non–data–warehouse applications. These antipatterns simplify reading but compromise the ability of database structure to enforce quality. Hence, these antipatterns are acceptable for data warehouses, but you should avoid them otherwise. A data warehouse is skewed towards reading and its database structure does not enforce data quality—that is the responsibility of the loading programs. Data warehouses forego enforcement of data quality in order to simplify database structure so that it is easier to write queries. A simple structure also reduces the difficulty of integrating disparate data sources.

Many of antipatterns are relatively simple so we just present the UML notation. For the more complex antipatterns, we use both UML and IDEF1X notations.

8

Universal Antipatterns

An *antipattern* is a characterization of a common software flaw. When you find an antipattern, substitute the correction. *Universal antipatterns* are antipatterns that you should avoid for all applications.

8.1 Symmetric Relationship Antipattern

8.1.1 Observation

An entity type has a self relationship with the same multiplicity and role names on each end. Typically this is a many-to-many self relationship. Symmetric relationships can be troublesome for programming and are always troublesome for relational databases.

8.1.2 Exceptions

There are no exceptions for relational database designs. Avoid symmetric relationships.

8.1.3 Resolution

Promote the relationship to an entity type in its own right. The improved model not only resolves the symmetry but is often more expressive.

8.1.4 Examples

Consider Figure 8.1a and Figure 8.2a. *RelatedContract* involves two contracts but the symmetry is troublesome. If each pairing is entered once, it is not clear which contract should be first and which second. If each pairing is entered twice, the amount of storage increases and any change requires double update. If more than two contracts are related, the situation is messier yet (for three contracts that are double stored: C1-C2, C2-C1, C1-C3, C3-C1, C2-

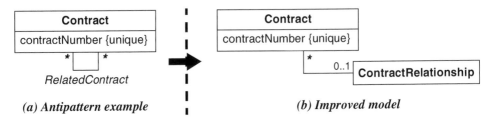

Figure 8.1 Symmetric relationship: UML contract model. Promote symmetric relationships to an entity type.

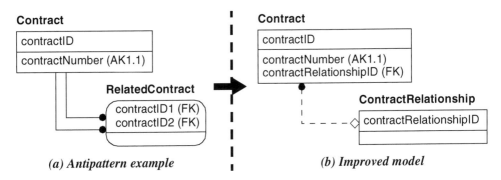

Figure 8.2 Symmetric relationship: IDEF1X contract model.

C3, C3-C2). Furthermore, the antipattern does not require that the related contracts be different. None of this is desirable.

The improved model (Figure 8.1b and Figure 8.2b) breaks the symmetry. To find related contracts traverse as follows: start with a *Contract*, find the possible *ContractRelationship*, then traverse back to *Contract* (excluding the initial contract) to obtain the related *Contracts*. Figure 8.3 shows the corresponding SQL Server code; the code is efficient if the join fields are indexed. (The SQL code presumes existence-based identity; see Chapter 16.)

The revised model has further advantages. The coupling is no longer binary and can readily support three or more related contracts. The model could be extended to make *Contract* to *ContractRelationship* many-to-many with different relationship types. For example, one relationship type could be successor contracts (one contract replacing another). A second relationship type could be alternative contracts (several contracts being considered as alternatives for purchase).

For another example, consider the words in a dictionary (Figure 8.4). An inferior model relates word meanings directly. Also the inferior model cannot handle a group of interchangeable words. Looking in the Framemaker 8 online thesaurus, the first definition of "account" has four synonyms (chronicle, history, annals, and report). The *SynonymSet* supports a group of word meanings.

```
SELECT C2.contractNumber
FROM Contract AS C1
   INNER JOIN ContractRelationship AS CR
      ON C1.contractRelationshipID =
         CR.contractRelationshipID
   INNER JOIN Contract AS C2
      ON CR.contractRelationshipID =
         C2.contractRelationshipID
WHERE C1.contractNumber = :aContractNumber AND
      C2.contractID <> C1.contractID
ORDER BY C2.contractNumber;
```

Figure 8.3 Symmetric relationship: Sample SQL traversal code. The
code is efficient if the join fields are indexed.

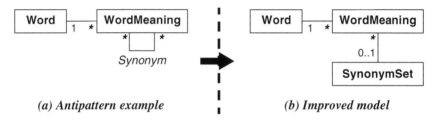

(a) Antipattern example   *(b) Improved model*

Figure 8.4 Symmetric relationship: UML synonym model. The improved model is more expressive.

8.2 Dead Elements Antipattern

8.2.1 Observation

A model has obsolete elements (entity types, relationships, attributes). They may have been
relevant in the past but are extraneous now.

8.2.2 Exceptions

It is acceptable for a model to have small amounts (no more than a few percent of the total)
of dead elements. Large amounts of junk cause confusion and complicate maintenance.

8.2.3 Resolution

Either cut the dead elements from the model or place them in isolation. For example, some
commercial products have a special documentation section for deprecated database tables
that will be removed in future releases.

8.2.4 Examples

Some databases have relic tables from past releases. It is acceptable to keep deprecated tables for a while, but eventually they should be removed. You should be suspicious of tables with zero records.

8.3 Disguised Fields Antipattern

8.3.1 Observation

The name and documentation for a field do not indicate the kind of data that is stored.

8.3.2 Exceptions

A few user-defined fields as well as miscellaneous comments are acceptable as an extensibility mechanism. Otherwise disguised fields are seldom justified.

8.3.3 Resolution

A relational database is supposed to be declarative. A field name should be informative and describe the data that is stored.

8.3.4 Examples

Disguised fields can arise in several ways.

- **User defined fields**. Many vendor packages have *user-defined fields*—anonymous fields for miscellaneous data. Vendors cannot anticipate all customer needs and user-defined fields provide flexibility.

- **Mislabeled fields**. Software is constructed with an original purpose that meets business needs. With subsequent releases, developers may store different data without updating the schema. With user-defined fields, data lacks a description of its meaning. Mislabeled fields are worse, as the description is misleading.

- **Binary fields**. Some databases have binary fields whose interpretation is left to programming code. For example, the MS-Access system catalog has binary fields, such as the *Lv*, *LvExtra*, and *LvProp* fields in *MSysObjects*. These are rarely a good idea.

- **Anonymous fields**. Figure 8.5 shows an excerpt from a legacy application with anonymous address fields. Figure 8.6 shows some corresponding data. To find a city, you must search multiple fields. Worse yet, it could be difficult to distinguish the city of *Chicago* from *Chicago* street. You may need to parse a field to separate city, state, and postal code. It would be much better to put address information in distinct fields that are clearly named.

- **Overloaded fields**. A column of a table can store alternative kinds of values. Sometimes the kind of value is indicated by a switch in another column. Other times the values are distinguished by their format or contextual knowledge buried in programming code.

```
CREATE TABLE Location
  (location_num                DECIMAL(3)
  ,location_name               VARCHAR(15)
  ,location_address_1          VARCHAR(30)
  ,location_address_2          VARCHAR(30)
  ,location_address_3          VARCHAR(30)
  ,location_address_4          VARCHAR(30)
  ,location_address_5          VARCHAR(30)
  ,location_group_code         DECIMAL(2)
  ,location_business_type      VARCHAR(1)
  ,location_tot_bus_sales_dol  DECIMAL(11,2)
  ,location_gross_profit_dol   DECIMAL(11,2)
  ,CONSTRAINT PK_Location PRIMARY KEY (location_num ) ) ;
```

Figure 8.5 Disguised fields: Sample SQL code. Creating a table with anonymous address fields.

location_address_1	location_address_2	location_address_3
456 Chicago Street	Decatur, IL xxxxx	
198 Broadway Dr.	Suite 201	Chicago, IL xxxxx
123 Main Street	Cairo, IL xxxxx	
Chicago, IL xxxxx		

Figure 8.6 Disguised fields: Sample data. Anonymous address fields.

8.4 Artificial Hardcoded Levels Antipattern

8.4.1 Observation

Chapter 2 presented hardcoded trees with a different entity type for each level. Such an approach can be justified for models where the structure does not vary and it is important to enforce the sequence of types.

The antipattern also involves a fixed hierarchy but one with little difference between the entity types. Such a model is brittle, permits duplicate and contradictory data, and is difficult to maintain and extend.

8.4.2 Exceptions

Sometimes the hardcoding of artificial levels is desirable for its simplicity. For example, I needed to convert bill-of-material formats for a past project. The source was a hierarchical indented list and the target was parent–child pairings. One program generated the hierarchy as output and another required the pairings as input. I did not want to program the recursive descent of a tree. Instead I hardcoded a fixed number of levels and quickly wrote a SQL query. Hardcoded levels can be acceptable for a prototype or throwaway code.

8.4.3 Resolution

Abstract and consolidate the levels. Use one of the tree patterns to relate the levels.

8.4.4 Example

Figure 8.7a shows a three-level hierarchy from a legacy application where an individual contributor has a supervisor who in turn has a manager. The limitation to three levels is arbitrary. Many questions come to mind. How should the software deal with an individual contributor who becomes a supervisor and then becomes a manager? Should there be three different records? Does the user multiply enter data, such as names, phone numbers, and addresses (omitted in the example)?

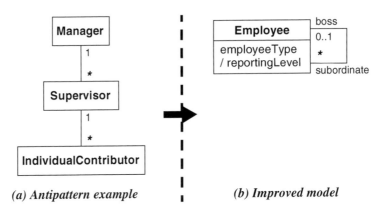

(a) Antipattern example   *(b) Improved model*

Figure 8.7 Artificial hardcoded levels: UML management hierarchy model. Abstract and consolidate the levels.

The improved model (Figure 8.7b) is simpler, more expressive, and avoids these issues. There can be an arbitrary number of management levels. An employee reports to a boss who is also an employee. The boss reports to his or her boss continuing up the reporting hierarchy. The field *employeeType* is an enumeration with the values of "Manager," "Supervisor," and "IndividualContributor." A boss can manage many subordinates and a subordinate has at most one boss. The highest ranking employee in the database has no boss. The '/' prefix is UML notation for derived data (see the Appendix for further explanation).

8.5 Excessive Generalization Antipattern

8.5.1 Observation

A model has a deep generalization. In many cases extensive taxonomies are motivated by object-oriented programming and are inadvisable.

8.5.2 Exceptions

If there is a formal standard for a taxonomy (such as for biological organisms) you should use it. Otherwise I cannot think of a justification. Normally, it is best to avoid deep generalization.

As an example, [Americazoo] presents a taxonomy for mammals, including Figure 8.8 for wolves. Each indentation is a lower level in the taxonomy. Figure 8.8 corresponds to a generalization that is seven levels deep.

```
Class: Mammalia
    Subclass: Theria
        Infraclass: Eutheria
            Order: Carnivora
                Family: Canidae
                    Genus: Canis
                        Species: lupus
```

Figure 8.8   Excessive generalization: Taxonomy for wolves. Normally it is best to avoid deep generalization; formal standards are an exception.

8.5.3 Resolution

As a guideline a database taxonomy should be no more than four levels deep. (A programming taxonomy should be no more than five levels deep.)

8.5.4 Examples

Many years ago at GE Global Research, we built a software modeling tool, called OMTool. The tool was based on a metamodel with a taxonomy that was seven levels deep. Even though the taxonomy was sound, we found it difficult to remember all the levels complicating development. In retrospect we regretted using such a deep taxonomy.

On another project we prepared a large equipment taxonomy (50 pages long!). [Blaha-2003] We understood the problem well and had access to domain experts. Nevertheless, we had trouble with modeling. The taxonomy was so extensive that it was difficult to determine where to place equipment. Also the various types of equipment had many fields and we kept discovering additional data. For this project, it would have been better to forego a hardcoded taxonomy and instead use a softcoding approach. [Blaha-2006]

Section 10.2 shows a sound taxonomy that is three levels deep.

8.6 Disconnected Entity Types Antipattern

8.6.1 Observation

A model has a number of free-standing entity types. From the problem understanding, it would seem that they should be related.

8.6.2 Exceptions

Some disconnected entity types can be acceptable (as a guideline, no more than 10% of the entity types). But it is suspicious when a model has many of them.

8.6.3 Resolution

Recognize that the model is likely to be incomplete. Determine the missing relationships and add them.

8.6.4 Example

Many Eclipse (www.eclipse.org) applications generate XML files for storing persistent data. An application may also have a database that developers populate apart from Eclipse. If you reverse engineer the database, the resulting model can appear to be incomplete. Ideally the database should store both the added data and the Eclipse data.

8.7 Modeling Errors Antipattern

8.7.1 Observations

A model has one or more serious conceptual flaws. Modeling errors lead to bugs in the finished software, complicate development and maintenance, and can impair performance.

8.7.2 Exceptions

Errors in models become errors in the finished software. Errors are never acceptable, but sometimes you have to live with them, such as with legacy systems and vendor software.

8.7.3 Resolution

Understand the flaw and how it may have come about. If possible, correct the model.

8.7.4 Examples

Over the years I have reverse engineered several modeling tools and inspected their internal metamodels. One would expect tool developers to have excellent models, but that is not always the case. Some data modeling tools have the deep flaw of directed relationships.

As Figure 8.9 shows, a directed relationship has "from" and "to" entity types. Using such a tool to construct Figure 8.1b, *Contract* would be "from" and *ContractRelationship*

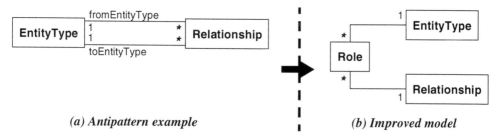

| (a) Antipattern example | (b) Improved model |

Figure 8.9 Modeling error: UML relationship model. Repair modeling errors.

would be "to" or vice versa. This is nonsense. The model simply states that *Contract* and *ContractRelationship* are related. An improved model (Figure 8.9b) introduces the notion of a role which is the intersection of an entity type and a relationship. As a side benefit, the improved model can support ternary relationships.

For another example, I reverse engineered a vendor product for a library catalog system and found that the database implemented a linked list. There is no such thing as a "linked list" in a conceptual model of a library. Someone did not abstract properly and misguidedly put implementation concepts in a conceptual model.

8.8 Multiple Inheritance Antipattern

8.8.1 Observation

A model has multiple inheritance. **Multiple inheritance** is a generalization for which an entity type inherits information from multiple supertypes.

8.8.2 Exceptions

Multiple inheritance is not appropriate for data models. It can be acceptable as a mechanism for programming reuse and for other kinds of models.

8.8.3 Resolutions

Avoid multiple inheritance in data models. Degrade the model if necessary. There is no clean way to implement multiple inheritance with a database. In practice I have found that multiple inheritance seldom occurs with databases and is not worth the bother.

8.8.4 Example

In Figure 8.10a and Figure 8.11a *FullTimeUnionEmployee* is both *FullTimeEmployee* and *UnionEmployee*. The model does not show it, but an extended model could define three additional combinations: *FullTimeNonUnionEmployee*, *PartTimeUnionEmployee*, and *PartTimeNonUnionEmployee*. Figure 8.10b and Figure 8.11b use a workaround (others are possible) to eliminate the multiple inheritance.

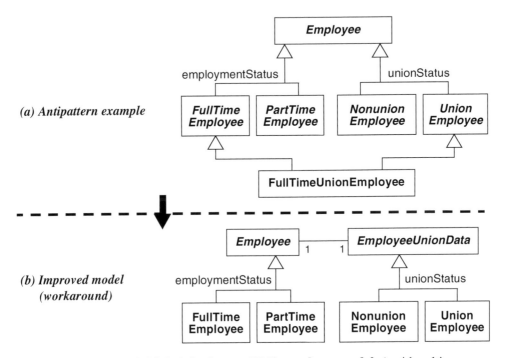

Figure 8.10 Multiple inheritance: UML employee model. Avoid multiple inheritance in conceptual data models.

8.9 Paradigm Degradation Antipattern

8.9.1 Observation
A relational database is degraded to fit some other paradigm.

8.9.2 Exceptions
Such a technique is highly questionable.

8.9.3 Resolution
Rework the model and architecture to avoid such degradation.

8.9.4 Examples
Many years ago, I was reverse engineering the database of a commercial product and was perplexed. The resulting model had many disconnected entity types with only a smattering of relationships. I could not understand how so much information could be missing and suspected that many relationships were disguised. I decided to cross check the schema with the

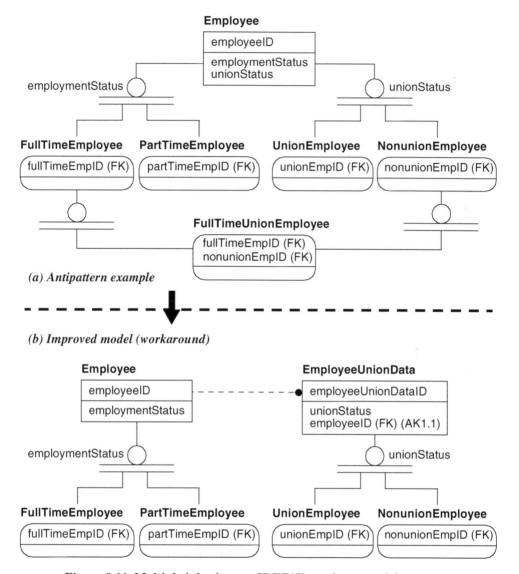

Figure 8.11 Multiple inheritance: IDEF1X employee model.

hierarchical screen layout and discovered the missing relationships. The software vendor confirmed my understanding.

The product supported a fixed hierarchy of depth three. Apparently the vendor created the original product with a proprietary hierarchical database. Then the vendor migrated to client-server technology and devised an isomorphic hierarchical database using a relational database for the server. Figure 8.12 shows the structure for level 1, 2, and 3 tables. The pointer fields are hidden parent pointers.

Antipattern example

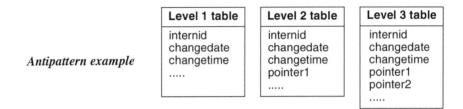

Figure 8.12 Paradigm degradation: Fixed three-level hierarchy.

Figure 8.13 shows a table from another application. I am not sure what the attributes mean. My best guess is that this table was being used for populating a spreadsheet.

Antipattern example

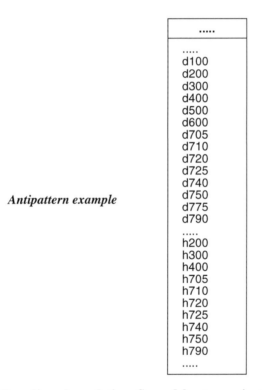

Figure 8.13 Paradigm degradation: Spreadsheet as a giant table.
Avoid distortions of a relational database.

8.10 Chapter Summary

An **antipattern** is a characterization of a common software flaw. As you construct models, you should be alert for antipatterns and correct them. Table 8.1 summarizes universal antipatterns—antipatterns to always avoid—along with their exceptions and resolution.

Table 8.1 Summary of Universal Antipatterns

Antipattern name	Observation	Exceptions	Resolution	Frequency
Symmetric relationship	A self relationship has the same multiplicity and roles on each end.	None	Promote the relationship to an entity type.	Common
Dead elements	A model has unused elements.	Acceptable in small amounts.	Delete them or isolate them.	Common
Disguised fields	Field names do not describe data.	A few user-defined fields.	Use meaningful names.	Common
Artificial hardcoded levels	There is a fixed hierarchy of similar entity types.	Use only with great caution.	Consolidate the levels and use a tree pattern.	Occasional
Excessive generalization	There is a deep generalization.	None	A db taxonomy should be at most four levels deep.	Occasional
Disconnected entity types	A model has free-standing entity types.	A few can be acceptable.	Add the missing relationships.	Occasional
Modeling errors	There is a serious conceptual flaw.	None	Fix the model.	Occasional
Multiple inheritance	A model has multiple inheritance.	Avoid for data models.	Use a work-around.	Seldom
Paradigm degradation	A relational db is degraded to some other paradigm.	Highly questionable.	Rework the model and architecture.	Seldom

Bibliographic Notes

[Brown-1998] discusses antipatterns for programming, architecture, and management. The book is informative, but the authors oversell the technology—antipatterns are not a panacea for the difficulties of software development. As [Brooks-1987] notes, there is no silver bullet for improving software quality. [Laplante-2006] builds on [Brown-1998] and adds further management antipatterns as well as cultural antipatterns.

Many of the examples in this chapter came from my experiences with database reverse engineering — starting with existing database structures and inferring the underlying models. [Premerlani-1994] and [Blaha-1995] present unusual database designs that were found during reverse engineering.

References

[Americazoo] http://www.americazoo.com/goto/index/mammals/classification.htm

[Blaha-1995] Michael Blaha and William Premerlani. Observed idiosyncrasies of relational database designs. *Second Working Conference on Reverse Engineering*, July 1995, Toronto, Ontario, 116–125.

[Blaha-2003] Michael Blaha. Data store models are different than data interchange models. *Proceedings of the International Workshop on Meta-Models and Schemas for Reverse Engineering (ateM 2003)*, November 2003, Victoria, BC.

[Blaha-2006] Michael Blaha. *Designing and Implementing Softcoded Values.* IEEE Computer Society ReadyNote, 2006.

[Brown-1998] William J. Brown, Raphael C. Malveau, Hays W. "Skip" McCormick, and Thomas J. Mowbray. *AntiPatterns: Refactoring Software, Architectures, and Projects in Crisis.* New York: John Wiley & Sons, Ltd, 1998.

[Brooks-1987] Frederick P. Brooks, Jr. No silver bullet: Essence and accidents of software engineering. *IEEE Computer 20*, 4 (April 1987), 10–19.

[Laplante-2006] Phillip A. Laplante and Colin J. Neill. *Antipatterns: Identification, Refactoring, and Management.* Boca Raton, FL: Auerbach Publications, 2006.

[Premerlani-1994] William Premerlani and Michael Blaha. An approach for reverse engineering of relational databases. *Communications ACM 37*, 5 (May 1994), 42–49.

9

Non-Data-Warehouse Antipatterns

Most applications rely on their database structure to help enforce data quality. Data warehouse applications are an exception—a data warehouse emphasizes the reading of data and makes data quality the responsibility of loading programs. The antipatterns in this chapter simplify reading but compromise the ability of database structure to enforce quality. Hence, these antipatterns are acceptable for data warehouses, but you should avoid them otherwise.

9.1 Derived Data Antipattern

9.1.1 Observation
A model has elements (entity types, relationships, attributes) that are not fundamental. These elements can be computed from other elements and lack substance in their own right. Derived data can complicate development and increases the likelihood of data corruption.

9.1.2 Exceptions
Consider using derived data for critical application elements or to resolve performance bottlenecks. For example, it is faster to store the current security positions for a broker account, than to compute them by processing past transactions. Derived data is often used for data warehouses to speed performance and ease the writing of queries.

9.1.3 Resolution
When possible, rework the model to eliminate derived elements. Otherwise carefully document derived data and pay special attention to checking for inconsistencies in your test plan. Sometimes it is helpful to use a generic mechanism to keep derived data consistent with base data—for example, it is entirely acceptable to have derived data that is computed via a database view.

9.1.4 Examples

In Figure 9.1 it is much better to include a person's birthdate rather than age which changes over time. The original model is also undesirable for a data warehouse.

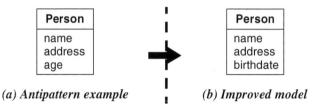

(a) Antipattern example   (b) Improved model

Figure 9.1 Derived data: UML person model. Try to avoid derived data
and focus on fundamental data.

Figure 9.2 and Figure 9.3 show a partial model for a library. The slash prefix in Figure 9.2 is UML notation for derived data. The *dueDate* can be computed from *checkoutDate* and *checkoutPeriod*. The *calculatedFine* is computed according to the formula. Figure 9.4 shows SQL Server code for the calculations.

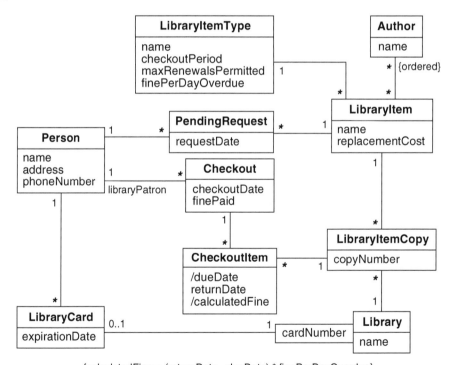

{calculatedFine = (returnDate - dueDate) * finePerDayOverdue}

Figure 9.2 Derived data: UML library model. If you do use derived data,
then carefully document it.

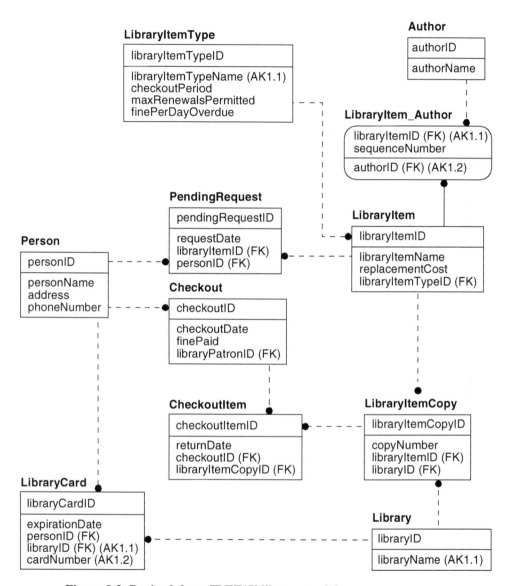

Figure 9.3 Derived data: IDEF1X library model.

Figure 9.5 shows a proper use of derived data for a fact table of a simple data warehouse. The gross profit is the retail price less the wholesale cost.

```
SELECT C.checkoutDate + LIT.checkoutPeriod AS dueDate,
    'calculatedFine' = CASE
        WHEN CAST (CI.returnDate -
            (C.checkoutDate + LIT.checkoutPeriod) AS int) > 0
            THEN CAST (CI.returnDate -
            (C.checkoutDate + LIT.checkoutPeriod) AS int) *
            LIT.finePerDayOverdue
        ELSE 0
        END
FROM CheckoutItem AS CI
    INNER JOIN LibraryItemCopy AS LIC
        ON CI.libraryItemCopyID = LIC.libraryItemCopyID
    INNER JOIN LibraryItem AS LI
        ON LIC.libraryItemID = LI.libraryItemID
    INNER JOIN LibraryItemType AS LIT
        ON LI.libraryItemTypeID = LIT.libraryItemTypeID
    INNER JOIN Checkout AS C
        ON CI.checkoutID = C.checkoutID
WHERE CI.checkoutItemID = :aCheckoutItem;
```

Figure 9.4 Derived data: Sample SQL code.

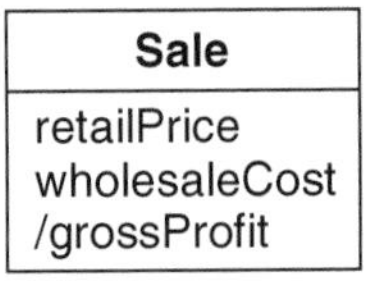

Sale
retailPrice
wholesaleCost
/grossProfit

Figure 9.5 Derived data: Sale fact in a data warehouse. Derived data
is often acceptable for data warehouses.

9.2 Parallel Attributes Antipattern

9.2.1 Observation

An entity type has groups of similar attributes. Such a model can be brittle, verbose, and
awkward to extend.

9.2.2 Exceptions

Parallel attributes are often used for data warehouses to ease data retrieval. Data warehouses
forego the enforcement of data quality, leaving that responsibility to the feeder applications
and scripts that load data.

9.2.3 Resolution

Abstract and factor out commonality.

9.2.4 Examples

Figure 9.6a is taken from a legacy application. The repetition is obvious. An organization has different kinds of products for which both sales and profit are recorded. Figure 9.6b avoids the repetition and readily extends to new products and financial metrics. The original model is also undesirable for a data warehouse.

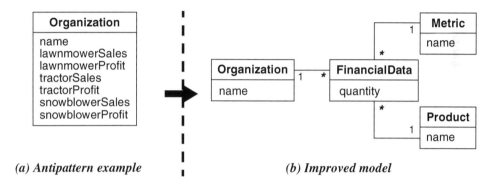

(a) Antipattern example   *(b) Improved model*

Figure 9.6 Parallel attributes: UML financial model. Abstract and factor out commonality.

Dimensions and facts of data warehouses often have parallel attributes. For example, *saleQuantity* and *salePrice* in Figure 6.6 are parallel attributes. Figure 9.7 shows a *Customer* dimension with parallel attributes for address and phone number.

Customer
customerName
dateOfBirth
billingStreetAddress
billingCityName
billingStateName
billingPostalCode
shippingStreetAddress
shippingCityName
shippingStateName
shippingPostalCode
homePhoneNumber
workPhoneNumber
cellPhoneNumber
faxPhoneNumber

Figure 9.7 Parallel attributes: Customer dimension. Parallel attributes are often acceptable for data warehouses.

9.3 Parallel Relationships Antipattern

9.3.1 Observation
Two entity types have several (at least three) similar relationships.

9.3.2 Exceptions
As with parallel attributes, parallel relationships can be acceptable for a data warehouse in order to simplify queries for retrieving data.

9.3.3 Resolution
Abstract and factor out commonality.

9.3.4 Example
In Figure 9.8, a person can participate in making a movie in various ways. The left model shows five movie roles. The right model permits any number of roles.

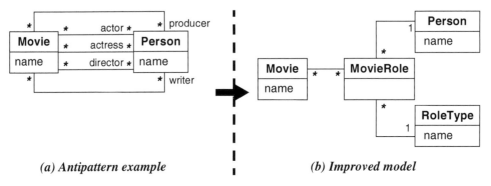

(a) Antipattern example   *(b) Improved model*

Figure 9.8 Parallel relationships: UML movie model. Abstract and
factor out commonality.

Figure 9.9 shows another representation for a *Customer* dimension. The various addresses can be noted via parallel relationships. The use of parallel relationships could be preferred to Figure 9.7 if there were extensive *Address* fields to record.

9.4 Combined Entity Types Antipattern

9.4.1 Observation
An entity type has disparate attributes and lacks cohesion.

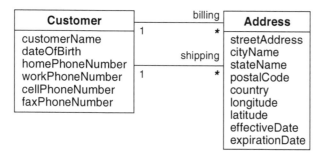

Figure 9.9 Parallel relationships: Customer dimension. Parallel relationships are often acceptable for data warehouses.

9.4.2 Exceptions

Giant tables are reasonable for input/output staging. It is also acceptable to combine entity types for the dimension tables of data warehouses.

9.4.3 Resolution

Make each concept its own entity type.

9.4.4 Example

In Figure 9.10 the contact position and contact phone depend on the contact name which in turn depends on the account. In the left model, several account records could have the same contact name with inconsistent positions and phone numbers. Note that the left model violates third normal form.

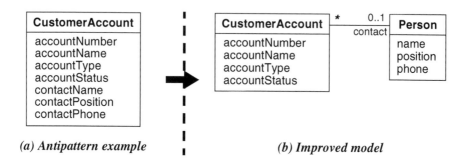

(a) Antipattern example   *(b) Improved model*

Figure 9.10 Combined entity types: UML customer account model. Make each concept its own entity type.

As a counterexample, it can be appropriate to combine entity types for a data warehouse. Specifically, such a combination can flatten a dimension. Many dimensions, when logically modeled, consist of several related entities. Data warehouses often collapse such snowflakes into a single dimension entity. For example, Figure 9.11 collapses the *Product* dimension of Figure 6.6 into a single entity.

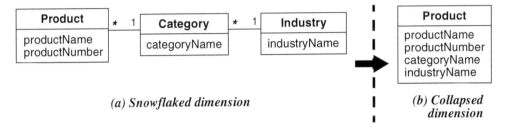

(a) *Snowflaked dimension*   (b) *Collapsed dimension*

Figure 9.11 Combined entity types: Collapsing a snowflaked dimension. It is acceptable to combine entity types for a dimension of a data warehouse.

9.5 Chapter Summary

An antipattern is a characterization of a common software flaw. The antipatterns in Table 9.1 simplify reading but compromise the ability of database structure to enforce quality. These antipatterns are often acceptable for data warehouses, but you should avoid them otherwise.

Table 9.1   Summary of Non-Data-Warehouse Antipatterns

Antipattern name	Observation	Exceptions	Resolution	Frequency
Derived data	A model has elements that are not fundamental.	OK for critical elements, bottlenecks, and data warehouses.	Rework the model to eliminate derived data.	Common
Parallel attributes	An entity type has groups of similar attributes.	Often used for data warehouses.	Abstract and factor out commonality.	Occasional
Parallel relationships	Two entity types have several similar relationships.	Can be acceptable for a data warehouse.	Abstract and factor out commonality.	Occasional
Combined entity types	An entity type has disparate attributes.	OK for I/O staging and data warehouses.	Make each concept its own entity type.	Occasional

Part III

Archetypes

Archetypes are deep abstractions that often occur and transcend individual applications. You should keep them in mind as you construct models.

   This chapter presents both UML and IDEF1X diagrams so that the meaning of the archetypes is clear for readers who prefer one or the other notation.

10

Archetypes

Archetypes are abstractions that often occur and transcend individual applications. You should keep them in mind as you construct models. The use of an archetype can lead to a breakthrough. By necessity, the list in this chapter is arbitrary and incomplete. The archetypes themselves are also incomplete so you will need to add detail as you include them.

Many of the archetypes relate to each other. This chapter uses an entity type icon (UML—no attribute section, IDEF1X—ellipsis for attributes) for references to entity types that are defined elsewhere in the chapter.

Throughout the chapter the shaded boxes are metadata and the white boxes are data.

10.1 Account

An *Account* is a label for recording, reporting, and managing a quantity of something. Applications involve a variety of account types:

- accounting applications — general ledger account, account payable, account receivable
- business applications — bank account, credit card account, customer account, expense account, purchase account, sales account
- computing applications — computing account, email account
- travel applications — frequent flyer account, travel account

Each *Account* has an *owner* (a *TangibleActor*, in this case a person or organization, see Section 10.2). Typically an owner can have multiple accounts for an account type (Figure 10.1, Figure 10.2). Some of these accounts might be unwanted duplicates and remain undetected until after data has been posted. The notion of *AccountEquivalence* can logically combine accounts without having to move data (see the *Symmetric Relationship Antipattern*). In addition, since the merge is logical and not physical, it can be undone.

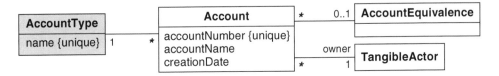

Figure 10.1 Archetype Account: UML model. An *Account* is a label for
recording, reporting, and managing a quantity of something.

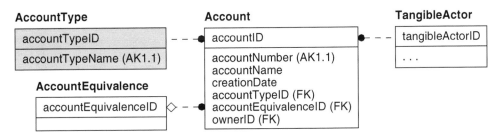

Figure 10.2 Archetype Account: IDEF1X model.

10.2 Actor

An *Actor* is someone or something that is notable in terms of data or relationships. An actor
is not the real world thing but is the computing counterpart for attaching information.

An actor provides a "hook" for interchangeable data (Figure 10.3, Figure 10.4). An *Actor* is a *Person*, *Application*, *Organization*, *ActorRole*, or *ActorRoleType*. An application includes this model and relates relevant entities. As an example, an actor can provide the basis for assigning permissions. Sales documents may be accessible by Joe Smith (a *Person*), the sales department (an *Organization*), and the head of marketing (an *ActorRoleType*). Additional examples involve approval and logging. For many business processes, the efforts of *Persons*, *Applications*, *Organizations*, *ActorRoles*, and *ActorRoleTypes* are interchangeable and *Actor* can abstract across them.

A *Person* is someone who is important to an application. An *Application* is a reference to software — an intelligent *Application* can take the place of a *Person* in some situations. For example, expert system logic can determine whether to grant approval for a credit card charge. An *Organization* can be a business entity, a grouping of organizations, or a part of an organization. A *TangibleActor* is a *Person*, *Application*, or *Organization*.

An *ActorRoleType* is a job function that a *TangibleActor* can perform; examples include clerk, manager, administrator, customer, and vendor. An *ActorRole* is the combination of a *TangibleActor* and an *ActorRoleType* (see Section 10.18). Examples include John Doe the manager and John Doe the user. You can think of an *ActorRole* as a *TangibleActor* wearing a hat (the hat is an *ActorRoleType*).

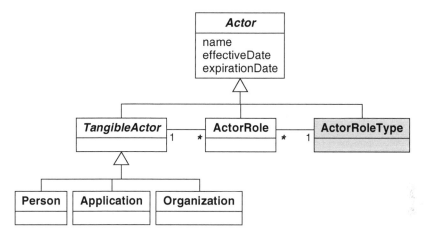

Figure 10.3 Archetype Actor: UML model. An *Actor* is someone or
something that is notable in terms of data or relationships.

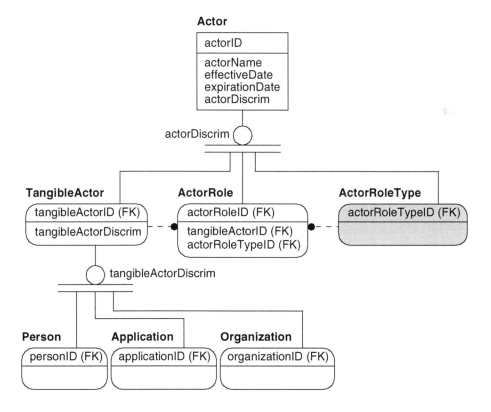

Figure 10.4 Archetype Actor: IDEF1X model.

The *Actor* archetype is highly generic. You can capture data for individual actors either by using softcoded values (see Chapter 13) or by creating specific entity types as this chapter does for customer (Section 10.7) and vendor (Section 10.20).

10.3 Address

An *Address* is a means for communicating with an *Actor* (Figure 10.5, Figure 10.6). An address can be a postal address, email address, phone number, or URL. An address can serve various purposes (*AddressRoleTypes*, see Section 10.18) such as shipping, billing, business, and home. Thus the same address might be used both as a business address and a home address.

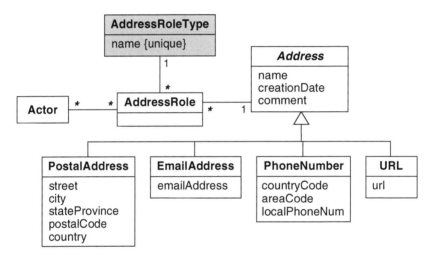

Figure 10.5 Archetype Address: UML model. An *Address* is a means
for communicating with an actor.

10.4 Asset

An *Asset* is something of value (Figure 10.7, Figure 10.8). An *OwnedAsset* is an asset that is owned outright. A *RentedAsset* is the use of an *OwnedAsset* for some time period. Thus, for example, a bicycle that is owned is an *OwnedAsset*. A bicycle that is rented for some time period is a *RentedAsset*. An *OwnedAsset* may or may not be individually identified — if an *OwnedAsset* lacks identity, *AssetOwnership* can involve a multiple quantity.

For another example, consider a timeshare. The underlying property is an *OwnedAsset*. The timeshare itself is a *RentedAsset* available for some time interval. Timeshares can be issued for a particular unit but are often tradeable and substitutable by a comparable unit.

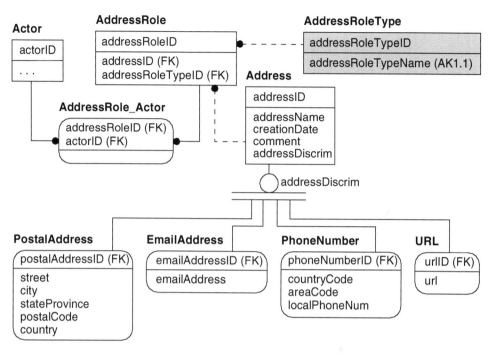

Figure 10.6 Archetype Address: IDEF1X model.

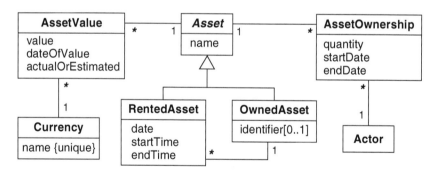

Figure 10.7 Archetype Asset: UML model. An *Asset* is something of value.

10.5 Contract

A *Contract* is an agreement for the supply of products (Figure 10.9, Figure 10.10). (Section 10.17 discusses *Product*.) Many *Actors* (various persons and organizations in a variety of roles) can participate in a contract. Businesses use contracts as a means for conducting com-

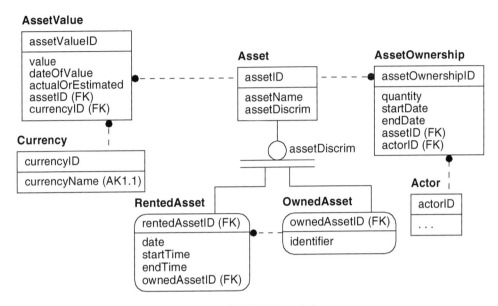

Figure 10.8   Archetype Asset: IDEF1X model.

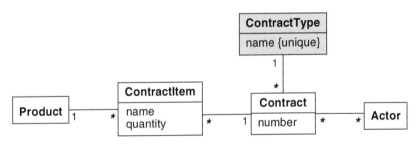

Figure 10.9 Archetype Contract: UML model. A *Contract* is an agreement for the supply of products.

merce. The financial markets use contracts for trading and capture specialized details, such as various kinds of securities, long and short quantities, as well as bid and ask price ranges.

There are various *ContractTypes* including purchase order, sales order, construction, lease, advertising, and employment.

10.6 Course

A *Course* is a series of lessons about a subject (Figure 10.11, Figure 10.12). A *ListedCourse* is an entry in a course catalog and is sponsored by a *SchoolDistrict* or some other education forum. A *ScheduledCourse* is a specific offering of a *ListedCourse* and is delivered by a

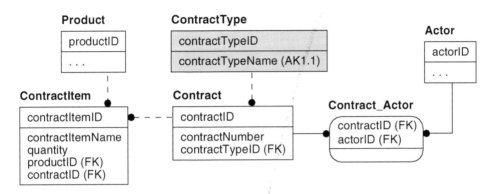

Figure 10.10 Archetype Contract: IDEF1X model.

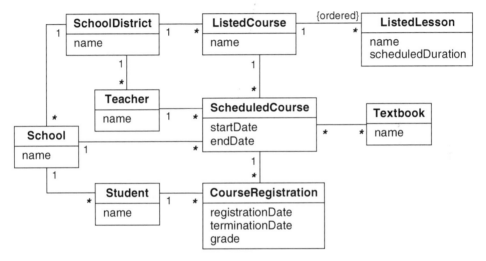

Figure 10.11 Archetype Course: UML model. A *Course* is a series of
lessons about a subject.

Teacher at a *School* using any number of *Textbooks*. There is a *CourseRegistration* for each
Student who participates in a *ScheduledCourse*. Note that the *Course* archetype has two *Item
Description* templates (see Chapter 5). *ListedCourse* corresponds to *ItemDescription* and
ScheduledCourse corresponds to *Item*. Similarly, *ScheduledCourse* corresponds to *ItemDe-
scription* and *CourseRegistration* corresponds to *Item*.

10.7 Customer

A **Customer** is someone involved in the purchase of products (Figure 10.13, Figure 10.14).
Customer reifies the customer role for a *TangibleActor* (in this case a person or organization,

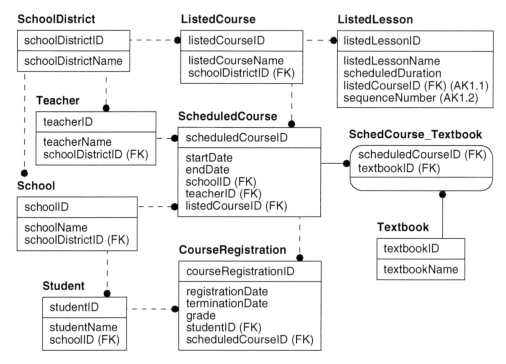

Figure 10.12 Archetype Course: IDEF1X model.

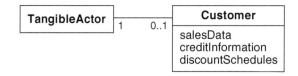

Figure 10.13 Archetype Customer: UML model. A *Customer* is someone involved in the purchase of products.

see Section 10.2). Customers are critically important to business and there is special data to collect for them, such as sales data, credit information, and discount schedules. You could use softcoding (see Chapter 13) to capture customer data, but an alternative is to define a distinct *Customer* entity type as shown here.

10.8 Document

A *Document* is a physical or electronic representation of a body of information (Figure 10.15, Figure 10.16).

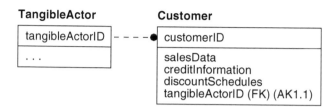

Figure 10.14 Archetype Customer: IDEF1X model.

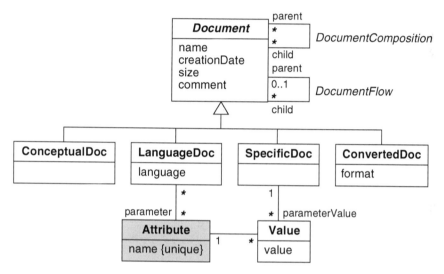

Figure 10.15 Archetype Document: UML model. A *Document* is a physical or electronic representation of a body of information.

DocumentComposition enables a document to combine lesser documents. For example, a product specification sheet may consist of various paragraphs, pictures, and tables. For a given document, there may be no decomposition, one level of decomposition, or multiple levels of decomposition. *DocumentComposition* is a directed acyclic graph as some documents are reusable in multiple contexts. Note that *DocumentComposition* avoids symmetry (see Chapter 8) with the distinction between *parent* and *child*.

There is also *DocumentFlow*. A *Document* starts out as a concept (*ConceptualDoc*) and is then expressed in one or more languages (*LanguageDoc*). For example, a product specification sheet may have English, German, and Japanese translations. *LanguageDocs* can be parameterized; a *SpecificDoc* assigns a value to each parameter. For example, a *LanguageDoc* may have a picture of an electric motor with placeholders (*parameters*) for length and diameter; the *SpecificDoc* specifies the actual length and diameter for each motor. And finally a *SpecificDoc* can be the basis for generating *ConvertedDocs* in formats such as PDF,

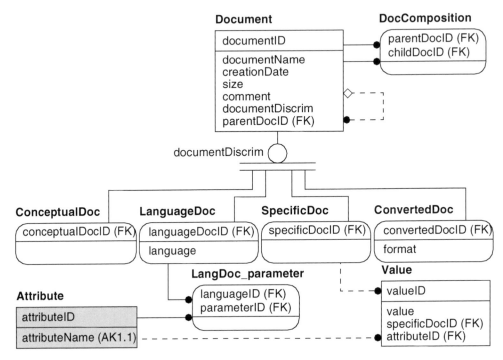

Figure 10.16 Archetype Document: IDEF1X model.

HTML, and XML. The model permits meaningless sequences, but this explanation describes the intended flow and application code must enforce a proper sequence.

Thus there is a flow to the progression of documents. Documents start out as concepts, are expressed in various languages, have parameters added, and then are converted into the desired formats.

10.9 Event

An **Event** is an occurrence at some point in time (Figure 10.17, Figure 10.18). The notion of an event often appears in application models. An *EventType* is a general category of *Events*. This archetype involves data and metadata and uses the shading convention from Chapter 5.

EventTypes can be organized into a generalization hierarchy. For example, a superevent could be pressing a key on a keyboard. A subevent would be pressing an alphanumeric key and a further subevent would be pressing the letter *X*. Sometimes it is helpful to organize the definition of events by their similarities and differences using generalization.

There is also a simple model of cause and effect. A group of causes might lead to a group of effects. By multiple traversals of *EventCausality* there can be a cascade of events.

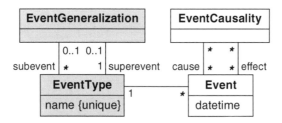

Figure 10.17 Archetype Event: UML model. An *Event* is an occurrence
at some point in time.

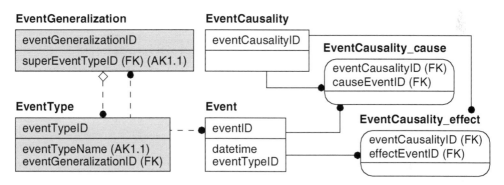

Figure 10.18 Archetype Event: IDEF1X model.

10.10 Flight

A ***Flight*** is the travel by an airplane between airports (Figure 10.19, Figure 10.20). The *Flight*
archetype is representative of many transportation routing problems. A published flight is the
planned travel and an actual flight is the realized travel. The *frequency* indicates the days of
the week for a *PublishedFlight*. The *effectiveDate* and *expirationDate* bracket the time period for which the *PublishedFlight* is in effect. A *PublishedFlightLeg* refers to the scheduled
travel between airports with one takeoff and landing. (A through flight has multiple legs.)

In contrast, an *ActualFlightLeg* refers to the actual travel made by an aircraft on a particular date. The actual origin, destination, departure time, and duration can vary because of
weather and equipment problems. Normally there is one *ActualFlightLeg* for a *Published-
FlightLeg* and *departureDate*, but flight problems can lead to multiple *ActualFlightLegs*.

Each *AircraftModel* has a manufacturer and model number. Each individual *Aircraft* has
a tail number and refers to an *AircraftModel*. Note that *PublishedFlightLeg* to *ActualFlight-
Leg* and *AircraftModel* to *Aircraft* illustrate the *Item Description* template (see Chapter 5).

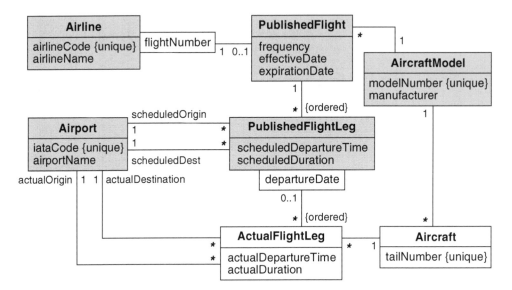

Figure 10.19 Archetype Flight: UML model. A *Flight* is the travel by
an airline between airports.

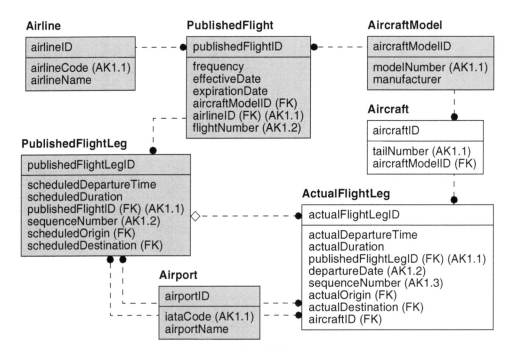

Figure 10.20 Archetype Flight: IDEF1X model.

10.11 Item

An *Item* is a part or a service (Figure 10.21, Figure 10.22). A *RenderedService* is a group of
tasks that are performed. In Section 10.14 many *PhysicalParts* can correspond to a *Catalog-
Part*. Similarly many *RenderedServices* can correspond to an *OfferedService*.

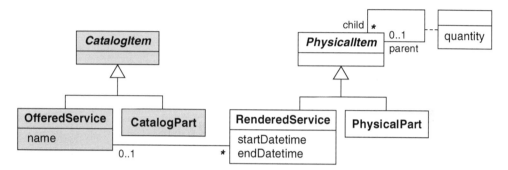

Figure 10.21 Archetype Item: UML model. An *Item* is a part or a service.

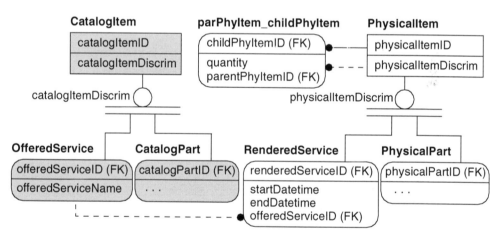

Figure 10.22 Archetype Item: IDEF1X model.

An example of an *OfferedService* is a business audit. Corresponding *RenderedServices*
would be business audits performed on particular dates.

A physical item can break down into lesser physical items, leading to a decomposition
tree. The *parent–child* relationship on *PhysicalItem* is redundant with the *Contains* relationship of *PhysicalPart* (Section 10.14). If *PhysicalItem* and *PhysicalPart* are in the same model, you should omit the *Contains* relationship on *PhysicalPart*. The *PhysicalItem*
decomposition is broader in scope and subsumes *PhysicalPart* decomposition. Section 10.14
shows relationships for *CatalogPart* and *PhysicalPart*.

10.12 Location

A *Location* is a physical place in space (Figure 10.23, Figure 10.24).

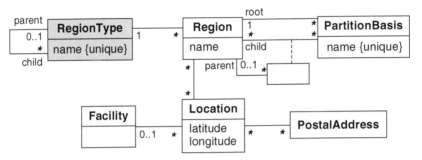

Figure 10.23 Archetype Location: UML model. A *Location* is a physical place in space.

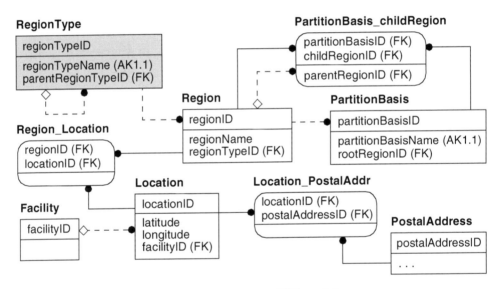

Figure 10.24 Archetype Location: IDEF1X model.

A *Region* is a geographical area. A parent *Region* may contain child *Regions*. For example, the United States can be divided into states and the states further divided into counties. Alternatively, the United States can be divided into time zones. The division into political units and time zones are two examples of *PartitionBasis*. Note the use of the *Overlapping Tree* template (see Chapter 2).

A *RegionType* is a kind of *Region*, such as a country, state/province, and county. *RegionTypes* can be organized into a hierarchy ranging from broad to fine categories.

A *Facility* is a building, a campus, or a part of a building where business can be conducted. The postal address for a location can change; an example is the creation of a new postal code. Furthermore a large building may have multiple postal addresses.

10.13 Opportunity

An ***Opportunity*** is an inquiry that can result in business (Figure 10.25, Figure 10.26). Opportunities often arise in the context of sales. Organizations devote many resources to cultivating sales and managing their response to them. Opportunities can be represented with a progression of steps as they progress in the sales cycle. Organizations collect data as an opportunity proceeds.

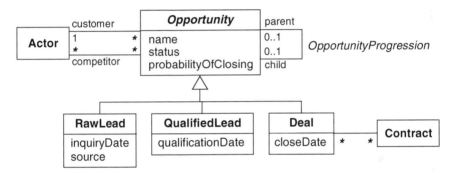

Figure 10.25 Archetype Opportunity: UML model. An *Opportunity* is
an inquiry that can result in business.

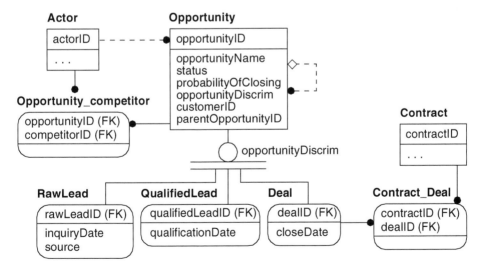

Figure 10.26 Archetype Opportunity: IDEF1X model.

The subtypes in the model show some possible steps. The precise steps vary by organization. A *RawLead* begins the sales cycle. After some investigation that the lead is bona fide it is called a *QualifiedLead*. An opportunity that has closed and culminated in business is called a *Deal*. *OpportunityProgression* connects the steps.

10.14 Part

A *Part* is a specific good that can be described (Figure 10.27, Figure 10.28). A *PhysicalPart* is a tangible thing while a *CatalogPart* is a description of a similar group of things. As an example, consider cars. Physical cars have individual serial numbers and each is a facsimile of a car model (Ford Escort, Mazda 626). Customer service records refer to physical cars, while design documents describe car models. A *PhysicalPart* may have a *Batch* specified (such as a batch of drugs) for manufacturing traceability.

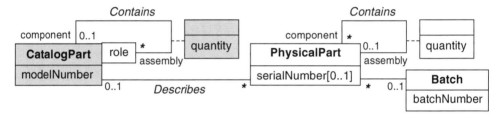

Figure 10.27 Archetype Part: UML model. A *Part* is a specific good
that can be described.

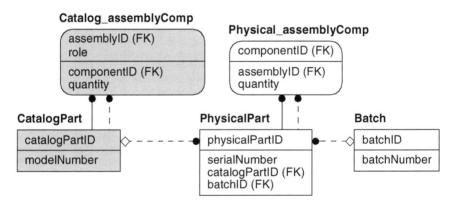

Figure 10.28 Archetype Part: IDEF1X model.

A catalog part may describe multiple physical parts. Each catalog part and physical part may contain lesser parts. A catalog part may belong to multiple assemblies (because the design of a part is reusable), but a physical part may belong to at most one assembly (because the individual part is consumed in constructing the assembly).

Catalog parts may have a quantity specified within a context of usage. For example, there are left and right windshield wipers and there may also be a wiper on the rear window. A role, such as left windshield, right windshield, and rear window, may be specified to differentiate the various uses of a wiper.

Physical parts may also have a quantity. Parts with serial numbers always have a quantity of one, since each part is individually noted. In contrast, other parts are interchangeable, such as nuts and bolts taken from a bin. Interchangeable parts lack a serial number.

The occurrences for physical parts form a collection of trees. The part at the root of a tree does not belong to any assembly, and all other parts within a tree belong to exactly one assembly.

In contrast, the occurrences for catalog parts form a directed acyclic graph. (See Chapter 3.) An assembly may have multiple components and a component may belong to multiple assemblies.

10.15 Payment

A *Payment* is the assignment of money in return for something of value (Figure 10.29, Figure 10.30). There are different kinds of payment, each with their own associated data. A check is written against a bank account (see Section 10.1).

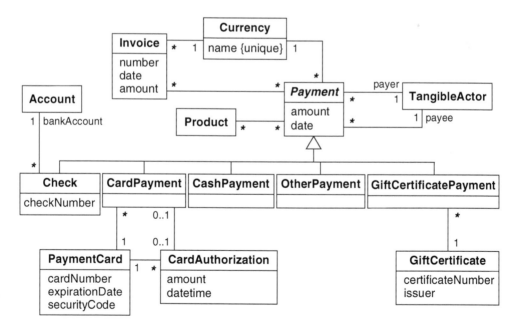

Figure 10.29 Archetype Payment: UML model. A *Payment* is the assignment of money in return for something of value.

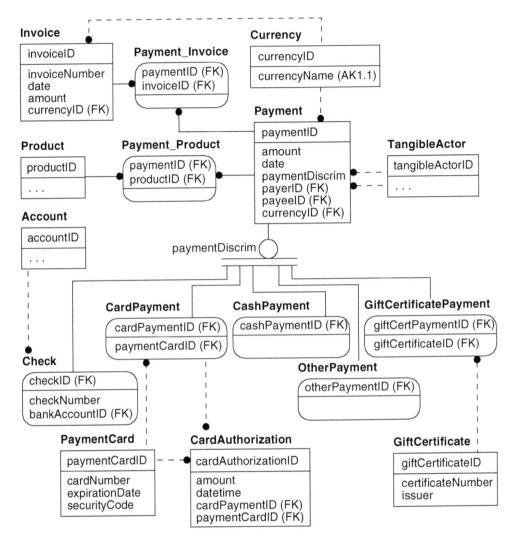

Figure 10.30 Archetype Payment: IDEF1X model.

10.16 Position

A **Position** is a job held by someone in an organization (Figure 10.31, Figure 10.32). An *Organization* can have many *Positions* and each *Position* is for a specific *Organization*.

A *Person* may hold multiple *Positions* over time and a *Position* may be held by multiple *Persons*. Furthermore, the model permits a *Person* to hold multiple *Positions* at the same time (intended) and also allows a *Position* to be held by multiple *Persons* at the same time (unin-

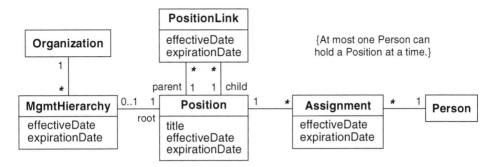

Figure 10.31 Archetype Position: UML model. A *Position* is a job held
by someone in an organization.

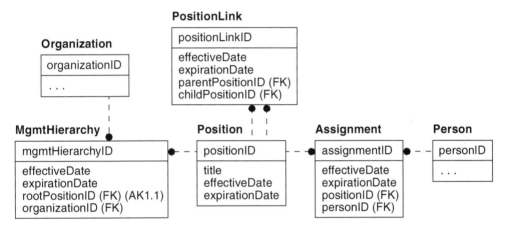

Figure 10.32 Archetype Position: IDEF1X model.

tended). In reality, at most one *Person* can hold a *Position* at a time and application code must
enforce this constraint.

The model does not require that the position structure be a hierarchy, although that is the
usual case. The model instead supports matrix management (a *Position* may report to multiple parent *Positions*).

10.17 Product

A ***Product*** is the packaging of a physical item for a particular marketplace (Figure 10.33,
Figure 10.34). For example, a bank can have a checking account service and tailor the service
into products for various markets. One product might be an interest-bearing checking account. Another might couple a checking account with discounts for various businesses. A
third product might have low fees for students. A product can consist of multiple items.

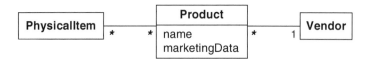

Figure 10.33 Archetype Product: UML model. A *Product* is the packaging of a physical item for a particular marketplace.

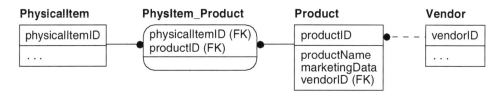

Figure 10.34 Archetype Product: IDEF1X model.

10.18 Role

A *Role* is a function played by someone or something (Figure 10.35, Figure 10.36). Each *Role* corresponds to one *Entity* and can also have a *Relationship*. Similarly, each *RoleType* corresponds to one *EntityType* and can also have a *RelationshipType*.

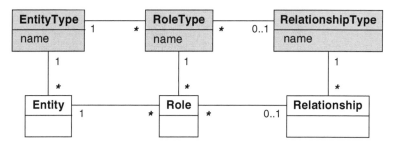

Figure 10.35 Archetype Role: UML model. A *Role* is a function played by someone or something.

This archetype is an excerpt from a metamodel but the notion of a role often arises for application models. Sometimes it is helpful to have explicit role tables as the *Actor* and *Address* archetypes illustrate.

Note that the role archetype has two homomorphisms.

- *EntityType* to *Entity* corresponds to *RoleType* to *Role*.
- *RelationshipType* to *Relationship* corresponds to *RoleType* to *Role*.

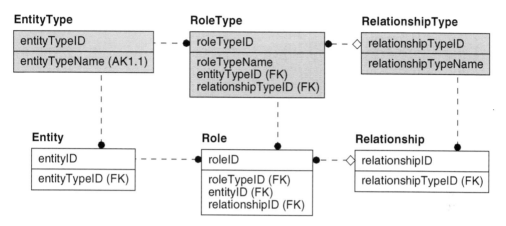

Figure 10.36 Archetype Role: IDEF1X model.

10.19 Transaction

A *Transaction* is an exchange that must be completed in its entirety or not at all (Figure 10.37, Figure 10.38). There are two major usages — in finance and in computing.

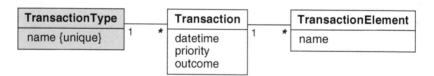

Figure 10.37 Archetype Transaction: UML model. A *Transaction* is an exchange that must be completed in its entirety or not at all.

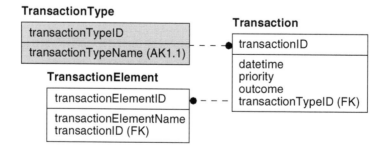

Figure 10.38 Archetype Transaction: IDEF1X model.

A financial transaction is an exchange of assets (information, goods, services, money) between two parties. For example, a stock holding might be sold on a stock exchange. A company may split its stock awarding additional shares to the owner as well as money in lieu of partial shares.

A computing transaction (often involving a database) is a group of commands that is treated as a unit of work. All commands must be completed before the transaction is successful. Partial work is not permitted; if the transaction cannot be completed all work is undone.

Each *Transaction* has a *TransactionType* that determines the precise processing. A transaction *outcome* is committed or rolled back. The *TransactionElements* are either the details of a financial transaction or the constituent commands for a computing transaction.

10.20 Vendor

A *Vendor* is someone involved in the sale of products (Figure 10.39, Figure 10.40). *Vendor* reifies the vendor role for a *TangibleActor* (usually an organization, see Section 10.2). Vendors often have special data to collect, such as supply data, credit information, and order lead time. You could use softcoding (see Chapter 13) to capture vendor data, but an alternative is to define a distinct entity type as shown here.

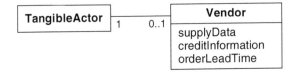

Figure 10.39 Archetype Vendor: UML model. A *Vendor* is someone involved in the sale of products.

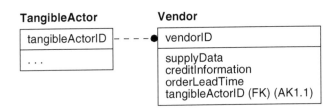

Figure 10.40 Archetype Vendor: IDEF1X model.

10.21 Chapter Summary

Archetypes are abstractions that often occur and transcend individual applications. You should keep them in mind as you construct models. Table 10.1 summarizes the archetypes.

Table 10.1 Summary of Archetypes

Archetype	Definition	Sample applications	Related terms
Account	a label for recording, reporting, and managing a quantity of something	• accounting • business • computing • financial • travel	• account payable • account receivable • credit card account • email account • expense account • frequent flyer account • general ledger account
Actor	someone or something that is notable in terms of data or relationships	widespread use across applications	• customer • organization • party • person • vendor
Address	a means for communicating with an actor		
Asset	something of value	• business • financial	• security
Contract	an agreement for the supply of products	• business • financial	• agreement • purchase order • sales order
Course	a series of lessons about a subject	• education	
Customer	someone involved in the purchase of products	CRM (customer relationship management)	
Document	a physical or electronic representation of a body of information		
Event	an occurrence at some point in time		
Flight	the travel by an airplane between airports	• aviation • shipping • trucking	• route
Item	a part or a service	• commerce • manufacturing	• part • product • service

Note: Keep them in mind as you construct models. The use of an archetype can lead to a breakthrough.

Table 10.1 Summary of Archetypes (continued)

Archetype	Definition	Sample applications	Related terms
Location	a physical place in space		• place • site • venue
Opportunity	an inquiry that can result in business	• marketing • sales	• campaign • lead
Part	a specific good that can be described	• manufacturing • engineering	• item • product
Payment	the assignment of money in return for something of value	• business • financial	
Position	a job held by someone in an organization	• human resources	• employee • employer • job • assignment
Product	the packaging of a physical item for a particular marketplace	• banking • mechanical parts • service companies	• item • part • service
Role	a function played by someone or something		
Transaction	an exchange that must be completed in its entirety or not at all	• computing • financial	
Vendor	someone involved in the sale of products		• seller • supplier

Bibliographic Notes

In some regards, this chapter is similar in style to other data pattern books and their emphasis on seed models. The difference is that this chapter emphasizes the core concepts rather than the details that applications add. My purpose is to call attention to concepts that often occur and can be overlooked.

The term *archetype* is taken from [Arlow-2004]. I had used *critical concept* in an earlier draft, but there is no point to creating a new term when the literature already has a suitable term.

The actor model is consistent with the literature but is more robust. [Arlow-2004], [Hay-1996], and [Silverston-2001a] define a party as a person or an organization. [Fowler-1997] defines a party as a person, organization, or role type (Fowler's term is *post*). The model in this book broadens the notion to include roles and applications. The term *actor* is also consistent with UML terminology.

Chapters 2 and 3 of [Silverston-2009] have an especially good discussion of *party* (comparable to *actor* in this book). The authors distinguish between a declarative role (a role that a person or organization plays within an entire enterprise) and a contextual role (a role in a specific relationship).

[Arlow-2004] discusses party roles, but their representation is flawed as there is no need to distinguish between a client and supplier in a party relationship, given that they have a role type. I suspect that the authors are thinking in terms of directed relationships, which is an inferior approach. (See Section 8.7.4.)

[Blaha-1998] has a further discussion of catalog parts and physical parts.

The Wikipedia Web site was helpful for constructing some definitions. Table 10.2 shows significant coverage by other books of the archetypes.

Table 10.2   Coverage of This Chapter's Archetypes in the Literature

Archetype	[Arlow-2004]	[Fowler-1997]	[Hay-1996]	[Silverston]
Account		p 97–132	p 118–121	p 260–277 [2001a]
Actor	p 119–155	p 18–33	p 23–28, 31–32	p 29–39 [2001a] p 35–131 [2009]
Address	p 132–137		p 33–36	p 49–57 [2001a] p 303–410 [2009]
Asset			p 149–150	
Contract	p 303–389	p 176–180	p 95–116	p 105–158 [2001a]
Course				
Customer	p 190–191			p 33–34 [2001a]
Document			p 205–234	
Event				
Flight				
Item	p 203–265		p 46–61	p 69–104 [2001a]
Location			p 36–40	p 380–410 [2009]
Opportunity				
Part	p 203–265		p 46–61	p 100–104 [2001a]
Payment	p 425–431			p 250–254 [2001a]
Position		p 32–33	p 28–31	p 303–314 [2001a]
Product	p 203–265		p 46–61	p 69–104 [2001a]
Role	p 160–179		p 106–108 p 242–243	p 33–47 [2001a] p 35–131 [2009]
Transaction		p 98–101	p 122–124	p 265–275 [2001a]
Vendor				

References

[Arlow-2004] Jim Arlow and Ila Neustadt. *Enterprise Patterns and MDA: Building Better Software with Archetype Patterns and UML*. Boston, Massachusetts: Addison-Wesley, 2004.

[Blaha-1998] Michael Blaha and William Premerlani. *Object-Oriented Modeling and Design for Database Applications*. Upper Saddle River, New Jersey: Prentice-Hall, 1998.

[Fowler-1997] Martin Fowler. *Analysis Patterns: Reusable Object Models*. Boston, Massachusetts: Addison-Wesley, 1997.

[Hay-1996] David C. Hay. *Data Model Patterns: Conventions of Thought*. New York, New York: Dorsett House, 1996.

[Silverston-2001a] Len Silverston. The *Data Model Resource Book, Volume 1*. New York, New York: Wiley, 2001.

[Silverston-2001b] Len Silverston. The *Data Model Resource Book, Volume 2*. New York, New York: Wiley, 2001.

[Silverston-2009] Len Silverston and Paul Agnew. *The Data Model Resource Book, Volume 3*. New York, New York: Wiley, 2009.

[Wikipedia] www.wikipedia.org

Part IV

Identity

Identity is the property that distinguishes an entity from all others. Identity is a prominent concern in databases because developers must be able to find and reference data. This chapter focuses on conceptual aspects of identity and minimizes the discussion of implementation.

Identity is relevant to patterns, because identity deeply pervades models and thinking about models. There are three purposes of data models: to define data structure, to constrain data, and to provide a blueprint for accessing data. Identity is important for all three. Identifying fields are prominent in the declaration of data structure. Identity is by its very nature a constraint on uniqueness. And finally, unique fields and unique combinations of fields are anchor points for starting navigation of a database to access data.

I debated whether or not to include a chapter on identity. I decided to include the chapter because identity is such an important aspect of modeling. Identity pervades both conceptual models (unique keys and traversals of models—this chapter) as well as design models (different approaches to defining primary keys—Chapter 16).

11

Identity

Identity is the property that distinguishes an entity from all others. In concept, an entity has intrinsic identity apart from how the entity may happen to be implemented. Users must be able to find data in a database or the database is compromised.

11.1 Intrinsic Identity

Intrinsic identity is the ability to find data with fields that have meaning. Starting from outside a database, a user specifies real-world fields to find one or more entities and then navigates the database to find the desired data. Intrinsic identity has no bearing on how identity is implemented. Rather intrinsic identity provides a way for logically finding entities when searching a database.

11.1.1 Candidate Keys

Candidate keys provide one aspect of intrinsic identity. A *candidate key* is a combination of one or more fields that uniquely identify the records in a table. The set of fields in a candidate key must be minimal; no field can be discarded from the candidate key without destroying uniqueness. No field in a candidate key can be null. When a candidate key is defined, the DBMS guarantees that the combination of fields will be unique. I strongly encourage the use of candidate keys. After all, the purpose of a database is not only to store data but also to assure data's quality. When you use a candidate key as the starting point for a search, you are guaranteed to obtain no more than one entity.

The UML lacks a notation for candidate keys. This book uses the notation *{unique}* to flag a unique field. In Figure 11.1 *Airline* has two candidate keys, each of which consists of one field. Thus, for example, the name American Airlines and the code AA both denote the same airline.

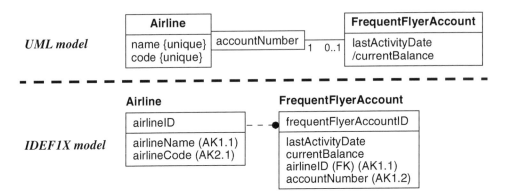

Figure 11.1 Intrinsic identity in a model. There are unique combinations of
fields that provide starting points for finding data in a database.

IDEF1X uses the *AKn.m* annotation to indicate unique combinations of fields (alternate
keys). The "n" is the number of the alternate key. The "m" is the sequence of fields within
the alternate key. Thus in Figure 11.1 the *airlineName* and *airlineCode* each individually denote an *Airline*. The combination of *airlineID* and *accountNumber* is also unique for a *FrequentFlyerAccount*.

11.1.2 UML Qualifiers

UML qualifiers are also helpful for specifying intrinsic identity. A ***qualifier*** is an attribute
that distinguishes among the entities at a "many" relationship end. A qualifier selects among
the entities, reducing the effective multiplicity, often from "many" to "one". For example, in
Figure 11.1 the UML model and IDEF1X models have the same meaning. They specify that
an *Airline* plus an *accountNumber* yield at most one *FrequentFlyerAccount*. In contrast, if
the *accountNumber* is omitted, an *Airline* yields many *FrequentFlyerAccounts*. A qualifier
specifies an important path for traversing a model and finding data.

11.1.3 Logical Horizon

Traversal is a third aspect of intrinsic identity. Applications can navigate a model and its corresponding database by traversing relationships and generalizations. Traversals of a model
become SQL joins in an implementation.

The ***logical horizon*** [Feldman-1986] of an entity type is the set of entity types reachable
by one or more paths terminating in a cumulative multiplicity of one. A ***path*** is a sequence
of traversals of relationships and generalization levels. The purpose of the logical horizon is
to compute the specific entities that can be inferred from a starting entity.

First I will explain Figure 11.2 and then give some examples for logical horizon. A *Person* may have multiple *FrequentFlyerAccounts*, each of which is offered by an *Airline*. An
accountNumber is unique within the context of an *Airline*. Each *FrequentFlyerAccount* can
have *Activities* posted of various *ActivityTypes*. For example, a frequent flyer account can
have credits posted for actual flight miles, bonus miles, dining activity, and car rentals.

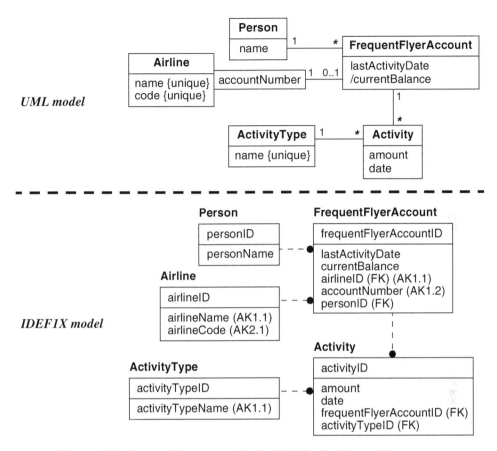

Figure 11.2 Names. Names are often helpful for finding entities.

The logical horizon of *Person* is null; the only relationship is to *FrequentFlyerAccount* and the multiplicity is "many." The logical horizon of *FrequentFlyerAccount* is *Person* and *Airline*. The logical horizon of *Activity* is *FrequentFlyerAccount*, *Person*, *Airline*, and *ActivityType*.

11.2 Names

Names are prominent in models and often helpful for finding entities. Webster's dictionary defines a name as "a word or phrase that constitutes the distinctive designation of a person or thing." There are four scenarios for how names can be used to find entities.

- **Unique names**. Some names are unique and resolve to a single entity. For example, the name of a country corresponds to a specific country. In Figure 11.2 *Airline name*, *Airline code*, and *ActivityType name* are globally unique.

- **Unique names within a context**. Other names are not unique on their own but are unique when combined with a parent entity. For example, the names of provinces are unique within the context of a country. UML qualifiers (and their equivalent in IDEF1X alternate keys) provide a notation for specifying fields that are unique within a context. In Figure 11.2 *accountNumber* provides the unique name for a *FrequentFlyerAccount* within the context of an *Airline*.

- **Non-unique names**. Still other names provide important description but alone cannot find an entity. For example, person names are important, but insufficient for finding an individual person. Sometimes non-unique names can be augmented with additional details to find a specific entity.

- **Multiple unique names**. Some entities have multiple names. Figure 11.3 promotes the *substanceName* attribute to an entity type because each chemical substance may have multiple aliases. For example, propylene is known as *propylene* and C_3H_6.

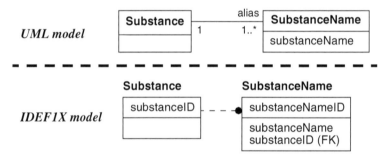

Figure 11.3 Multiple unique names. Chemical substances can have multiple names that identify the substance.

11.3 Surrogate Identity

Sometimes entities can be identified via other entities with which they are closely related. For example, you cannot reliably identify a person with his or her name. However, in some applications you can identify a person via a passport, driver's license, or identity card.

11.4 Structured Fields

Some entities, especially mechanical parts and items for commerce, have structured fields that provide identity. A **structured field** is a field that is composed from constituent pieces with a specified grammar. Structured fields are synthetic but when parsed the pieces have meaning. Many structured fields are backed by standard protocols.

As an example, consider the UPC, EAN, and GTIN codes for consumer packaged goods. The UPC (Universal Product Code) originated in the United States in the early 1970s and has twelve digits. The first digit is the system digit and indicates the kind of item—general merchandise, random-weight item, health item, in-house item, and coupon. The next five digits denotes the vendor. Digits seven through eleven are called the item code—a unique code for an item within the context of a vendor. The last digit is a check digit.

The UPC was followed by the EAN (European Article Number) which has thirteen digits. The EAN has the following sequence: two system digits, five vendor digits, five item digits, and one check digit.

Most recently the UPC and EAN have both been replaced by the GTIN (Global Trade Item Number). The GTIN has fourteen digits with the following sequence: item digit, two system digits, five vendor digits, five item digits, and one check digit. Note that there are a total of six item digits, one at the start of the sequence and the other five later in the sequence. The extra item digit is often used to distinguish individual items from multiple items that are packaged into cases and pallets.

Many manufacturers have product codes that embody information about the major components, location of manufacture, and date of manufacture.

11.5 Master Applications

Some organizations have dedicated applications (called *master applications*) that enforce the identity of occurrences of crucial concepts and unify their data across an organization's applications. All requests for creating, modifying, and deleting such occurrences must be coordinated via the corresponding master application. For example, customers, parts, locations, securities, and contracts are often good candidates for master applications. An organization should have no more than a handful of master applications and the subject concepts should pervade the organization.

Consider a *Customer* master application. If each application names customers, there could be many variations, such as AT&T, A.T.&T., and American Telephone and Telegraph. One application might have the current mailing address and another might have a stale address from the past. With this kind of chaos, it is difficult to have a global perspective for data. In contrast, a *Customer* master application would dictate the precise name for a company for use throughout an organization and serve as a centralized source for its data.

11.6 Merging Data

Duplicate copies of data can arise in various ways, such as through flaws in business processes. For example, an airline may create two frequent flyer accounts for a person and not realize that they are dealing with the same customer. Duplicate copies can also arise through business acquisitions that cause databases to be merged. For example, the merger of Delta Airlines and Northwest Airlines created a need to merge frequent flyer databases.

The tricky part of merging data is determining if one entity is the same thing as another. The entities being compared must have matching real-world data that can identify them or there must be an algorithm to deduce a match (such as by equating the various AT&T names in Section 11.5). Sometimes the information required to make the determination is missing from a database; then a person has to investigate to reach a decision. Once a match is established the mechanics of combination are straightforward but can still be tedious to accomplish without disrupting a business.

There is no merge technique that is clearly superior. The appropriate solution depends on the situation as Table 11.1 explains.

Table 11.1 Summary of Approaches to Merging Data

Merge approach	Definition	Advantages	Drawbacks
Combine entities	Copy data from one entity to the other. Then discard the rejected entity.	• Fully consolidates the data.	• There can be much data to migrate, especially if there are many foreign keys. • May have to remap foreign keys and revise foreign key definitions. • It is easy to overlook a foreign key, causing a stale reference.
Favor an entity	Mark one entity as deprecated and the other as active. Both entities remain in the database. Gradually migrate data to the active entity.	• Eventually consolidates the data. • There is less risk of stale references as obsolete data can persist for awhile.	• In the meantime there is database clutter, possible confusion, and indirection in accessing data. • There can be much data to migrate, especially if there are many foreign keys.
Logical merge	Use a binding table to logically combine entities. (See Section 10.1.) One entity could be favored for new data.	• Can readily merge data as well as unmerge. • There is no risk of stale references.	• Causes indirection in accessing data, complicating queries and slowing performance. • The database schema remains fragmented by multiple aspects of an entity.

Note: The appropriate solution depends on the situation.

11.7 Chapter Summary

Identity is the property that distinguishes an entity from all others. In concept, an entity has intrinsic identity apart from how the entity may happen to be implemented. Candidate keys and UML qualifiers are important aspects of intrinsic identity. Names are prominent in models and can be helpful for finding specific data.

Bibliographic Notes

[Khoshafian-1986] is a classic reference on identity, but the ideas in the paper reach beyond programming languages and also pertain to databases.

Chapter 5 of [Fowler-1997] has a good discussion of identity.

Chapter 4 of [Arlow-2004] discusses identity for persons and organizations. Chapter 7 discusses identity for products.

References

[Arlow-2004] Jim Arlow and Ila Neustadt. *Enterprise Patterns and MDA: Building Better Software with Archetype Patterns and UML.* Boston, Massachusetts: Addison-Wesley, 2004.

[Feldman-1986] P. Feldman and D. Miller. Entity model clustering: Structuring a data model by abstraction. *Computer Journal 29*, 4 (1986), 348–360.

[Fowler-1997] Martin Fowler. *Analysis Patterns: Reusable Object Models.* Boston, Massachusetts: Addison-Wesley, 1997.

[Khoshafian-1986] S.N. Khoshafian and G.P. Copeland. Object identity. *OOPSLA '86 as ACM SIG-PLAN 21*, 11 (November 1986), 406–416.

Part V

Canonical Models

Part V presents several canonical models — models that often appear and cut across individual applications. These models are services with logic that stands apart from the various applications that use them. The canonical models contrast with the archetypes, in that archetypes revolve around a basic concept found in models, while canonical models are complete models that can be used as part of a larger application.

Chapter 12 presents several approaches to the translation of human languages. Software that is written for international markets must be able to support multiple languages such as English, Spanish, and Chinese. Data can often be stored in the language of entry, but there is a need to translate metadata, such as labels in forms and reports.

Chapter 13 covers softcoded values. The usual approach is to hardcode attributes in entity types and the resulting tables. As an alternative, values can be softcoded — metadata specifies the intended model and generic tables store the values. Softcoded values are appropriate for applications with uncertain data structure; softcoding adds stability to the data representation, minimizes changes to application logic, and reduces the likelihood of data conversion. On the downside, softcoded values add complexity and incur a modest performance penalty.

Chapter 14 discusses generic diagrams, diagrams that display as a picture and have underlying semantic content. The generic diagram model provides a starting point for various kinds of diagrams such as data structure diagrams, data flow diagrams, state diagrams, and equipment flow diagrams.

Chapter 15 explains state diagrams for specifying states and stimuli that cause changes of state. State diagrams are helpful for applications with a lifecycle or a sequence of steps to enforce. Such information can be declared in database tables, rather than encoded via programming. One group of tables specifies state diagrams that generic code interprets. Another set of tables can store data from an application's execution of state diagrams.

The canonical models have some complexity that illustrates the power of modeling. They leverage some of the patterns shown in earlier chapters.

12

Language Translation

Much of today's software is written for an international market. Worldwide sales enable vendors to maximize profits. In addition multinational companies often must build systems that cut across countries, cultures, and languages. Language translation can be a difficult issue. Data often is stored in the language of entry, but there can be a need to translate metadata, such as labels in forms and reports. This chapter presents the nucleus of a string translation model.

12.1 Alternative Architectures

Table 12.1 summarizes several approaches to language translation. It is convenient to consider abbreviation along with translation.

One option is to add parallel columns for translations and abbreviations. This approach is certainly simple, but it is verbose (many columns could be needed) and brittle (each added translation or abbreviation causes modification of the schema).

A dedicated lookup table can convert a phrase from a base to a translated language and handle abbreviations. The advantage is that there are no disruptions to application schema. The downside is that phrases can be translated out of context leading to errors. For example, there are multiple meanings of the word *bank*.

The language–neutral translation service is a robust choice. This also uses a lookup table, but a concept ID represents the source idea. This approach separates the multiple meaning of words and phrases for a clean translation. The drawback is that application databases must replace translatable strings with concept IDs. Consequently this approach is normally limited to new applications.

Some Web sites implement the last option. For example, Babel Fish and Google Language Tools can both translate a phrase from a source to a target language. Such an approach is not viable for most applications as translation quality is often poor.

The next sections elaborate the first three options.

Table 12.1 Language Translation Approaches

Approach	Synopsis	Advantages	Disadvantages
Attribute translation in place	Each translated or abbreviated attribute has multiple parallel fields.	• Simplicity. • Precise translation. • No language bias. • Supports abbreviation.	• Must add fields. • Translations can be inconsistent. • A person must provide the translations.
Phrase–to–phrase translation	A lookup mechanism converts a source phrase into a target language and abbreviation.	• No disruption to applications. • Supports abbreviation.	• Multiple meanings can lead to translation errors. • Language bias. • A person must provide the translations.
Language–neutral translation	Applications store concept IDs. A lookup table maps IDs to phrases.	• Precise translation. • No language bias. • Supports abbreviation.	• Translated application fields must be stored as IDs. • A person must provide the translations.
Automated translation	A software algorithm translates a phrase from one language into another.	• Persons do not make any translations.	• Poor translation quality. • May not handle abbreviation.

12.2 Attribute Translation In Place

The simplest approach is to add columns for translations and abbreviations. Figure 12.1 shows an example. The birth place, hair color, and eye color strings are stored in both English and Spanish. The other fields are not translated. This approach is vulnerable to inconsistencies. For example, one person could have brown hair with a Spanish translation and another person could also have brown hair with a different translation.

Consider this approach when only a few fields must be translated. Also consider this approach when XML files store data. XML files can handle parallel fields with nested elements (unlike relational database tables).

12.3 Phrase–to–Phrase Translation

Figure 12.2 and Figure 12.3 model the lookup mechanism for phrase–to–phrase translation. The advantage of this approach is that there is no disruption to any existing application schema. Consider this approach when you can limit the phrase vocabulary and avoid multiple meanings.

Figure 12.1 Attribute translation in place: Person model. Consider when few fields must be translated and for XML files.

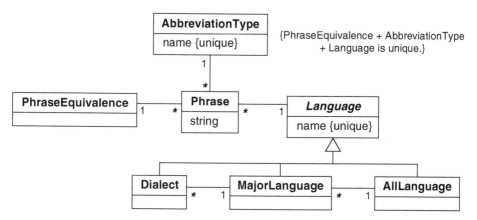

Figure 12.2 Phrase–to–phrase translation: UML model. Consider when you can limit the phrase vocabulary and avoid multiple meanings.

A ***Phrase*** is a string with a specific *Language* and *AbbreviationType*. The ***Language*** for a string can be a *Dialect*, a *MajorLanguage*, or *AllLanguage*. A ***MajorLanguage*** is a natural language, such as French, English, and Japanese. A ***Dialect*** is a variation of a *MajorLanguage*, such as UK English, US English, and Australian English. ***AllLanguage*** has a single record for strings do not vary across languages.

Each *Phrase* has an ***AbbreviationType*** which is the maximum length for a string. For example, there may be a short name (5 characters), a medium name (10 characters), a long name (20 characters), and an extra long name (80 characters). Abbreviations are especially handy for reports and user interface forms.

PhraseEquivalence cross references *Phrases* with the same meaning. (See the *Symmetric relationship* antipattern in Chapter 8.) There are synonymous *Phrases* across *Languages* and *AbbreviationTypes* but not for the same *Language* and *AbbreviationType* (hence the uniqueness constraint).

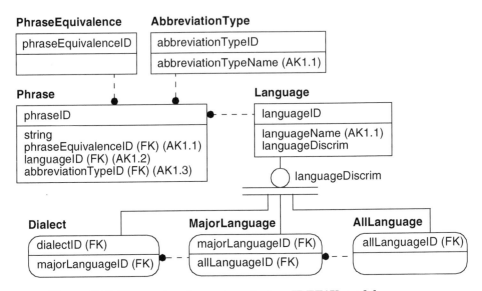

Figure 12.3 Phrase–to–phrase translation: IDEF1X model.

The translation service is dedicated software that runs apart from client applications. The translation database stores corresponding *Phrases* for various *Languages* and *AbbreviationTypes*. (A person must populate the translation database.) Upon request, the service finds the translation given a source *Phrase*, target *Language*, and target *AbbreviationType*.

Figure 12.4 shows a sample application table that could be subject to the translation mechanism. The phrase–to–phrase approach has a language bias. For example, the source data may be stored in English and converted to another language only upon translation mapping. Architecturally, a language bias is undesirable because users may detect the favored language.

Person
familyName
personalName
birthdate
birthPlace_English
hairColor_English
eyeColor_English
height
weight

Figure 12.4 Phrase-to-phrase translation: Person model.

The pseudocode in Figure 12.5 illustrates the logic for finding a translation. (The pseudocode is written using the UML's Object Constraint Language [Warmer-1999].) The basic logic is to first look for an exact match to the target language. Otherwise, if a *Dialect* is specified, look for the corresponding *MajorLanguage*. If that fails, then make one more try to look for the *AllLanguage* record.

Phrase::getTargetPhrase (aTargetAbbrevType, aTargetLanguage) RETURNS aPhrase

```
/* Start with all possible phrases for a source Phrase */
aSetOfPhrases := self.PhraseEquivalence.Phrase

/* Second, restrict phrases to matching the target abbreviation type */
aSetOfPhrases := aSetOfPhrases->SELECT (abbreviationType == aTargetAbbrevType)

/* Third, look for an exact match to the target language */
card := Cardinality (aSetOfPhrases=>SELECT(language==aTargetLanguage));
IF card == 1 THEN RETURN aSetOfPhrases->SELECT(language == aTargetLanguage)
ELSEIF card > 1 THEN RETURN "Error: Ambiguous"
ENDIF

/* Otherwise for a dialect look for a major language */
IF TypeOf(aTargetLanguage) == "Dialect" THEN RETURN
    self.getTargetPhrase (aTargetAbbrevType, aTargetLanguage.MajorLanguage);
ENDIF

/* Otherwise for a major language look for a default */
IF TypeOf(aTargetLanguage) == "MajorLanguage" THEN RETURN
    self.getTargetPhrase (aTargetAbbrevType, aTargetLanguage.AllLanguage);
ENDIF

/* Else failure. Could not find a translation. */
RETURN "Error: No translation found"

END getTargetPhrase
```

Figure 12.5 Phrase–to–phrase translation: Pseudocode for finding a phrase.

12.4 Language–Neutral Translation

Figure 12.6 and Figure 12.7 show a model for a language–neutral translation service. This approach separates the multiple meaning of words and phrases for a clean translation. However, you replace translatable strings with concepts IDs, limiting this approach to new applications.

A ***Phrase*** is a string with a specific *Language* and *AbbreviationType*. The **Language** for a string can be a *Dialect*, a *MajorLanguage*, or *AllLanguage*. A ***MajorLanguage*** is a natural language, such as French, English, and Japanese. A ***Dialect*** is a variation of a *MajorLanguage*, such as UK English, US English, and Australian English. ***AllLanguage*** has a single record for strings that do not vary across languages.

Each *Phrase* has an ***AbbreviationType*** which is the maximum length for a string. For example, a name may be short (5 characters), medium (10 characters), long (20 characters), and extra long (80 characters). Abbreviations are especially handy for reports and forms.

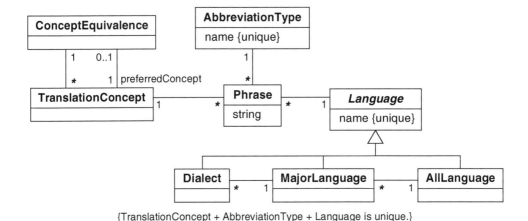

{TranslationConcept + AbbreviationType + Language is unique.}

Figure 12.6 Language–neutral translation: UML model. Consider for
new applications that require a robust translation approach.

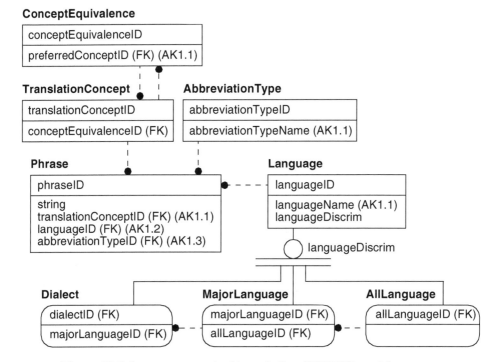

Figure 12.7 Language–neutral translation: IDEF1X model.

A ***TranslationConcept*** is the idea in a person's mind that underlies a group of related *Phrases*. The premise of language–neutral translation is that an idea can be precisely expressed in any *Language*. Of course, this assumption is not exactly true as each language has its nuances. However, it is a good approximation for translating short phrases such as those that occur in user interface screens and reports. The translation service is not intended for long passages such as those in documents and books.

Table 12.2 shows a simple example. A person has the concept "truck" in mind with a *translationConceptID* of 2054.

Table 12.2   Language–Neutral Translation: Sample Phrases

translationConceptID	Language	AbbreviationType	Phrase
2054	*MajorLanguage* = English	long	truck
	MajorLanguage = French	long	camion
	MajorLanguage = English	short	trk
	Dialect = British English	long	lorry

- A *MajorLanguage* of English and long *AbbreviationType* yields a *Phrase* of "truck."
- A *MajorLanguage* of French and long *AbbreviationType* yields a *Phrase* of "camion."
- A *MajorLanguage* of English and short *AbbreviationType* yields a *Phrase* of "trk."
- A *Dialect* of British English and long *AbbreviationType* yields a *Phrase* of "lorry."

In practice, many persons could populate data and define redundant *TranslationConcepts*. Multiple definitions are undesirable but difficult to avoid. These multiple definitions ripple throughout application databases and are difficult to consolidate.

ConceptEquivalence provides a cross reference for synonymous *TranslationConcepts* and effects a logical merge. (See Chapter 11.) The application tables store *translationConceptIDs*. *ConceptEquivalence* serves only as a cross-reference and is not referenced by application tables. (See the *Symmetric relationship* antipattern in Chapter 8.) Each occurrence of *ConceptEquivalence* has a *preferred TranslationConcept*.

The translation service is dedicated software that runs apart from client applications. To use the service, an application database substitutes a *translationConceptID* for each translatable phrase. For each *TranslationConcept*, the translation database stores the corresponding *Phrases* for the pertinent *Languages* and *AbbreviationTypes*. (A person must populate the translation database.) Upon request, the service finds the *Phrase* for the specified *TranslationConcept*, *Language*, and *AbbreviationType*.

Figure 12.8 shows a sample application table that is subject to language–neutral translation. The use of concept IDs works well for a new application. But it would be disruptive for an existing application to change strings to IDs.

The pseudocode in Figure 12.9 illustrates the logic for finding a phrase, given a *TranslationConcept*, *AbbreviationType*, and *Language*. The basic logic is to first look for an exact

```
+-----------------------------+
|           Person            |
+-----------------------------+
| familyName                  |
| personalName                |
| birthdate                   |
| birthPlace_conceptID        |
| hairColor_conceptID         |
| eyeColor_conceptID          |
| height                      |
| weight                      |
+-----------------------------+
```

Figure 12.8 Language–neutral translation: Person model.

TranslationConcept::getPhrase (aTargetAbbrevType, aTargetLanguage)
     RETURNS aPhrase

/* Start with all possible phrases for a TranslationConcept */
aSetOfPhrases := self.ConceptEquivalence.preferredConcept.Phrase

/* Second, restrict phrases to matching the target abbreviation type */
aSetOfPhrases := aSetOfPhrases->SELECT (abbreviationType == aTargetAbbrevType)

/* Third, look for an exact match to the target language */
card := Cardinality (aSetOfPhrases=>SELECT(language==aTargetLanguage));
IF card == 1 THEN RETURN aSetOfPhrases->SELECT(language == aTargetLanguage)
ELSEIF card > 1 THEN RETURN "Error: Ambiguous"
ENDIF

/* Otherwise for a dialect look for a major language */
IF TypeOf(aTargetLanguage) == "Dialect" THENI RETURN
     self.getPhrase (aTargetAbbrevType, aTargetLanguage.MajorLanguage);
ENDIF

/* Otherwise for a major language look for a default */
IF TypeOf(aTargetLanguage) == "MajorLanguage" THEN RETURN
     self.getPhrase (aTargetAbbrevType, aTargetLanguage.AllLanguage);
ENDIF

/* Else failure. Could not find a translation. */
RETURN "Error: No translation found"

END getPhrase

Figure 12.9 Language–neutral translation: Pseudocode for finding a phrase.

match to the target language. Otherwise, if a *Dialect* is specified, look for the corresponding *MajorLanguage*. If that fails, then make one more try to look for the *AllLanguage* record.

12.5 Chapter Summary

A translation service is helpful when software must support multiple languages such as English, French, and Japanese. The need for such a capability often arises and can be delivered as a service apart from any particular application. This chapter presents several approaches to language translation.

Bibliographic Notes

Several commercial products have language translation capabilities including Multilizer, Schaudin, Lionbridge, and Xataface.

The terms internationalization and localization are prominent in the literature. "Internationalization is the process of designing a software application so that it can be adapted to various languages and regions without engineering changes. Localization is the process of adapting software for a specific region or language by adding locale-specific components and translating text." [Wikipedia] The models in this chapter deal with internationalization. The population of data addresses localization.

References

[Warmer-1999] Jos Warmer and Anneke Kleppe. *The Object Constraint Language*. Boston: Addison-Wesley, 1999.

13

Softcoded Values

Most database applications directly map concepts to tables. The direct approach is effective for applications with well-defined entity types and attributes. However, it fails for applications with open-ended requirements.

Consider person data. Persons are prominent in applications and can involve much data. For example, a police database could have a lengthy description of suspects including height, weight, eye color, and hair color. The top of Figure 13.1 shows a database table for *Person*, using a direct representation (hardcoding). The bottom shows an alternative representation using softcoding. The columns in boldface are primary keys.

If the requirements are uncertain, the hardcoding of person data will be fragile. New attributes will be likely to arise, requiring model extensions and disrupting the application code. Softcoding decreases efficiency and increases storage space, but the cost is tolerable for many applications.

Hardcoding builds many constraints into the database structure. For example, a person has one height and one weight. With softcoding, metadata can declare that each person has a single value of height and weight. (Figure 13.1 omits metadata.) Careful programming must ensure that data satisfies the constraints specified by the metadata.

Hardcoding is easier to visualize and develop. Softcoding involves queries and programming that are more complex. Given that applications hide behind a user interface, softcoding implies more work for the developer, but need not complicate the application for the end user. The database and application code can be softcoded for flexibility with the user interface being hardcoded for usability.

13.1 UML Model

Figure 13.2 presents a UML model for softcoded values. The model combines data and metadata. The top entity types shaded in gray (*EntityType*, *Attribute*, *EnumValue*) concern metadata. The bottom (*Entity*, *SoftcodedValue*) concern data. Ordinary users may enter data

Person table

personID	height	weight	eyeColor	hairColor
1	180	90	brown	black
2	190	95	blue	brown

Hardcoding

Softcoding

Person table

personID
1
2

Attribute table

attribID	name
1	height
2	weight
3	eyeColor
4	hairColor

SoftcodedValue table

value ID	value Number	value String	person ID	attrib ID
1	180		1	1
2	90		1	2
3		brown	1	3
4		black	1	4
5	190		2	1
6	95		2	2
7		blue	2	3
8		brown	2	4

Figure 13.1 Database tables for hardcoding vs. softcoding.

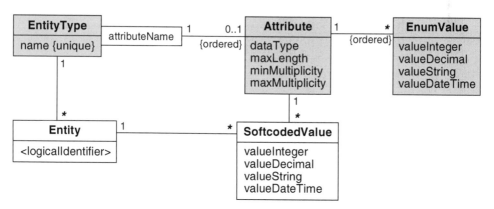

Figure 13.2 Softcoded values: UML model. The model combines data and metadata.

but only privileged users should enter metadata. Softcoded values extend the *Homomorphism* template. (See Chapter 5.)

13.1.1 Data

An **Entity** is a placeholder for things that can have *SoftcodedValues*.

A *SoftcodedValue* is a piece of data for an *Entity* and has parallel fields for different data types. A *SoftcodedValue* can have one of four data types—integer, decimal, string, or date-Time. Exactly one of these four fields must be filled in (and the other three set to NULL) for each *SoftcodedValue* record. If additional data types are needed (such as money), you can add more fields. Note the following subtleties of the model.

- **Multivalues**. An *Entity* can have multiple *SoftcodedValues* for the same *Attribute* (*Attribute* is to be explained).

- **Flexible data entry**. By default, any *SoftcodedValue* can be stored. Alternatively, you may restrict the possible *SoftcodedValues* with enumerations (to be explained).

13.1.2 Metadata

An **EntityType** describes a group of *Entities* with the same attributes, behavior, kinds of relationships, and semantics. An *EntityType* can have many *Attributes*. An **Attribute** is a named property of an *EntityType* that describes *SoftcodedValues* that can be held by each *Entity* of the *EntityType*.

Thus each *Entity* has an *EntityType* that defines *Attributes* for which *SoftcodedValues* can be stored. Another way of thinking about the model is that an *Entity* can have any number of *SoftcodedValues*. The *EntityType* constrains the *SoftcodedValues* by specifying the *Attributes* that can be populated.

Each *Attribute* has a specified **dataType** (integer, decimal, string, or datetime) indicating the appropriate field to fill in for each *SoftcodedValue*. *Attributes* with a *dataType* of 'string' have a maximum length to which *SoftcodedValues* must conform.

The box enclosing *attributeName* is a UML qualifier specifying that each *Attribute* has a unique **attributeName** for its *EntityType*. Since the model does not specify otherwise, an *attributeName* is not globally unique and may be reused across multiple *EntityTypes*. The *Attributes* are ordered within an *EntityType* just as you would find for a hardcoded model.

Note that the model's structure permits an *Entity* and *Attribute* combination to have no *SoftcodedValue* or multiple *SoftcodedValues*. The **minMultiplicity** indicates if an *Attribute* is optional (*minMultiplicity* = 0) or required (*minMultiplicity* = 1) for each *Entity* of an *EntityType*. Similarly, the **maxMultiplicity** indicates if an *Attribute* is single valued (*maxMultiplicity* = 1) or multi valued (*maxMultiplicity* = *) for each *Entity* of an *EntityType*. The *maxMultiplicity* is intended to be a set—if an *Entity* has multiple *SoftcodedValues* for an *Attribute*, they are not ordered and there can be no duplicates.

Some *Attributes* have a set of possible values. For example, the permissible colors for a lawn mower might be red, green, and blue. An **EnumValue** defines an enumeration value for an *Attribute*. If *EnumValues* are specified for an *Attribute*, the *SoftcodedValues* must conform to the list. The *EnumValues* for an *Attribute* have a defined order.

EnumValue also has parallel fields for the different data types. An *EnumValue* can have one of four data types—integer, decimal, string, or dateTime—corresponding to its *Attribute*. Exactly one of these four fields must be filled in (and the other three set to NULL) for each *EnumValue*. If additional data types were needed (such as money), it would be a simple matter to add more fields.

13.2 IDEF1X Model

Figure 13.3 restates Figure 13.2 with the IDEF1X notation. The IDEF1X model uses existence-based identity. (See Chapter 16.)

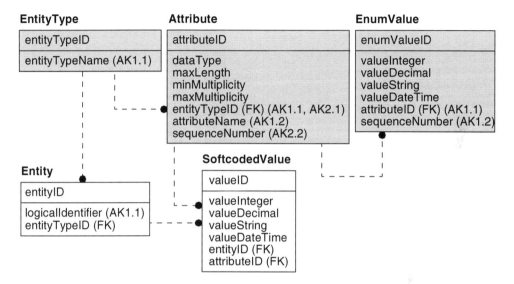

Figure 13.3 Softcoded values: IDEF1X model.

An *Entity* can have one or more fields that serve as a logical identifier (alternate keys, see Chapter 11). For example, taxpayer number could identify *Persons*. Given a logical identifier, a user can find an *Entity* and then traverse the model to retrieve associated data.

13.3 Architecture

13.3.1 Using Softcoded Values in an Application

There are two ways that an application can use softcoded values.

- **Inherit softcoding**. In Figure 13.4 and Figure 13.5 *Person* and *Document* inherit from *Entity*. Thus, for example, all *Persons* are *Entities* with an *EntityType* of "Person" that determines *Attributes* for which softcoded values can be stored. [Blaha-2006] shows how to write *Entity* stored procedures that *Person* and *Document* can reuse. The example shows only *Person* and *Document*, but the inheritance approach is best when several *EntityTypes* have softcoded values.

- **Clone softcoding**. Figure 13.6 and Figure 13.7 clone softcoding tables, once for *Person* and once for *Document*. With this approach an application not only clones schema, but also repeats data manipulation logic. Cloning provides a simple approach when few entity types have softcoded values.

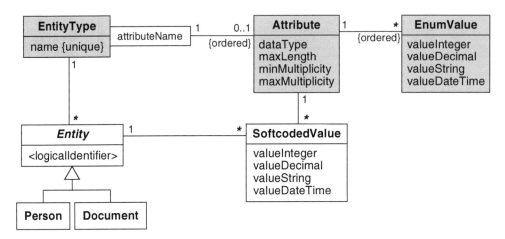

Figure 13.4 Inheriting softcoding: UML model. *Person* and *Document* inherit from *Entity* to have softcoded values.

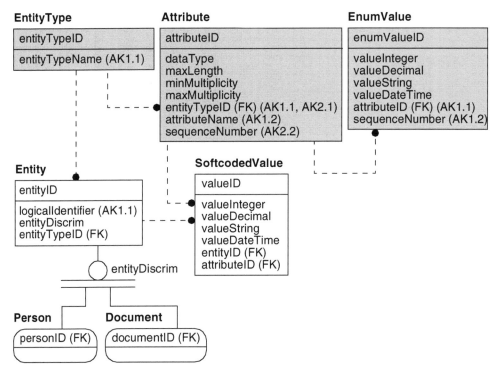

Figure 13.5 Inheriting softcoding: IDEF1X model.

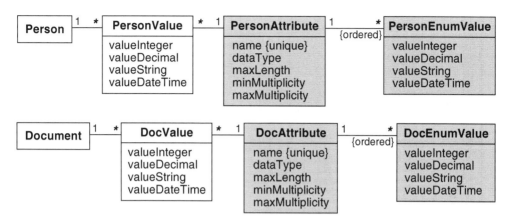

Figure 13.6 Cloning softcoding: UML model. The pertinent *EntityTypes* repeat softcoding concepts.

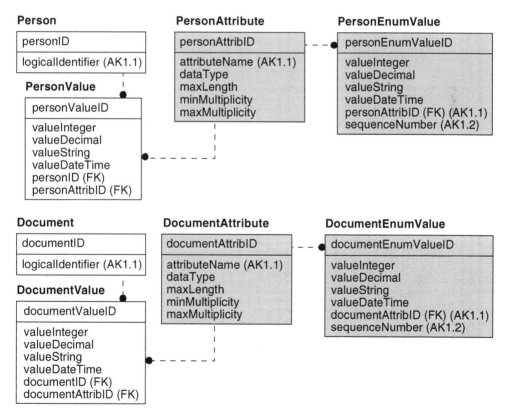

Figure 13.7 Cloning softcoding: IDEF1X model.

13.3.2 Hardcoded Model for Populating Metadata

Metadata can be difficult to grasp. It is often helpful to first prepare a hardcoded model (such as Figure 13.8) as an intermediate step and use it to populate the metadata. Domain experts understand hardcoded models better, because they can see the concepts, relationships, and constraints.

Person
name taxpayerNumber height weight eyeColor hairColor

Figure 13.8 Hardcoded model. A hardcoded model can ease discussions with application experts for acquiring metadata.

13.3.3 Mixing Hardcoded and Softcoded Attributes

Application entities can have both hardcoded and softcoded values. For example, the name and taxpayer number of a *Person* may be hardcoded. Miscellaneous data (such as weight, height, eye color, and hair color) can be softcoded. Figure 13.2 and Figure 13.3 define softcoded attributes. In contrast, each hardcoded attribute becomes a field in an application entity type.

Since there are two ways of defining attributes, there must be a way for choosing between them. My convention is to hardcode system attributes and softcode other attributes, as Table 13.1 explains.

Table 13.1 Hardcoding vs. Softcoding

	System values (hardcoded)	**Other values (softcoded)**
Certainty	Hardcode attributes that are certain	Softcode attributes that are uncertain or may be added during or after development
Indexing	Hardcode attributes that are desirable to index	Cannot index with softcoding
Multivalues	Limited to at most one value for an entity–attribute combination	Permits multiple values for an entity–attribute combination
Value metadata	Awkward to record	Straightforward to record
Examples	name, timestamp	descriptive data

Note: An entity may have both hardcoded and softcoded values.

Given the rationale for softcoding, it is clear that you should softcode attributes that may not be known until run time. For simplicity and improved performance, you can hardcode attributes that are certain.

Some attributes have a critical effect on queries and if you hardcode them you can improve performance. In particular, database indexes for important hardcoded values can boost performance by orders of magnitude. Softcoding is not amenable to database indexes because values from different entities and attributes are mixed together.

Softcoding can be desirable when there are multiple values for an entity–attribute combination. Relational database tables are flat, and hardcoding consequentially limits an entity–attribute combination to at most one value.

Softcoding also facilitates value metadata. Each value has its own record so it is easy to attach incidental data. In contrast, value metadata is clumsy with hardcoded values. For example, Figure 13.8 could have the additional attributes *heightDataSource*, *heightUnitsOfMeasure*, *heightLastUpdate*, *weightDataSource*, and so forth. The number of added attributes can quickly become unwieldy.

13.3.4 Database Performance

You do have to pay attention to performance to obtain good softcoding results.

Softcoding disperses the values of an entity across multiple records and it is important to avoid database thrashing. Therefore if you update several fields for an entity, it is normally best to enclose the updates within a database transaction. Then the group of records incurs the transaction overhead once, rather than for each update, one at a time.

Another database technique is to collocate records for an entity on the physical disc. Many DBMSs (such as Oracle and SQL Server) have commands to define the physical ordering of records for a table. If you organize the disc so that an entity's softcoded records are physically contiguous and define transactions as described above, disc activity is comparable to that of a hardcoded record type.

13.3.5 User Interface

Softcoding in a database does not imply softcoding in a user interface. As Figure 13.9 shows, it is best to adopt a hybrid approach where known attributes (both hardcoded and softcoded) have specific placement on a screen and miscellaneous softcoded values are in a generic panel. This gives you the best of both worlds—a softcoded database handles volatile data; hardcoded screens ease user understanding. Then a change to softcoded values does not affect database structure, but could require user interface revisions. Given that it is much easier and less disruptive to change a user interface than a database, the combination of a softcoded database with a hardcoded user interface can be an effective compromise.

13.4 Softcoding Variations

Figure 13.2 and Figure 13.3 provide one approach to softcoding, but others are possible.

Person data		
Person name: John Doe		
Taxpayer number: 123-45-6789		
Height: 1.85 meters	**Weight:** 90 kg	
Eye color: blue	**Hair color:** brown	

Field name	Value	Unit of measure
user defined 1	xxx	ppp
user defined 2	yyy	qqq

Figure 13.9 Sample screen for viewing person data in a hybrid format. Soft-coding in a database need not imply softcoding in a user interface.

13.4.1 Add Value Metadata

One rationale for softcoding is support for value metadata. By promoting *SoftcodedValue* to an entity type, a model can readily store information about it. For example, each value has a source — whether it is obtained from a person, the literature, calculations, an estimate, or somewhere else. Some values may have a unit of measure (such as inches, meters, seconds, and joules) — a value may override the default for its attribute. A value can also have a time of entry. Figure 13.10 and Figure 13.11 show such a revised model.

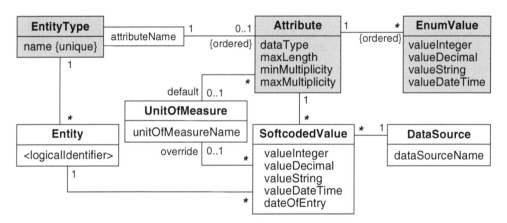

Figure 13.10 Softcoded values—add value metadata: UML model.

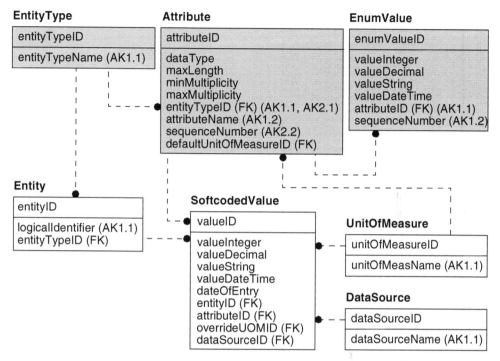

Figure 13.11 Softcoded values—add value metadata: IDEF1X model.

13.4.2 Cut Metadata

A simplification is to forego metadata. This is essentially what the UML does with tagged values. Figure 13.12 and Figure 13.13 show the corresponding revision. In essence the model stores values without metadata. The advantage of omitting metadata is simplicity. The downside is that the values are less structured, less controlled, and more vulnerable to errors. This approach can be useful for a small amount of miscellaneous data, but is not suitable for large quantities.

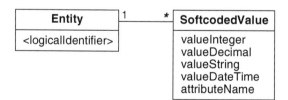

Figure 13.12 Softcoded values—cut metadata: UML model.

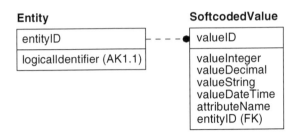

Figure 13.13 Softcoded values—cut metadata: IDEF1X model.

13.4.3 Store All SoftcodedValues as Strings

Figure 13.14 and Figure 13.15 show the option of storing all values as strings and converting them to the appropriate data type upon access. This simplifies the model at the cost of type conversions. Type conversions complicate programming and can introduce round-off errors.

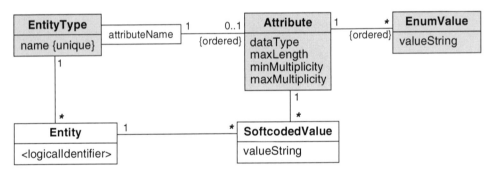

Figure 13.14 Softcoded values—store all values as strings: UML model.

13.4.4 Subtype by Data Type

An implementation can subtype *SoftcodedValue*, *Attribute*, and *EnumValue* according to the *dataType* (Figure 13.16, Figure 13.17). Note that the model's structure does not enforce that *SoftcodedValue* and *Attribute* subtypes must correspond. For example, *ValueInteger* should only be associated with *AttributeInteger*. Programming code must enforce this intent.

13.4.5 Require All Attributes to be Enumerated

Another possibility is to require that all softcoded values be enumerated (Figure 13.18, Figure 13.19). Enumerations control data entry so there should be approval for new *EnumValues*. The resulting database has clean data since users can not introduce variations such as alternate spellings, abbreviations, and upper/lower case combinations for the same thing.

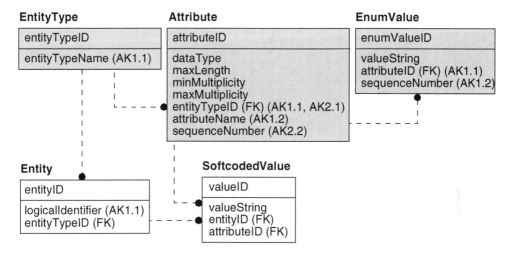

Figure 13.15 Softcoded values—store all values as strings: IDEF1X model.

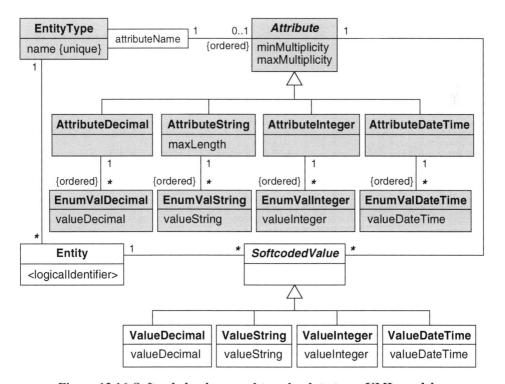

Figure 13.16 Softcoded values—subtype by data type: UML model.

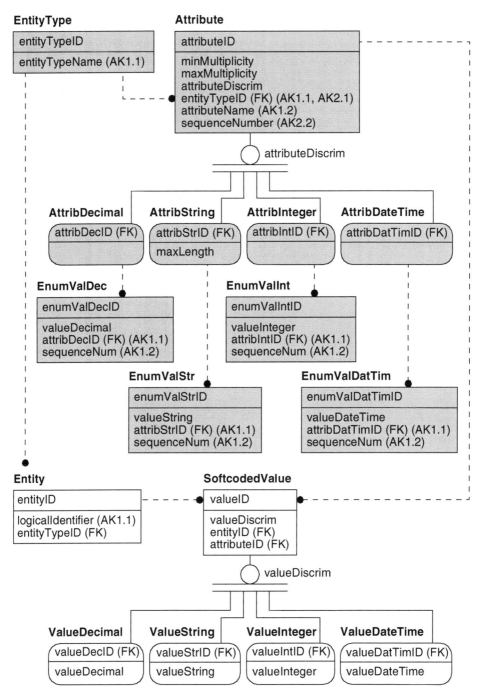

Figure 13.17 Softcoded values—subtype by data type: IDEF1X model.

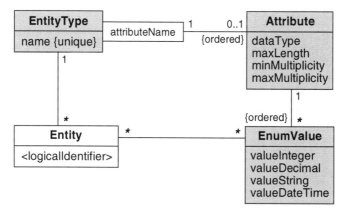

Figure 13.18 Softcoded values—all values are enumerated: UML model.

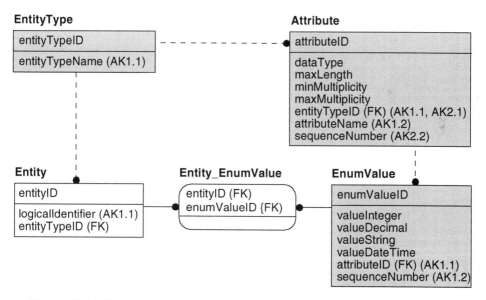

Figure 13.19 Softcoded values—all values are enumerated: IDEF1X model.

13.4.6 Enable Time History

The previous softcoded value models have treated data and metadata as invariant. An extension is to let data change over time. For example, each *SoftcodedValue* could have effective and expiration dates to track its history. Then a database can record a *SoftcodedValue* in advance of when it is needed. It can also keep a *SoftcodedValue* after it becomes obsolete. Similarly, *Attributes* and *EnumValues* could have effective and expiration dates.

The addition of time history greatly complicates the model, more so than it might seem at first. For example, what is the meaning of *minMultiplicity* when *SoftcodedValues* change over time? If *minMultiplicity* is '0', there is no problem. If *minMultiplicity* is '1' then a *SoftcodedValue* must exist for the *Attribute* at all times, extending indefinitely into the past as well as the future.

Time history also complicates enforcement of *maxMultiplicity*. If *maxMultiplicity* is '*', there is no problem. If *maxMultiplicity* is '1' then software must ensure that the constraint is satisfied at all times. The enforcement of *minMultiplicity* and *maxMultiplicity* leads to tricky programming that can degrade performance. Also, it is difficult to explain errors. In practice, it is better to omit *minMultiplicity* and *maxMultiplicity* from a model with time history.

Another concern is coordinating *Attribute* time intervals with *SoftcodedValue* time intervals. An *Attribute's* change cannot conflict with its *SoftcodedValues*. For example, a reduction in the *maxLength* for a string cannot conflict with pre-existing *SoftcodedValues*. Some changes are not permitted. For example, if *SoftcodedValues* are stored it probably does not make sense to change the *dataType* from *dateTime* to *integer*.

Given the semantic questions, performance concerns, development effort, and likelihood of bugs, Figure 13.20 and Figure 13.21 simplify the model with time history. Note that the *minMultiplicity* is implicitly '0' and *maxMultiplicity* is '*'. The *Attribute name* can vary. So too can the *dataType* as long as there is no conflict. Changes to *maxLength* are permitted.

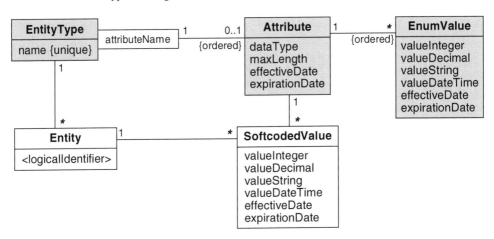

Figure 13.20 Softcoded values—with time history: UML model.

13.4.7 Support Weakly Typed Entities

The typical application assigns each entity a type that determines its attributes. However, sometimes it is helpful to define an entity on its own and then assign it multiple types that determine sets of attributes that can be populated. For example, there can be different perspectives of persons. For example, person data can include identification, physical description, and personal preferences.

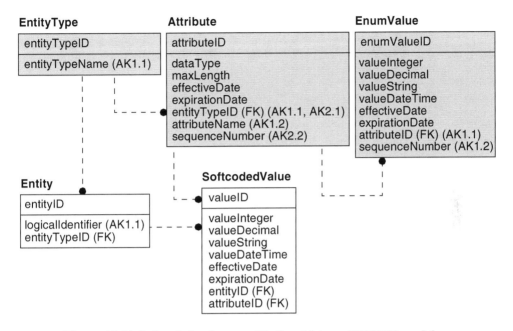

Figure 13.21 Softcoded values—with time history: IDEF1X model.

Another way of thinking is to regard entities as independent things. Each entity can be assigned multiple entity types, and the entity types can vary over time. This is the mathematical perspective. Consider a four-sided polygon on a screen (Figure 13.22). The dragging of one vertex can make it a parallelogram. Then the dragging of two vertices can make it into a rectangle. The dragging of a side can turn it into a square. All the time the same entity is being manipulated, but its entity type progressively changes from *Polygon* to *Parallelogram* to *Rectangle* to *Square*.

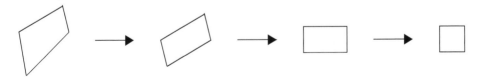

Figure 13.22 Evolution of a mathematical entity.

Figure 13.23 and Figure 13.24 permit an *Entity* to have multiple *EntityTypes*. A *Entity-Type* can be added to an *Entity*. Similarly, an *EntityType* can be removed from an *Entity*, if there are no dependent *SoftcodedValues*. The union of *EntityTypes* determines the *Attributes* for which *SoftcodedValues* can be stored. This model makes *Attributes* globally unique, so that there is no confusion among the various *EntityTypes*.

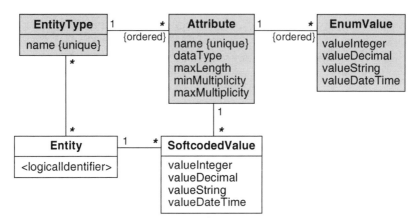

Figure 13.23 Softcoded values—weakly-typed entities: UML model.

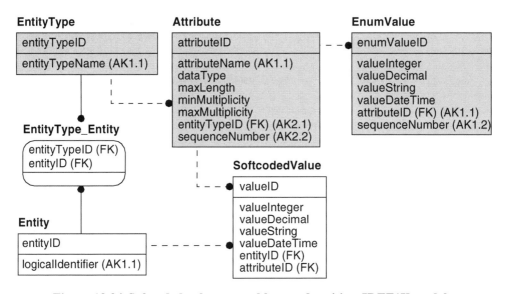

Figure 13.24 Softcoded values—weakly-typed entities: IDEF1X model.

13.4.8 Combine Variations

This chapter has presented the variations individually, but of course, you can combine many of them. For example, you might add value metadata and represent all data as strings.

13.5 Chapter Summary

I know of several industrial applications of softcoded values that have worked well in practice. The resulting applications are flexible and their performance is only moderately slower (about 20% slower) than with hardcoded data. Of course, writing the software was more difficult than with hardcoding and required skilled developers.

You should consider using softcoded values for an application with uncertain data structure. For volatile applications, softcoding adds stability to the data representation, minimizes changes to application logic, and reduces the likelihood of data conversion. A softcoded model is more abstract than a hardcoded model, hence it is more resilient in the face of application changes.

The cost of using softcoded values is additional complexity as well as a modest performance penalty. You must be careful with your use of SQL to obtain good database performance.

Bibliographic Notes

This chapter is based on an IEEE Computer Society ReadyNote (an electronic mini-book) [Blaha-2006]. The ReadyNote has a more detailed explanation of softcoded values and provides a SQL Server implementation.

[Kopaliani-2007] presents a case study of using softcoded values for a library information system. He has also implemented softcoded values using SQL Server and reports excellent performance. Softcoded values provide a robust infrastructure for his employer's software product architecture in the mechanical parts industry.

References

[Blaha-2006] Michael Blaha. *Designing and Implementing Softcoded Values*. IEEE Computer Society ReadyNote, 2006.

[Kopaliani-2007] Dimitri Kopaliani. *Architecture of Digital Asset Systems for Libraries*. Dissertation at Lawrence Technological University, 2007.

14

Generic Diagrams

A generic diagram is a picture for viewing an underlying model. I use the term *generic* diagram because it is a starting point for various kinds of diagrams such as data structure diagrams, data flow diagrams, state diagrams, and equipment flow diagrams.

Generic diagrams have a number of features.

- A diagram is a picture with underlying semantics.
- The user clicks through an icon to access semantic content from the background model.
- Lines connect icons and arrowheads indicate the direction of flow.
- Some diagrams restrict connections to discrete locations on icons. Other diagrams permit connections anywhere on an icon.
- An icon can expand into subdiagrams.
- A diagram can be rendered through different notations.

The next section presents some examples and the subsequent four sections explain the generic diagram model by splitting it into four subject areas. The final section then revisits one of the initial examples.

This chapter users an entity type icon (UML—no attribute section, IDEF1X—ellipsis for attributes) for references to entity types that are defined in other subject areas.

14.1 Generic Diagram Examples

Figure 14.1 shows a data flow diagram. The large contour is a high-level diagram that encompasses the internal detail. Figure 14.2 shows an equipment flow diagram for an air conditioning cycle. Figure 14.1 lacks ports and Figure 14.2 has ports (ports are to be explained).

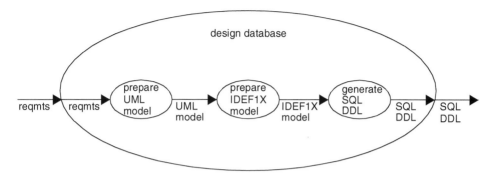

Figure 14.1 Example: Data flow diagram for designing a database (no ports).

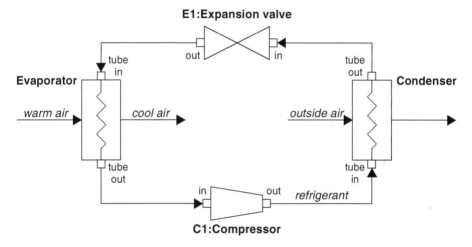

Figure 14.2 Example: Equipment flow diagram for an air conditioner (with ports).

14.2 Diagram Subject Area

A generic diagram is a picture that conveys the meaning of the underlying model. Figure 14.3 and Figure 14.4 support discrete tabs for attaching lines. The gray shading is for entity types that involve metadata.

An **Icon** is a picture that is symbolic of something. Examples of *Icons* include an oval in a data flow diagram and a compressor symbol in an equipment flow diagram. Each *Icon* has a *name*, as well as a *scale* and *position* that are applied to its corresponding *IconType*. For example, Figure 14.2 has two *Icons* for heat exchangers (*IconTypes*). One *Icon* is named "Evaporator" and the other *Icon* is named "Condenser". Each *Icon* belongs to a specific *Diagram*.

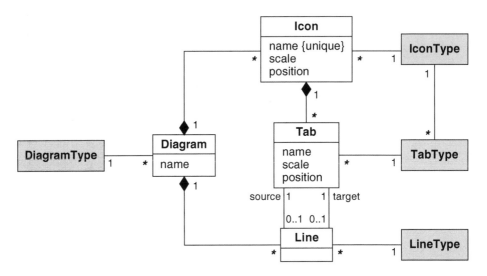

Figure 14.3 Diagram subject area, with tabs: UML model. A generic diagram is a picture that suggests the meaning of the underlying model.

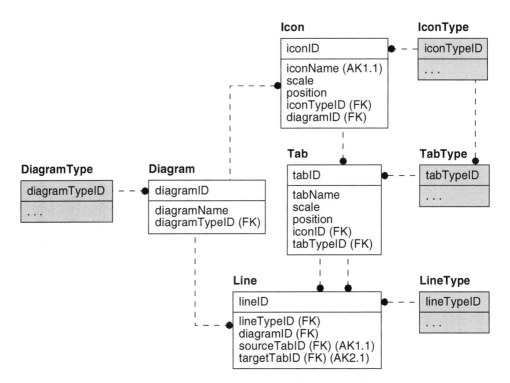

Figure 14.4 Diagram subject area, with tabs: IDEF1X model.

A **Tab** is a discrete position on an *Icon* for attaching a *Line*. A *Tab* has a *name*, as well as a *scale* and *position* that are applied to its corresponding *TabType*. The relationships between *Tab* and *Line* illustrate the *Node–Edge* directed graph (see Chapter 3). The relationships between *Icon*, *IconType*, *Tab*, and *TabType* form a homomorphism (see Chapter 5).

A **Line** is a means for coupling two *Tabs*. A **Diagram** is a set of *Icons* and *Lines*. Section 14.5 defines *DiagramType*, *IconType*, *TabType*, and *LineType*.

Figure 14.5 and Figure 14.6 forego *Tabs* and permit lines to connect anywhere on an *Icon*.

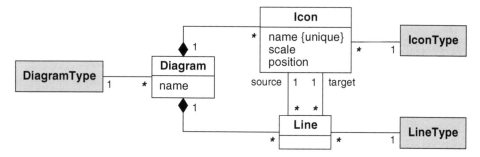

Figure 14.5 Diagram subject area, no tabs: UML model.

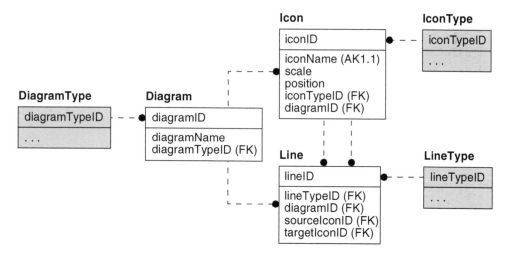

Figure 14.6 Diagram subject area, no tabs: IDEF1X model.

14.3 Model Subject Area

A semantic diagram has a model that expresses the meaning. Figure 14.7 and Figure 14.8 show the model with discrete ports.

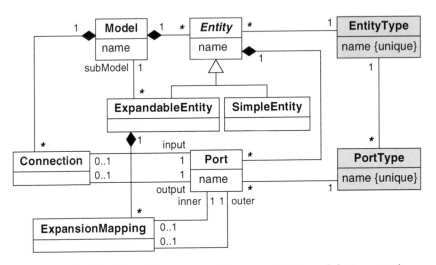

Figure 14.7 Model subject area, with ports: UML model. A semantic
diagram has an underlying model that expresses the meaning.

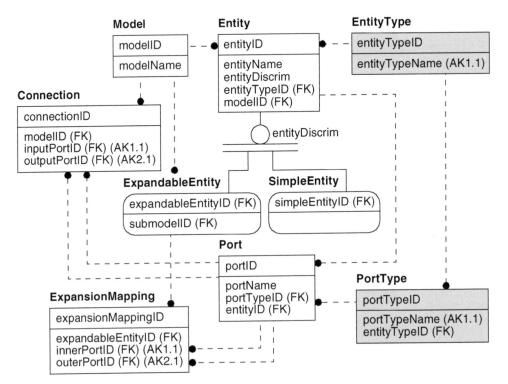

Figure 14.8 Model subject area, with ports: IDEF1X model.

An **Entity** is a thing with semantic meaning. Examples of *Entities* include a data flow in a data flow diagram and a piece of equipment in an equipment flow diagram. An *Entity* can be represented by an *Icon* in a generic diagram. An *Entity* name may or may not be unique within a model.

A **Port** is a defined place for an *Entity*, available for a connection. Just as *Icons* have *Tabs*, so too *Entities* have *Ports*. For example, an expansion valve has inlet and outlet ports. An *Entity* has many *Ports* and each *Port* belongs to a specific *Entity*.

An *Entity* may have multiple *Ports* with the same name. For example, a piping tee has two outputs that are interchangeable (and consequently have the same name). A minimum value function could have up to ten inputs and one output that is the minimum value.

Ports are helpful for some kinds of models and unnecessary for others. If a diagram omits *Ports*, then connections go directly to *Entities*.

An **EntityType** is a classification of *Entities*. For example, E101 (an *Entity*) is a heat exchanger (an *EntityType*). The *EntityType* specifies the kinds of ports (*PortType*) that apply.

It would be clumsy to define ports individually. It is better to define them for an *Entity-Type*. Thus, an *EntityType* can have *PortTypes*. A **PortType** is a classification of *Ports*. Each *PortType* belongs to a specific *EntityType*. Then each *Entity* defines *Ports* corresponding to the *PortTypes* for its *EntityType*. Such a mechanism enforces uniformity. Note that the relationships among *Entity*, *EntityType*, *Port*, and *PortType* form a homomorphism (see Chapter 5).

A **Model** is a set of *Entities* and *Connections* and has a meaning that a diagram illustrates. Each *Entity* and *Connection* belong to a single *Model*. Some of the *Entities* in a *Model* are *ExpandableEntities* and lead to *submodels*. Hence *Models* can be structured as a hierarchy of arbitrary depth.

There are two kinds of *Entities*: *ExpandableEntities* and *SimpleEntities*. An **ExpandableEntity** provides a placeholder for a submodel. In an implementation, double clicking the corresponding icon leads to the expansion into a lower-level diagram. As Figure 14.1 illustrates, some *Entities* can be expanded into submodels with a finer level of detail. A submodel is reusable and can be embedded in multiple places. A **SimpleEntity** encompasses all other *Entities* that do not lead to a submodel.

A **Connection** is a binding between an *input Port* and an *output Port*. A *Port* may, or may not, have a *Connection*. The various *Connections* establish the direction of flow through *Ports*. *Port* and *Connection* illustrate the *Node–Edge* directed graph (see Chapter 3).

The **ExpansionMapping** takes a *Port* on an interface (*outer Port* for an *ExpandableEn-tity*) and couples it to a *Port* (an *inner Port*) within the corresponding *subModel*. A *Port* may participate in one *ExpansionMapping* as an *inner Port*, one *ExpansionMapping* as an *outer Port*, or in no *ExpansionMapping* at all. The *inner Port* must belong to an *Entity* that is directly contained within the *subModel*.

Figure 14.9 and Figure 14.10 simplify the *Model* subject area and permit *Connections* anywhere on an *Entity*.

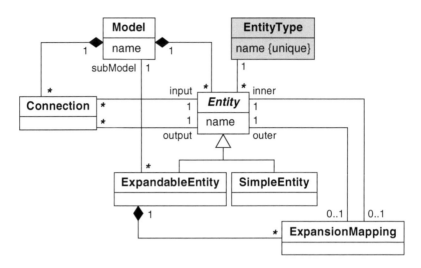

Figure 14.9 Model subject area, no ports: UML model.

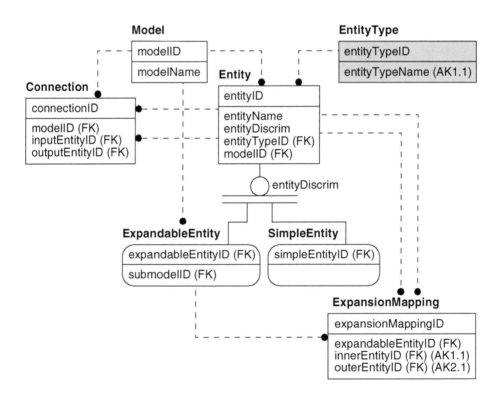

Figure 14.10 Model subject area, no ports: IDEF1X model.

14.4 Model–Diagram Binding Subject Area

Figure 14.11 and Figure 14.12 map diagram constructs to model constructs. Each diagram construct corresponds to one model construct. A model construct can appear in multiple places. These additional relationships lead to three more homomorphisms (considering also the previous subject areas).

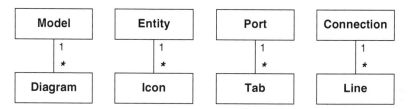

Figure 14.11 Model–diagram binding subject area: UML model.
Diagram constructs correspond to model constructs.

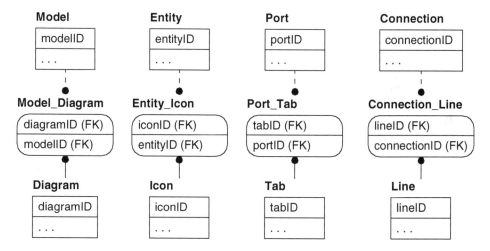

Figure 14.12 Model–diagram binding subject area: IDEF1X model.

14.5 DiagramType Subject Area

Figure 14.13 and Figure 14.14 determine the kind of diagram construct from the *Diagram-Type* and kind of model construct. For example, the combination of a *DiagramType* and an *EntityType* determine the *IconType*. Thus North America and Europe may have different *DiagramTypes* leading to different *IconTypes* for a heat exchanger.

A ***DiagramType*** specifies the kind of notation for a *Diagram*. For example, IDEF1X and IE are alternative *DiagramTypes* for a data structure model.

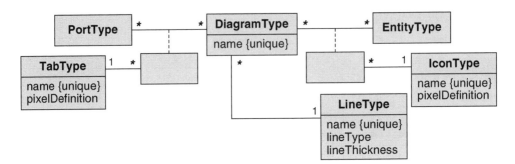

Figure 14.13 Diagram type subject area: UML model. The kind of model
construct determines the kind of diagram construct.

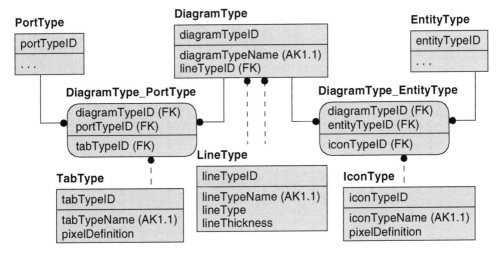

Figure 14.14 Diagram type subject area: IDEF1X model.

An *IconType* is the graphical shape for an *Icon*. The *IconType* can be determined as follows. An *Icon* corresponds to an *Entity* and an *Entity* has an *EntityType*. An *Icon* also belongs
to a *Diagram* of a specific *DiagramType*. The combination of a *DiagramType* and an *Entity-
Type* determines an *IconType* for the *Icon*.

A *TabType* is the graphical shape for a *Tab*. *TabType* can be determined in a similar manner to *IconType*.

A *LineType* is the graphical representation for a *Line* that renders a *Connection*.

14.6 Diagram Example, Revisited

Figure 14.15 shows populated relational database tables for the equipment example at the
start of the chapter (Figure 14.2).

Icon table

icon ID	iconName	scale	position	icon TypeID	diagram ID
1	Compressor			1	1
2	Condenser			2	1
3	Expansion valve			3	1
4	Evaporator			2	1

IconType table

icon TypeID	iconType Name	pixel Definition
1	compressor	
2	air heat exchanger	
3	expansion valve	

Tab table

tab ID	tab Name	scale	position	icon ID	tab TypeID
1	in			1	1
2	out			1	1
3	tube in			2	1
4	tube out			2	1
5	in			3	1
6	out			3	1
7	tube in			4	1
8	tube out			4	1

TabType table

tab TypeID	tabType Name	pixel Definition
1	standard	

LineType table

line Type ID	line Type Name	line Type	line Thickness
1	standard	solid	medium

Line table

line ID	line TypeID	diagram ID	inlet TabID	outlet TabID
1	1	1	8	1
2	1	1	2	3
3	1	1	4	5
4	1	1	6	7

Diagram table

diagram ID	diagram Name	diagram TypeID
1	air conditioner	1

Port_Tab table

tab ID	portID
1	1
2	2
3	3
4	4
5	5
6	6
7	7
8	8

Entity_Icon table

iconID	entityID
1	1
2	2
3	3
4	4

DiagramType table

diagram TypeID	diagram TypeName	line TypeID
1	equipment flow diagram	1

Figure 14.15 Populated tables for air conditioner example.

Entity table

entity ID	entityName	entity Discrim	entity TypeID	model ID
1	Compressor	simple	1	1
2	Condenser	simple	2	1
3	Expansion valve	simple	3	1
4	Evaporator	simple	4	1

EntityType table

entity TypeID	entityType Name
1	compressor
2	condenser
3	expansion valve
4	evaporator

Port table

port ID	port Name	port TypeID	entity ID
1	in	1	1
2	out	1	1
3	tube in	1	2
4	tube out	1	2
5	in	1	3
6	out	1	3
7	tube in	1	4
8	tube out	1	4

PortType table

tabTypeID	tabTypeName	pixelDefinition
1	standard	

Model table

modelID	modelName
1	air conditioner

ExpandableEntity table

expandable EntityID	submodel ID

SimpleEntity table

simple EntityID
1
2
3
4

Connection table

connection ID	input PortID	output PortID	model ID
1	8	1	1
2	2	3	1
3	4	5	1
4	6	7	1

ExpansionMapping table

expansion MappingID	expandable EntityID	inner PortID	outer PortID

DiagramType_PortType table

diagramTypeID	portTypeID	tabTypeID
1	1	1

DiagramType_EntityType table

diagram TypeID	entity TypeID	icon TypeID
1	1	1
1	2	2
1	3	3
1	4	2

Model_Diagram table

diagramID	modelID
1	1

Connection_Line table

lineID	connectionID
1	1
2	2
3	3
4	4

Figure 14.15 Populated tables for air conditioner example (continued).

14.7 Chapter Summary

This chapter presents a model of generic diagrams. A generic diagram appears as a picture but has semantic content that lies behind the graphics. The model is too large to fit on a single page, so the chapter divides the model into four subject areas. The generic diagram model provides a starting point for various kinds of diagrams such as data structure diagrams, data flow diagrams, state diagrams, and equipment flow diagrams.

I have used the technology in this chapter on several consulting projects.

Bibliographic Notes

This chapter is motivated by my personal experiences with consulting projects. The following notions have been especially useful in practice.

- The uniform mapping of diagram constructs to model constructs.
- The ability to hierarchically nest diagrams and models.
- The ability to display graphical constructs based on the type of diagram.
- The ability to include or omit ports and tabs.

15

State Diagrams

A state diagram specifies states and stimuli that cause changes of state. State diagrams are often used for control and managing user interaction. They are also helpful for enforcing business policies and constraining data — the reason for coverage in this chapter.

Figure 15.1 shows a simple state diagram for processing orders. A customer places an order and it is quickly acknowledged. Some further processing assigns a customer number and order number and the order is then confirmed. The desired product may or may not be available. If inventory is lacking, the order can be back ordered or if the customer cannot wait, the order is cancelled. Once inventory is available, the customer's payment is processed. Upon payment approval, the order is considered complete. The product is then shipped and the customer signs for delivery. This completes order processing and the order is considered fulfilled.

One way to realize state diagrams is by writing the equivalent procedural code. Another option is to have a generalized interpreter based on declarations in database tables as this chapter explains. An interpreter is especially useful for simple state diagrams.

15.1 State Diagrams

The UML not only has a notation for data structure (the class diagram) but also has one for state diagrams (as well as other kinds of diagrams). In Figure 15.1 the rounded boxes denote *StateTypes*. The solid circle is an initial *StateType* and the bull's-eye is a final *StateType*. The directed lines connecting a source *StateType* to a target *StateType* are *TransitionTypes*. A *Stimulus* causes a change of state and is shown as a label on a transition. The full UML notation for state diagrams is more complex than presented here, but this simple notation suffices for many database applications.

Figure 15.2 and Figure 15.3 show a model for state diagrams that can store the data of Figure 15.1. As with earlier chapters, a gray shading denotes entity types that concern metadata.

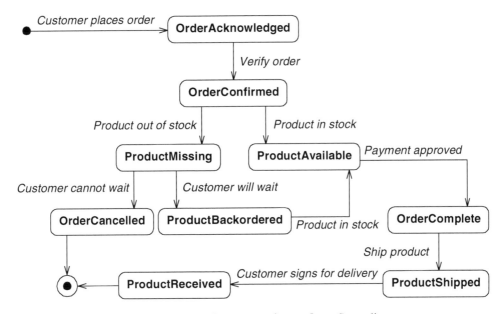

Figure 15.1 State diagram for processing orders. State diagrams are
helpful for enforcing business policies and constraining data.

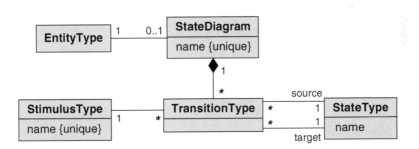

Figure 15.2 State diagram: UML model. State diagrams can enforce a lifecycle or a meaningful sequence of steps for an *EntityType*.

In Figure 15.2 and Figure 15.3 a ***StateDiagram*** specifies the permissible *StateTypes* and
the *StimulusTypes* that cause changes of state. State diagrams are helpful for situations where
there is a lifecycle or a meaningful sequence of steps to enforce. An *EntityType* has a *State-
Diagram* if there is a process to enforce. An application can involve multiple *StateDiagrams*
via multiple *EntityTypes*. The individual *StateDiagrams* interact through common stimuli.

A *StateDiagram* has no memory of the past and responds to stimuli solely on the basis
of an entity's current state. *StimulusType* names must be unique for an application. *StateType*
names must be unique within the scope of a *StateDiagram*.

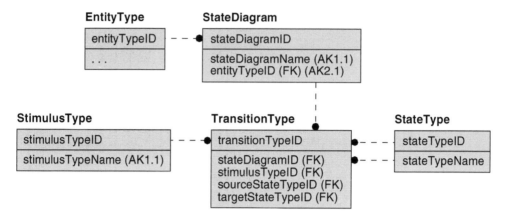

Figure 15.3 State diagram: IDEF1X model.

A ***StimulusType*** is a category for similar occurrences that can cause changes in *State-Diagrams*. In Figure 15.1 *Customer places order*, *Verify order*, and *Product in stock* are examples of *StimulusTypes*. Each entity proceeds at its own pace and a *StimulusType* provides a means for grouping together occurrences with similar behavior. (In the UML a stimulus can be an event — see Chapter 10 — and/or a boolean guard condition that must be true for a transition to occur.)

A ***StateType*** is a category for similar states in which an entity awaits further stimulus. In Figure 15.1 *OrderAcknowledged*, *OrderCancelled*, and *ProductBackordered* are examples of *StateTypes*. Each entity has its individual state but is governed by the *StateDiagram* for its *EntityType*. A *StateType* defines the context for processing stimuli. The same stimulus can have different effects (or no effect) for different *StateTypes*.

A ***TransitionType*** is a change from a *source StateType* to a *target StateType*. The *source* and *target* usually differ but can be the same *StateType*. In Figure 15.1 one *TransitionType* is from *OrderAcknowledged* to *OrderConfirmed*. Another *TransitionType* is from *OrderConfirmed* to *ProductAvailable*. The choice of next *StateType* depends on both the original *StateType* and the *Stimulus*.

The *StateDiagram* in Figure 15.1 has the following constructs:

- 11 *StateTypes* (the initial *StateType*, the final *StateType*, and 9 intermediate *StateTypes*).
- 9 *StimulusTypes* (*Product in stock* affects behavior in two different places).
- 12 *TransitionTypes*.

15.2 Scenarios

A *StateDiagram* defines the lifecycle for an *EntityType*. In contrast a ***Scenario*** executes a *StateDiagram* for an *Entity* of the *StateDiagram's EntityType*. Figure 15.4 and Figure 15.5 show a *Scenario* model that can store the history of execution as well as the current *State*. Via model traversal, a *Scenario* has an *Entity*; an *Entity* has an *EntityType*; and an *EntityType*

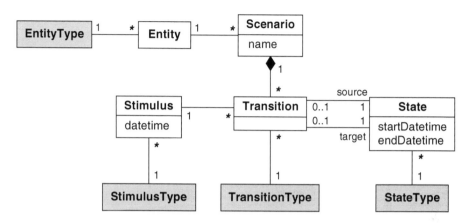

Figure 15.4 Scenario: UML model. A *Scenario* executes a *StateDiagram* for an *Entity* of the *StateDiagram's EntityType*.

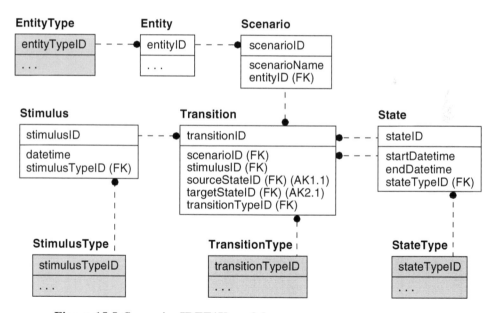

Figure 15.5 Scenario: IDEF1X model.

can have a *StateDiagram*; thus a *Scenario* corresponds to a *StateDiagram*. It is an architectural decision for what data should be stored, how long it is stored, when it is archived, and when it is discarded.

A **Stimulus** is something that happens at a point in time. An example of a *Stimulus* is Joe Smith the customer placing an order for a laptop computer on May 29, 2010 at 10:15

AM. Thus a *Stimulus* is a specific occurrence that conforms to the general description of its *StimulusType*.

A **State** is the period in which an *Entity* waits for the next *Stimulus*. For example, Joe Smith has placed his order and the order is in the *StateType* of *OrderAcknowledged* awaiting completion of verification. Similar *States* are described by a common *StateType*. All *Stimuli* are ignored in a *State*, except those for which a *StateDiagram* prescribes behavior. Each *Entity* can have many *States* over time, but has exactly one *State* at a time. A *StateDiagram* has no memory of the past and responds to *Stimuli* solely on the basis of an *Entity's* current *State*.

Note the contrast between *Stimulus* and *State*. A *Stimulus* represents a point in time. A *State* represents an interval of time.

A **Transition** is an instantaneous change from a *source State* to a *target State*. A *Transition* happens when a *Stimulus* occurs and the *Entity's* current *State* and the *Stimulus* matches the types specified for the *TransitionType*. The *Transition* causes the *Entity* to shift to the *target State*. Multiple *Entities* may be caused to *Transition* by the same *Stimulus*.

The *StateDiagram* and *Scenario* models use the *ItemDescription* and *Homomorphism* templates (see Chapter 5).

15.3 Chapter Summary

A state diagram specifies the permissible states and stimuli that cause changes of state. A scenario executes a state diagram and can store the current state as well as the past history. State diagrams are helpful for situations where there is a lifecycle or a meaningful sequence of steps to enforce. Developers typically realize state diagrams by writing the equivalent procedural code. But another option is to have a generalized interpreter based on the models in this chapter.

Bibliographic Notes

I have used declarative state diagrams on several industrial consulting projects. This chapter was motivated by Chapter 6 of [Silverston-2009]. Silverston and Agnew discuss the notion of data status which can be much more richly modeled with state diagrams.

[Blaha-2005] has a further explanation of UML state diagrams.

References

[Blaha-2005] Michael Blaha and James Rumbaugh. *Object-Oriented Modeling and Design with UML, 2nd Edition*. Upper Saddle River, NJ: Prentice Hall, 2005.

[Silverston-2009] Len Silverston and Paul Agnew. *The Data Model Resource Book, Volume 3*. New York, New York: Wiley, 2009.

Part VI

Relational Database Design

This book is about patterns and patterns are described via models. I have presented two notations — the UML data structure notation and the IDEF1X notation — to help readers familiar with either or both notations understand the nuances of patterns.

Chapter 16 elaborates this use of two modeling notations and presents an overview of my approach to the database design process. I begin constructing a model with the UML data structure notation and then flesh out the attributes. Next I drive the UML content into an IDEF1X model and add database design decisions. Finally I use a tool and generate the appropriate database DDL (data definition language) code.

16

Relational Database Design

This chapter summarizes my approach to database design. I start with a UML model of conceptual and logical intent and use that as the basis for preparing an IDEF1X model. Given an IDEF1X model, modern tools can readily generate SQL code to create the database structure. As a matter of software engineering discipline, I recommend a uniform policy for database design and deviate from the recommendations that follow only for good cause (such as demanding performance).

16.1 Mapping: Entity Types

As Figure 16.1 shows, each entity type normally maps to a table. Each attribute becomes a column in the table. There may be additional columns for existence-based identity, buried relationships, and generalization discriminators (to be explained).

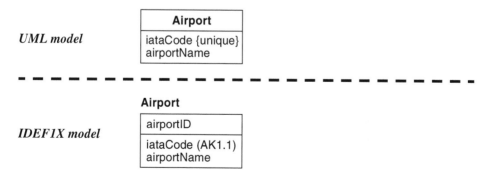

Figure 16.1 Entity type: Mapping. Map each entity type to a table.

Two alternative mappings are sometimes useful.

- **Fragmentation**. For distributed databases it may be helpful to split an entity type into vertical or horizontal fragments. A vertical split maps attributes to columns in different tables. A horizontal split apportions records across multiple tables with identical columns.
- **Elided table**. If an entity type has no attributes other than a primary key, it may not be mapped to a table and simply omitted. However, such an optimization seldom boosts performance. I discourage this option because it leads to an irregular schema. I prefer a strict correspondence between UML and IDEF1X models as a matter of software engineering rigor.

16.2 Mapping: Non-Qualified Relationships

Relationship mappings mostly depend on the multiplicity.

- **Many-to-many relationship**. Map a many-to-many relationship to a distinct table (Figure 16.2). The primary key of the relationship combines the primary keys of the entity types. Role names become part of foreign key attribute names.

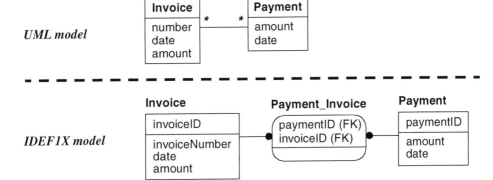

Figure 16.2 Many-to-many relationship: Mapping. Map a many-to-many relationship to a distinct table.

- **Simple one-to-many relationship**. Bury a foreign key in the "many" table (Figure 16.3). Role names become part of foreign key attribute names.
- **Simple optional-to-exactly-one relationship**. Bury a foreign key in the "optional" table (Figure 16.4). Role names become part of foreign key attribute names. The foreign key is unique in the buried table.
- **Other simple one-to-one relationship**. Bury a foreign key in either table.
- **Relationship with attributes**. Regardless of the multiplicity, map the relationship to a distinct table. Add relationship attributes to the distinct table.
- **Aggregation and composition**. Follow the same mappings as the underlying relationship.

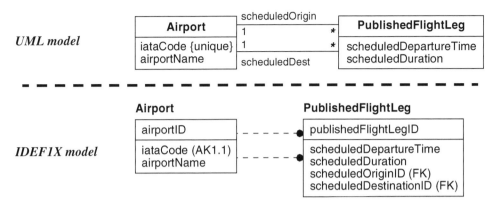

Figure 16.3 Simple one-to-many relationship: Mapping. Bury a foreign key in the "many" table.

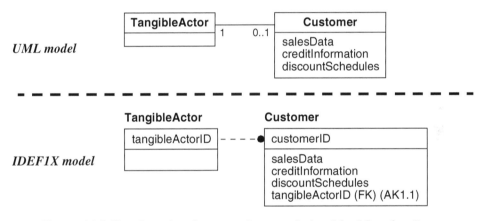

Figure 16.4 Simple optional-to-exactly-one relationship: Mapping. Bury a foreign key in the "optional" table.

- **Ordered relationship**. Use the same mapping as without ordering. Add a sequence number attribute and define a uniqueness constraint on the source entity type plus the sequence number (Figure 16.5).

- **Ternary and n-ary relationships**. These seldom occur and many database design tools do not support them. Where possible, restate them as binary relationships. Otherwise promote them to entity types and define the appropriate uniqueness constraints.

Sometimes it is desirable to disregard the recommended mappings and promote simple one-to-one and one-to-many relationships to distinct tables. For example, Chapter 14 had a separate table for the relationship between *Entity* and *Icon* even though it was one-to-many (as well as for the relationships between *Model–Diagram*, *Port–Tab*, and *Connection–Line*). It

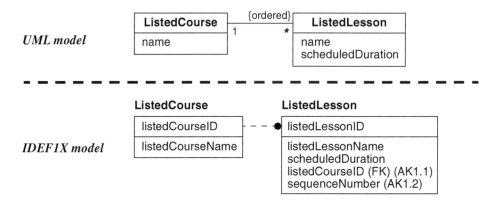

UML model

IDEF1X model

Figure 16.5 Ordered relationship: Mapping. Use the same mapping as without ordering. The source entity type plus a sequence number is unique.

would have been correct to bury the relationships, but from an architectural point of view I wanted to isolate dependencies between subject areas.

16.3 Mapping Qualified Relationships

There are four possible situations for qualified relationships.

- **One-to-optional after qualification.** This is the most common situation (Figure 16.6). The underlying relationship is one-to-many without the qualifier and you should bury the source entity type key and the qualifier in the "many" table. The combination of the source entity type plus the qualifier is unique.

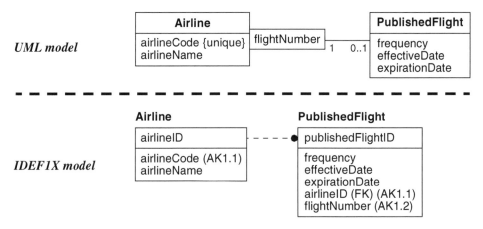

UML model

IDEF1X model

Figure 16.6 Qualified relationship, one-to-optional: Mapping. Bury fields in the "many" table. The source entity type plus the qualifier is unique.

- **Optional-to-optional after qualification**. This situation is also common (Figure 16.7). Bury the source entity type key and the qualifier in the table that is "many" without qualification. In the example, one record (the root of the tree has a null *parentID*) keeps the source entity type plus the qualifier from being unique. (As an alternative, you can promote the relationship to a table and then the qualified relationship has a unique key.)

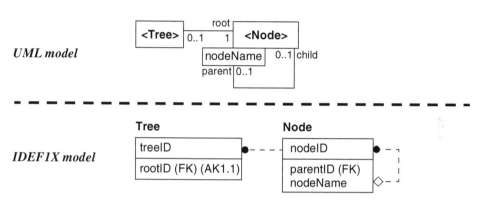

Figure 16.7 Qualified relationship, optional-to-optional: Mapping. Bury fields in the "many" table. The source entity type plus the qualifier is not unique.

- **Many-to-optional after qualification**. These qualified relationships seldom occur (Figure 16.8). Promote the relationship to a table with a primary key of the source entity type plus the qualifier. Note that the combination of the related entity types (*assemblyID* and *componentID* in Figure 16.8) need not be unique; the same component part may be used multiple times for the same assembly. For example, a wiper may be used for the left windshield, right windshield, and rear window.

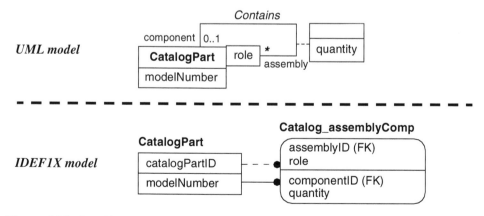

Figure 16.8 Qualified relationship, many-to-optional: Mapping. Promote the relationship to a table with a primary key of the source entity type plus the qualifier.

- **Optional-to-many after qualification**. These qualified relationships also seldom occur (Figure 16.9). Bury the source entity type key and the qualifier in the "many" table. In the example the "ordered" constraint yields an alternate key — the combination of the source entity type plus the qualifier plus a sequence number is unique. If "ordered" was omitted from the model, there would still be a buried source entity type key plus the qualifier, but no alternate key constraint.

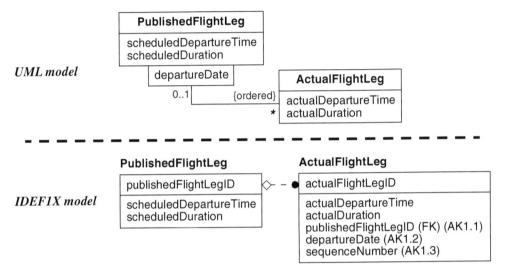

Figure 16.9 Qualified relationship, optional-to-many: Mapping. Bury fields in the "many" table. The source entity type plus the qualifier alone is not unique.

16.4 Mapping: Generalizations

Generalization organizes entity types by their similarities and differences. This book only considers single inheritance—a generalization for which a subtype has one supertype. (Chapter 8 recommends that data models avoid multiple inheritance—a generalization for which a subtype has multiple supertypes.)

As Figure 16.10 shows, I recommend that you map the supertype and each subtype to a table. The tables share common primary key values. The discriminator indicates the appropriate subtype table for each supertype record. Views can be helpful for consolidating the data of an entity across generalization levels.

Relational databases only partially support generalization. Relational databases cannot express the generalization partition, that each supertype record is further described by exactly one subtype. Also referential integrity is a one-way mechanism and cannot enforce the two-way correspondence between records of a supertype and a subtype. (Section 16.6 elaborates.) Applications must compensate with additional programming.

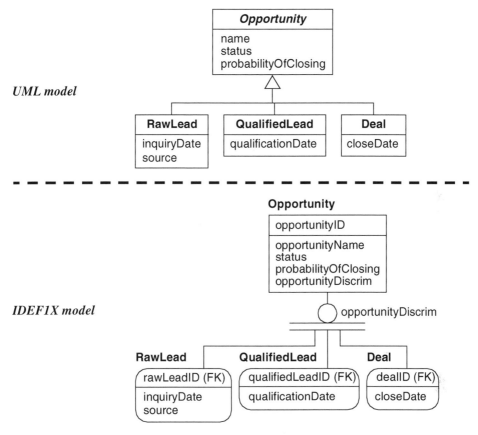

Figure 16.10 Generalization (single inheritance): Mapping: Map the supertype and each subtype to a table.

Several alternative mappings are sometimes helpful for generalization.

- **Elimination**. You can optimize away tables that have no attributes other than a primary key. This reduces the number of tables but provides an irregular implementation.

- **Push supertype attributes down**. You can eliminate the supertype table and duplicate supertype attributes for each subtype. This has the advantage of describing each entity in one table. However, it causes redundancy of structure and you may need to search multiple subtype tables to find an entity.

- **Push subtype attributes up**. As a third alternative, you can eliminate the subtype tables and store all subtype attributes in the supertype table. Each record populates the relevant columns. This describes each entity in one table, but violates third normal form.

- **Generalization table**. Use separate tables for the supertype and the subtypes and implement the generalization itself as a table. This can be helpful if you are merging two databases, one of which has the supertype and the other which has subtypes.

16.5 Design Identity

Chapter 11 discussed *intrinsic identity* — the ability to start from outside a database and find data with fields that have application meaning. In contrast, ***design identity*** is the ability to find data within a database. Databases implement design identity with primary keys. A ***primary key*** is a candidate key that is chosen for internal (foreign key) references. A table normally has a primary key, and has at most one primary key.

There are several approaches to implementing primary keys. Of these approaches I favor existence-based identity and existence-based identity + lookups.

- **Existence-based identity**. An artificial number (called an ID) is the primary key of each entity table (Figure 16.11). The major DBMS products can generate such numbers; examples include Oracle sequences and the SQL Server identity property. With existence-based identity all primary keys are single attribute, small, and uniform in size. One of the few downsides is that the IDs can complicate debugging. (When debugging you have to dereference IDs to see meaningful fields.)

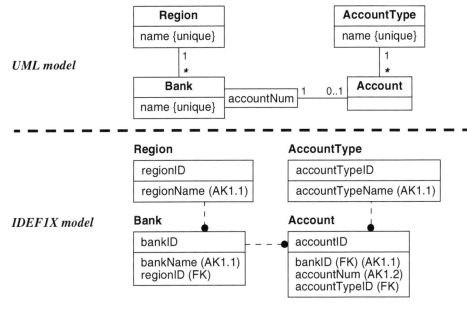

Figure 16.11 Existence-based identity (recommended): Example. A system-generated field is the primary key of the table for each entity.

- **Existence-based identity + lookups**. Another option (Figure 16.12) is to use a mnemonic abbreviation for lookup tables, and existence-based identity for everything else. "Lookup" data means metadata such as *AccountType* that is often implemented as a pick list in a user interface. Lookup tables have a small number of records (usually no more than tens of records) that are seldom updated.

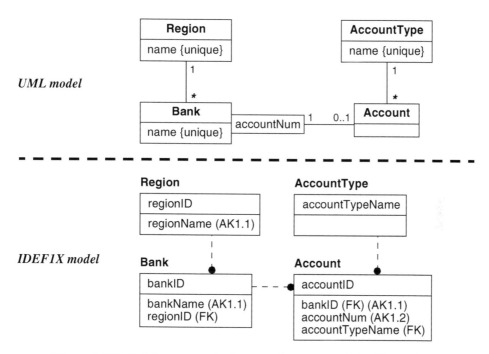

Figure 16.12 Existence-based + lookups (recommended): Example.
Another option is to use a mnemonic abbreviation for lookups and existence-based identity for everything else.

- **Value-based identity**. A combination of application attributes identify each entity. In Figure 16.13 names identify *Region, Bank,* and *AccountType. Account* is identified by *bankName* combined with *accountNum.* An advantage of value-based identity is that primary keys have intrinsic meaning.

  However primary key values can be difficult to change — a change to a primary key may require propagation to many foreign keys. Some entities lack natural real-world identifiers. Also primary keys can become lengthy, from the foreign keys of a series of related tables as Figure 16.14 illustrates. Figure 16.15 shows an awkward situation for *Transaction.* With value-based identity and referential integrity, the two paths lead to two copies of *bankID* and *accountNumber.* With value-based identity developers must abandon referential integrity to have a single copy of the fields.

- **Hybrid identity**. A schema can combine existence-based identity with value-based identity. In Figure 16.16 *Region, Bank,* and *AccountType* have artificial identity and *Account* has identity derived from a bank reference combined with an account number.

- **Propagated identity**. Identity can also propagate from one entity type to another. In Figure 16.17 the primary key of *Exercise* is also the primary key for *Answer.* (A book can have many exercises; an exercise may have an answer.) This is seldom a good idea as there is a "leakage" of information from one entity type to the other.

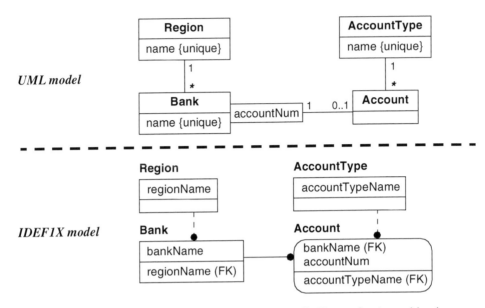

Figure 16.13 Value-based identity (discouraged): Example. A combination of application attributes identify each entity.

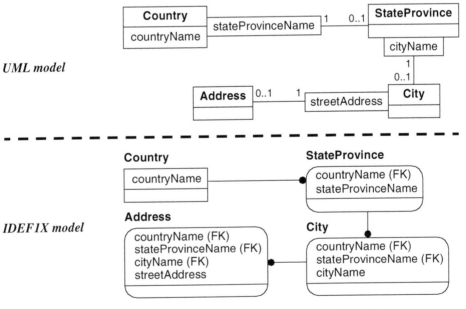

Figure 16.14 Value-based identity: Flaw. A sequence of foreign keys can lead to lengthy primary keys.

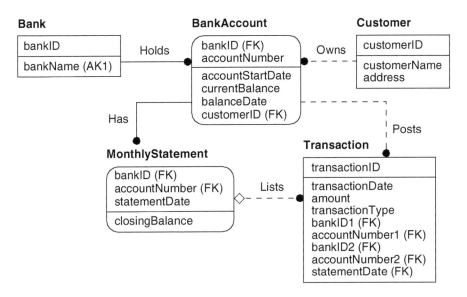

Figure 16.15 Value-based identity: Flaw. The two paths lead to two copies
of *bankID* and *accountNumber* for *Transaction*. You must
abandon referential integrity to have a single copy.

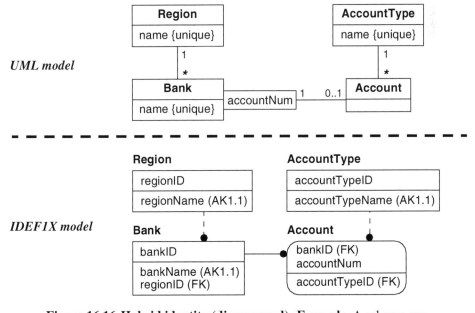

Figure 16.16 Hybrid identity (discouraged): Example. A schema can
combine existence-based identity with value-based identity.

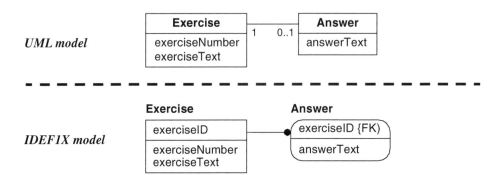

Figure 16.17 Propagated identity (discouraged): Example. Identity can also propagate from one entity type to another.

Table 16.1 summarizes the approaches to design identity and their trade-offs.

16.6 Referential Integrity

Once the IDEF1X model is in place, you should define referential integrity actions to enforce the model's meaning. Referential integrity is a database mechanism that ensures that references to data really exist and that there are no dangling foreign keys. Normally you should let a DBMS enforce referential integrity constraints rather than write custom application code. If you use existence-based identity, there are no primary key updates to propagate and referential integrity actions are only needed for deletions.

Neither the UML model nor the IDEF1X model specify referential integrity precisely, so you will have to rely on your application understanding. I recommend the following guidelines for deletions.

- **Generalization**. Cascade deletions for foreign keys that arise from generalization. For example, in Figure 16.18 *OwnedAsset* is a subtype of *Asset* and *ownedAssetID* references *assetID*. Upon deletion, an *Asset* record and an *OwnedAsset* record should both be deleted. Given separate supertype and subtype tables, there should be a on delete cascade clause for each subtype reference to the supertype.

  A relational DBMS can propagate deletion downward from the supertype to the subtypes. However, a relational DBMS cannot propagate deletion upward from a subtype toward the supertype. For example, the deletion of an *Asset* record could cause the deletion of the corresponding *OwnedAsset*. Then the deletion of an *OwnedAsset* could cause deletion of its *RentedAssets*. But deletion of a *RentedAsset* record cannot propagate upward to *Asset*. Consequently, it is necessary to first delete the *Asset* records that are *RentedAssets* and then delete the *Asset* record for the *OwnedAsset*.

  Some organizations forbid cascaded deletions as a matter of policy (fearful of inadvertent errors). In that case there will have to be additional programming code to propagate a deletion from a supertype record to descendant subtype records.

Table 16.1   Summary of Approaches to Design Identity

Identity approach	Definition	Advantages	Drawbacks	Recommendation
Existence-based	An artificial number is the primary key of each entity.	• PKs are single attribute, small, and uniform in size. • Handles entities without real-world identifiers.	• IDs can complicate debugging.	A good choice
Existence-based + lookups	A mnemonic for lookups and existence-based for everything else.	• PKs are single attribute, small, and uniform in size. • Handles entities without real-world identifiers.	• Simpler debugging than with existence-based identity alone.	A good choice
Value-based	A combination of application attributes identifies each entity.	• PKs have intrinsic meaning.	• Propagated PK values are difficult to change. • Some entities lack real-world identifiers. • Can have multiple paths for the same FK.	Seldom a good idea
Hybrid	Schema combines existence-based and value-based identity.		• Irregular approach that lacks rigor.	A poor option
Propagated	PK of an entity comes from a relationship.		• Awkward dependency between entities.	A poor option

Note: I recommend the use of existence-based identity or existence-based + lookups.

- **Buried relationship, minimum multiplicity of zero.** There are two choices — either set the foreign key to null or forbid deletion. The choice depends on a model's meaning. For example in Figure 10.23, upon deletion of a *Facility* the references in the corresponding *Locations* should be set to null. In contrast, it is appropriate to forbid the deletion of a *Document* with *child Documents* via *DocumentFlow* (Figure 10.15).

- **Buried relationship, minimum multiplicity of one.** Forbid the deletion or cascade the effect of a deletion. For example, in Figure 10.1 it should not be possible to delete an *AccountType* that is referenced by *Accounts*. In Figure 10.5 the deletion of an *Address*

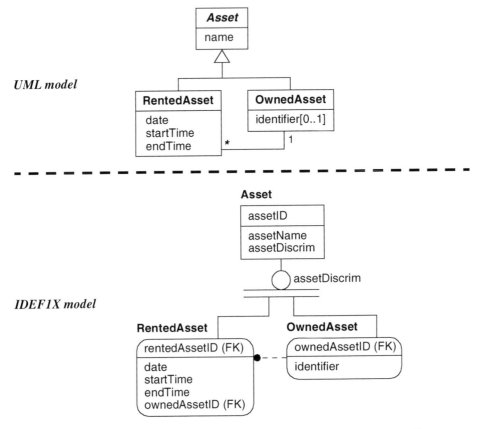

Figure 16.18 Referential integrity for generalization. A relational DBMS cannot propagate deletion upward from the subtype toward the supertype.

should cascade to deletion of its *AddressRoles* (*AddressRoles* are clearly secondary to *Address*).

- **Relationship table**. Cascade deletions to the records of a relationship table or forbid the deletions. For example, in Figure 10.5 deletion of an *Actor* could lead to deletion of the *AddressRole_Actor* records (thinking that the relationship records are incidental to an *Actor*). It would be reasonable to forbid deletion of an *AddressRole* with dependent *AddressRole_Actor* records (to avoid accidentally deleting important *Actor* data).

16.7 Miscellaneous Database Constraints

SQL has powerful constraint mechanisms that are part of the language. As much as possible, it is desirable to place declarative constraints in the database rather than write imperative constraints via programming code. The *not null* clause enforces that a column of a table must have a value. The previous section discussed referential integrity which ensures that there are no dangling referents. Unique indexes (next section) can enforce candidate keys. In addition SQL has triggers and general constraints.

16.7.1 SQL Triggers

A *trigger* performs a database command upon the occurrence of a specified event and satisfaction of a condition. [Elmasri-2006] Although it is a dangerous practice, triggers can be used to enforce database constraints. The concern is that careless use of triggers can lead to explosions of database activity — one trigger fires, causing other triggers to fire, leading to an extensive cascade. One trigger in isolation is straightforward to understand. However a database with numerous triggers can be inscrutable.

It is especially important not to use SQL triggers to implement referential integrity. This was done with some of the old DBMS products of the past. Modern SQL has declarative referential integrity that is well understood and efficient — you should use it. Triggers are several orders of magnitude slower for executing referential integrity and should not be used for that purpose.

A proper use of triggers is for propagating data — to update related applications, to synchronize distributed databases, or to feed data warehouses. Triggers can also be helpful for keeping derived data consistent with its underlying base data.

16.7.2 General SQL Constraints

SQL also supports general constraints with the *check* constraint. Models imply some of these constraints. Others are details that are lacking from the model and rely on your application understanding.

The purpose of the generalization discriminator is to indicate which subtype record elaborates each supertype record. Accordingly a discriminator must be an enumeration with one value for each of the subtypes. For example, in Figure 16.18 *assetDiscrim* is an enumeration with two values: *RentedAsset* and *OwnedAsset*. With SQL *assetDiscrim* would be stored as a string that is not null. A check constraint could enforce that the string value was in the list {'RentedAsset', 'OwnedAsset'}.

SQL check constraints are also useful for enforcing domains. A SQL table has many columns each of which has a domain. A domain specifies a datatype, constraints on the data, and semantic meaning of the data. Thus the domain for UPC codes may store data as a string of digits with a specified length and have a rule to verify the check digit at the end. (See Chapter 11 for a discussion of UPC codes.) As another example, in Figure 16.18 a *RentedAsset's endTime* must be greater than its *startTime*.

SQL check constraints can also enforce enumerations. Enumerations often arise and should be enforced by the database rather than application code. The following are enumerations: *actualOrEstimate* (Figure 10.7), *grade* (Figure 10.11), *format* (Figure 10.15), *priority* (Figure 10.37), and *outcome* (Figure 10.37).

16.8 Indexes

Indexes serve two purposes: enforcing uniqueness for primary and candidate keys as well as enabling fast database traversal. Most relational DBMSs create indexes as a side effect of declaring primary keys and candidate keys. I recommend that you also create an index for each foreign key that is not subsumed by a primary key or candidate key. These foreign key indexes are important because they enable the fast performance that users expect when they traverse a model. Joins often occur across relationships and across the levels of generalization hierarchies. Joins are orders of magnitude more efficient if foreign keys and primary keys have indexes.

You should incorporate foreign key indexes in your initial database design because they are straightforward to include and there is no good reason to defer them. The database administrator (DBA) may define additional indexes to fine-tune performance. The DBA may also use DBMS-specific features.

16.9 Generating SQL Code

If you have a modern tool, it is relatively easy to generate SQL code from a database design. With ERwin I pay attention to the following.

- **Domains**. Define pertinent domains for the application, giving each a datatype and relevant constraints.

- **Nulls**. Specify nullability. ERwin enforces that primary keys are not null. You can check the box so that candidate key fields and mandatory application fields are also not null. For flexibility, if you are unsure, you should permit a column to be null.

- **Default value**. Enter a default value for the appropriate columns. ERwin adds default values to create table statements.

- **Check constraints**. Enter miscellaneous constraints. I include check constraints in create table statements (instead of alter statements).

- **Keys**. I check the options to include primary keys and unique (candidate) keys as part of the create table statements.

- **Referential integrity**. Add referential integrity actions via relationship properties. Given the use of existence-based identity, there are no on-update clauses for foreign keys. I specify that alter statements be used to create on-delete clauses for foreign keys. (There can be problems with circular code if foreign key clauses are included with the create table statement.)

- **Indexes**. Check the flag to index foreign keys. ERwin does not consider if a foreign key index is subsumed by a primary key or candidate key index. The overhead of this duplicate indexing is usually trivial.

- **Storage**. You can set the initial size of each table and indicate how space should grow as records are added.

16.10 Chapter Summary

This chapter summarizes my approach to database design. I start with a UML model of conceptual and logical intent and use that as the basis for preparing an IDEF1X model. Modern tools, such as ERwin, can then generate SQL code to create the database design. Here is a summary of my preferred database design practices.

- **Entity type**. Map each entity type to a table and each attribute to a column. Define a primary key for each entity type and additional unique keys as needed. Make sure all primary-key and unique-key columns are not null.

- **Many-to-many relationships**. Promote each one to a table. The primary key of the relationship combines the primary keys of the entity types.

- **Simple one-to-x relationships**. Bury a foreign key in the table for the x entity type. If the one-end is mandatory, then the foreign key is not null.

- **Relationship with attributes**. Regardless of the multiplicity, promote each one to a table. Add relationship attributes to the table.

- **Aggregation and composition**. Use the same mappings as the underlying relationship.

- **Ordered relationship**. Use the same mapping as without ordering. Add a sequence number attribute and define a uniqueness constraint on the source entity type plus the sequence number.

- **Qualified relationship, one-to-optional**. Bury the source entity type key and the qualifier in the "many" table. The combination of the source entity type plus the qualifier is unique.

- **Qualified relationship, optional-to-optional**. Bury the source entity type key and the qualifier in the "many" table. The combination of the source entity type plus the qualifier is not unique.

- **Qualified relationship, many-to-optional**. Promote the relationship to a table with a primary key of the source entity type plus the qualifier. The combination of the related entity types need not be unique.

- **Qualified relationship, optional-to-many**. Bury the source entity type key and the qualifier in the "many" table. The source entity type key plus the qualifier is not unique.

- **Generalization**. Create separate tables for the supertype and each subtype. With my naming protocol the primary key names vary, but an entity should have the same primary key value throughout the levels of a generalization.

- **Identity**. Add an artificial number column to the table for each entity type and make it the primary key. Modern relational DBMSs can readily generate existence-based IDs. As an option it is acceptable to instead use a mnemonic abbreviation for lookup tables.

- **Referential integrity**. Enforce referential integrity for every foreign key (unless there is an unusual performance issue). Specify referential integrity actions for deletion.

- **General constraints**. Forego the use of triggers for constraints, but use SQL check constraints on domains and tables as needed.

- **Indexes**. Make sure that every foreign key is covered by an index. These indexes are important for searching and joining tables efficiently. Add other incidental indexes as required.

Table 16.2 summarizes the recommended mapping rules.

Table 16.2 Summary of Relational DBMS Mapping Rules

Concept	Model construct	Relational DBMS construct
Entity type	Entity type	Table
Non-qualified relationship	Many-to-many	Distinct table
	Simple one-to-many	Buried foreign key
	Simple one-to-one	
	Relationship with attributes	Distinct table
	Aggregation	Same as underlying relationship
	Composition	
	Ordered relationship	
Qualified relationship	One-to-optional	Buried foreign key + qualifier
	Optional-to-optional	Buried foreign key + qualifier
	Many-to-optional	Distinct table
	Optional-to-many	Buried foreign key + qualifier
Generalization		Separate supertype and subtype tables

Bibliographic Notes

Many of the ideas in this chapter come from my consulting and database reverse engineering experiences.

[Bruce-1992] is a good reference for IDEF1X. [Elmasri-2006] is a good general database reference.

References

[Bruce-1992] Thomas A. Bruce. *Designing Quality Databases with IDEF1X Information Models*. New York, New York: Dorset House, 1992.

[Elmasri-2006] Ramez Elmasri and Shamkant B. Navathe. *Fundamentals of Database Systems (5th Edition)*. Boston, Massachusetts: Addison-Wesley, 2006.

Appendix A

Explanation of the UML Notation

The UML (Unified Modeling Language) is a graphical language for modeling software development artifacts. The UML encompasses about a dozen notations of which one (the ***class model***) concerns data structure. The class model sets the scope of data and level of abstraction for subsequent development. The Object Management Group (www.omg.org) has been actively working towards standardizing all of the UML notations.

The UML class model is an object-oriented notation. Nevertheless, the class model is entirely suitable for databases and actually derives from the Chen notation [Chen-1976]. The Chen notation and its derivatives have been influential in the database community, but there are many dialects and a lack of consensus. This UML class model is just another Chen dialect, but one that has the backing of a standard. The class model also has several helpful features (such as ordering, qualifiers, aggregation, composition—to be discussed) not found in most other Chen dialects.

This appendix focuses on the class model; it ignores the other UML notations as they are less relevant to database applications. I try to avoid object-oriented jargon and use entity-relationship terminology where possible. The major concepts in the class model are entity types, relationships, and generalizations.

Entity Type

An ***entity*** (UML term is *object*) is a concept, abstraction, or thing that can be individually identified and has meaning for an application. An ***entity type*** (UML term is *class*) describes a group of entities with the same attributes, kinds of relationships, and intent. Figure A1.1 shows four entity types. The UML symbol for an entity type is a box with the name of the entity type in bold font toward the top.

The second portion of the box (the three entity types to the left of Figure A1.1) shows attribute names. An ***attribute*** describes a value held by each entity of an entity type. *Account* has three attributes, *Actor* has three attributes, and *PhysicalPart* has one attribute. By default

223

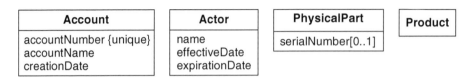

Figure A1.1   UML entity types.

an attribute has an unspecified number of possible values. Alternatively a trailing annotation within square brackets can indicate a specific number. Thus *serialNumber* can be null (lower limit of 0) and has at most one value (upper limit of 1).

In Figure A1.1 *Product* is also an entity type but the attributes are not shown. The convention of an entity type icon (an entity type box showing only the name) denotes a reference to an entity type that is defined elsewhere.

This book has several occurrences of derived attributes. A ***derived attribute*** is computed from other attributes. In Figure A1.2 the *grossProfit* is the *retailPrice* less the *wholesaleCost*. The UML notation for a derived attribute is a prefix of '/' before the attribute name.

Figure A1.2   UML derived attribute.

Relationships

A ***relationship*** (UML term is *link*) is a physical or conceptual connection among entities. A ***relationship type*** (UML term is *association*) is a description of a group of relationships with similar structure and meaning. A relationship type describes a set of potential relationships in the same way that an entity type describes a set of potential entities. The UML notation for a relationship type is a line (possibly with multiple line segments) between entity types. Figure A1.3 shows four relationship types. Data modelers often blur the distinction between relationship and relationship type with the distinction being apparent from context. The remainder of this appendix refers to both as relationship.

A binary relationship has two ends, each of which has a name and multiplicity. ***Multiplicity*** is the number of occurrences of one entity type that may connect to an occurrence of a related entity type. The most common UML multiplicities are "1", "0..1" (at most one), and "*" ("many", that is zero or more). In Figure A1.3 a *ContractItem* pertains to one *Product* and a *Product* can be the basis for many *ContractItems*.

Figure A1.4 illustrates relationship end names. For *Tree–Node*, the *Node* is the *root* of the *Tree*. For *Node–Node*, one *Node* is the *parent* and the other is a *child*. Thus a *parent Node* may have many *child Nodes*; a *child Node* has an optional *parent Node*.

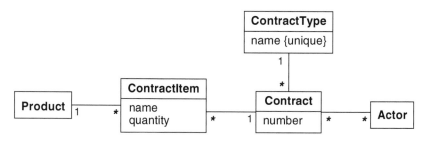

Figure A1.3 UML relationships.

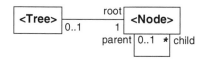

{All nodes have a parent except the root node. There can not be any cycles.}

Figure A1.4 UML relationships with end names and constraints.

Figure A1.4 also shows two constraints. The UML notation is to enclose constraints within curly braces. A **constraint** is a boolean condition that governs the validity of a model. Entity types, attributes, and relationships may all have constraints. One constraint specifies that all nodes have a parent except the root node. The other forbids cycles.

You can usually regard the entities on a "many" relationship end as a set. Sometimes, however, the entities have an explicit order. You can indicate an ordered set of entities by writing "{ordered}" next to the appropriate relationship end. In Figure A1.5 the *Published-FlightLegs* for a *PublishedFlight* are ordered. For example, a through flight could first go from St. Louis to Chicago and then from Chicago to Buffalo.

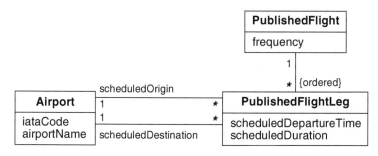

Figure A1.5 UML relationships with ordering and qualifier.

The UML supports a **relationship entity type** — an entity type that is also a relationship (UML term is *association class*). Like a relationship, the occurrences of a relationship entity type derive identity from the related entity types. Like an entity type, a relationship entity type can have attributes and participate in relationships. The UML notation is a box that connects to the relationship with a dotted line. Figure A1.6 has a relationship entity type, between *Tree* and *child Node*. The relationship entity type itself relates to *parent Node*. The meaning of the model is that the combination of a *Tree* and a *child Node* yields a *parent Node*. A *child Node* may have a different *parent Node*, depending on the *Tree*.

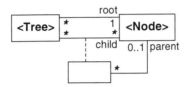

{All nodes have a parent in a tree except for the root node. There may not be any cycles of nodes.}
{A parent must only have children for trees to which the parent belongs.}

Figure A1.6 UML relationship entity type.

A *qualified relationship* (UML term is *qualified association*) is a relationship in which an attribute called the *qualifier* disambiguates the entities for a "many" relationship end. The qualifier selects among the target entities, reducing the effective multiplicity, often from "many" to "one". The notation for a qualifier is a small box on the end of the relationship line near the source entity type. The source entity type plus the qualifier yields the target entity type. In Figure A1.7 a *DirectoryFile* plus a *fileName* yields a specific *File*. The qualified relationship also indicates that a *DirectoryFile* has many (zero or more) *Files* if *fileName* is omitted. In Figure A1.8 a *Country* plus three qualifiers yields an *Address*.

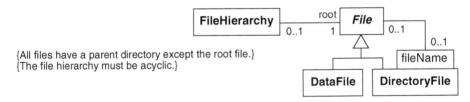

Figure A1.7 UML qualified relationship.

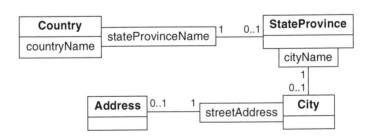

Figure A1.8 UML qualified relationships.

Aggregation is a strong form of relationship in which an aggregate entity is made of component parts. The most significant property of aggregation is transitivity (if A is part of B and B is part of C, then A is part of C) and anti symmetry (if A is part of B, then B is not part of A). This book does not have any aggregations.

Composition is a form of aggregation with two additional constraints. A constituent part can belong to at most one assembly. Furthermore, once a constituent part has been assigned an assembly, it has a coincident lifetime with the assembly. In Figure A1.9 *Icons* and *Lines* belong to a *Diagram*. If a *Diagram* is deleted, all of its *Icons* and *Lines* are also deleted.

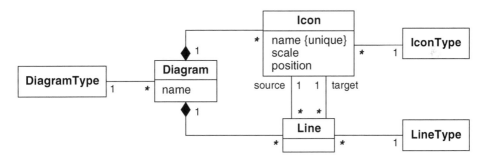

Figure A1.9 UML composition.

Generalization

Generalization is the relationship between an entity type (the ***supertype***) and one or more variations of the entity type (the ***subtypes***). Generalization organizes entity types by their similarities and differences, structuring the description of entities. The supertype holds common attributes and relationships; the subtypes add specific attributes and relationships. Each subtype inherits the attributes and relationships of its supertype. A hollow triangle denotes generalization. The apex of the triangle connects to the supertype. Lines connect the base of the triangle to the subtypes.

Figure A1.10 has two generalizations. One generalization has a supertype of *Actor* and subtypes of *TangibleActor*, *ActorRole*, and *ActorRoleType*. The other generalization has a supertype of *TangibleActor* and subtypes of *Person*, *Application*, and *Organization*.

Bibliographic Notes

[Chen-1976] is the classic reference for entity-relationship modeling. The other references give further information on the UML class modeling notation as well as other UML notations. The explanation of the UML class model here is abridged and only covers the constructs used in this book.

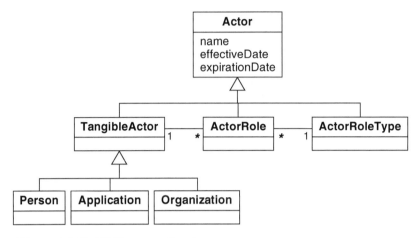

Figure A1.10 UML generalization.

References

[Blaha-2001] Michael Blaha. *A Manager's Guide to Database Technology.* Upper Saddle River, New Jersey: Prentice-Hall, 2001.

[Blaha-2005] Michael Blaha and James Rumbaugh. *Object-Oriented Modeling and Design with UML, 2nd Edition.* Upper Saddle River, NJ: Prentice Hall, 2005.

[Chen-1976] PPS Chen. The entity-relationship model—toward a unified view of data. *ACM Transactions on Database Systems 1*, 1 (March 1976).

[Hoberman-2010] Steve Hoberman. *Data Modeling Made Simple: A Practical Guide for Business and IT Professionals, 2nd Edition.* Bradley Beach, New Jersey: Technics Publications, 2010.

[Rumbaugh-2005] James Rumbaugh, Ivar Jacobson, and Grady Booch. *The Unified Modeling Language Reference Manual, Second Edition.* Boston, MA: Addison-Wesley, 2005.

Appendix B

Explanation of the IDEF1X Notation

IDEF1X is the successor notation to IDEF (Integrated Definition for Data Modeling). IDEF1X is a popular notation for modeling relational databases. The IDEF1X notation has been in use for two decades now and was effectively standardized through early adoption by the U.S. Air Force.

The major concepts in IDEF1X are entity types, relationships, and generalizations.

Entity Type

An *entity* is a concept, abstraction, or thing that can be individually identified and has meaning for an application. An *entity type* describes a group of entities with the same attributes, kinds of relationships, and intent. An entity type corresponds to a relational database table and an entity corresponds to a row in a table. The IDEF1X notation for an entity type is a box. IDEF1X differentiates between independent and dependent entity types.

Figure B1.1 shows three independent entity types. An *independent entity type* is an entity type that can exist on its own. Some authors call this a *strong entity type*. The IDEF1X symbol for an independent entity type is a square-corner box with the name of the entity type listed above the box. The top portion of the box contains primary key attributes and the lower portion contains the remaining attributes.

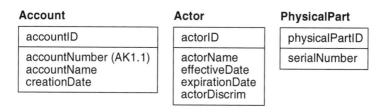

Figure B1.1 IDEF1X independent entity types.

An **attribute** describes a value held by each entity of an entity type. *Account* has four attributes—the primary key attribute and three non-primary key attributes. Similarly, *Actor* has five attributes and *PhysicalPart* has two attributes.

A **candidate key** is a combination of one or more attributes that uniquely identifies each entity of an entity type. The attributes in a candidate key must be minimal; no attribute can be discarded without destroying uniqueness. No attribute in a candidate key can be null. A database index is often used to enforce uniqueness for a candidate key.

A **primary key** is a candidate key that is chosen for cross-table references (see the discussion of foreign keys in the next section). Normally, an entity type should have a primary key; an entity type can have at most one primary key. The IDEF1X notation for a primary key is to list the primary key attributes in the top portion of the entity type box. All three entity types in Figure B1.1 have a single attribute as the primary key.

An **alternate key** is a candidate key that is not chosen as a primary key. Thus all candidate keys are either a primary key or an alternate key. An entity type can have any number of alternate keys. The IDEF1X notation for an alternate key is to append "AKn.m" after each constituent attribute. The 'n' denotes the nth alternate key and the 'm' indicates the sequence of attributes within the nth alternate key. Figure B1.1 has one alternate key—*accountNumber* for an *Account*. This alternate key consists of a single attribute.

Figure B1.2 shows two independent entity types and one dependent entity type. A **dependent entity type** is an entity type that can exist only if one or more other entity types also exist. Accordingly, the primary key of a dependent entity type incorporates one or more foreign keys. Some authors call this a *weak entity type*. The IDEF1X symbol is a rounded box with the name of the entity type listed above the box. In Figure B1.2 *AddressRole_Actor* is a dependent entity type whose primary key refers to the *Actor* and *AdressRole* entity types.

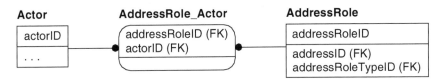

Figure B1.2   IDEF1X dependent entity type.

Relationships

A **relationship** is a physical or conceptual connection among entities. A **relationship type** is a description of a group of relationships with similar structure and meaning. A relationship type describes a set of potential relationships in the same way that an entity type describes a set of potential entities. The IDEF1X notation for a relationship type is a line (possibly with multiple line segments) between entity types. Data modelers often blur the distinction between relationship and relationship type with the distinction being apparent from context. The remainder of this appendix refers to both as relationship. IDEF1X differentiates between identifying and non-identifying relationships.

Figure B1.3 shows five relationships, two of which are identifying. Both relationships to *Contract_Actor* are identifying. An ***identifying relationship*** is a relationship that contributes to the primary key of a dependent entity type. The IDEF1X symbol for an identifying relationship is a solid line.

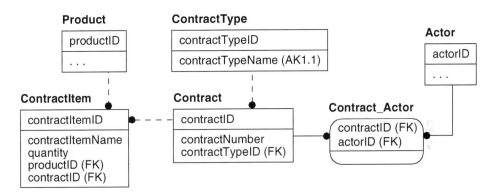

Figure B1.3   IDEF1X relationships.

The remaining three relationships in Figure B1.3 are non-identifying. A ***non-identifying relationship*** is a relationship that does not contribute to the primary key of an entity type. Consequently the foreign key appears in the lower portion of the entity type box. The IDEF1X symbol for a non-identifying relationship is a dotted line.

The suffix *(FK)* after an attribute name denotes a foreign key. Each foreign key corresponds to a relationship, either identifying or non-identifying. Thus IDEF1X shows relationships redundantly with both relationship lines and *(FK)* annotations. IDEF1X represents many-to-many relationships, such as *Contract_Actor*, with a dependent entity type and two identifying relationships.

Non-identifying relationships can involve both independent and dependent entity types as Figure B1.4 illustrates. *PartitionBasis_childRegion* has two identifying and one non-identifying relationships.

Although little used in this book, an IDEF1X relationship line can be labeled with a relationship name. Although IDEF1X does not show them on the diagram, relationship ends can also be named. Relationship end names are manifest via foreign keys. Thus in Figure B1.4 *PartitionBasis_childRegion* has an identifying relationship to *Region* with an end name of *child*. Furthermore, *PartitionBasis_childRegion* has a non-identifying relationship to *Region* with an end name of *parent*.

The ends of a binary relationship also have multiplicity. ***Multiplicity*** is the number of occurrences of one entity type that may connect to an occurrence of a related entity type. A small solid ball denotes "many" multiplicity (zero or more). A small diamond denotes "at most one" multiplicity (zero or one). The lack of a symbol indicates a multiplicity of exactly one.

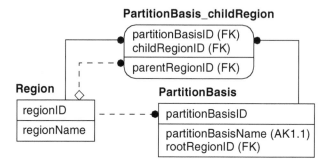

Figure B1.4 IDEF1X relationships. Non-identifying relationships can
involve both independent and dependent entity types.

The IDEF1X literature often uses the term "cardinality" incorrectly, instead of the proper term "multiplicity." Multiplicity is a constraint on the size of a collection; cardinality is
the count of elements that are actually in a collection. Therefore, multiplicity is a constraint
on the cardinality.

IDEF1X only permits certain combinations of multiplicity as Figure B1.5 shows.
(IDEF1X also supports a more precise specification of 'many' multiplicity with the 'P', 'Z',
and 'N' annotations, but this book does not use them.)

Figure B1.5 IDEF1X permitted multiplicity.

Note that all the prior relationships in this appendix attach to the contours of entity type
boxes. As Figure B1.6 shows, an IDEF1X relationship need not touch the contour.

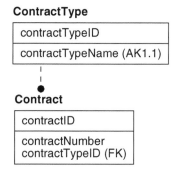

Figure B1.6 IDEF1X relationships. A relationship line need not attach
to an entity type box.

Generalization

Generalization is the organization of entity types by their similarities and differences. The *supertype* holds common attributes and relationships. The *subtypes* add specific attributes and relationships. Each subtype inherits the attributes and relationships of its supertype.

The IDEF1X notation for generalization is a circle with a double line underneath. The double line indicates that the generalization is exhaustive; each occurrence of a supertype must correspond to a subtype. (IDEF1X also supports a single horizontal line indicating that a generalization is not exhaustive. As a matter of style all the generalizations in this book are exhaustive.) The attribute next to the circle is called a discriminator and indicates the subtype that elaborates each supertype record.

Figure B1.7 shows two generalizations. One generalization has a supertype of *Actor* and subtypes of *TangibleActor*, *ActorRole*, and *ActorRoleType*. The other generalization has a supertype of *TangibleActor* and subtypes of *Person*, *Application*, and *Organization*. Note that as a matter of style we rename propagated keys for generalization so that the primary key name corresponds to the entity type name. Such a practice makes it easier to understand foreign keys for a large model where there are various relationships to different levels of a generalization.

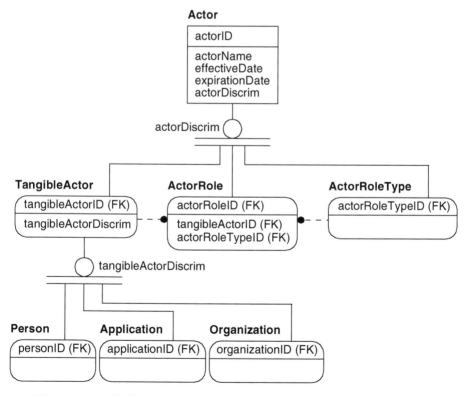

Figure B1.7 IDEF1X generalization.

Bibliographic Notes

The explanation of IDEF1X in this appendix is abridged and only covers the constructs used in this book. [Bruce-1992] has a more extensive discussion of IDEF1X. [Blaha-2001] compares IDEF1X to other notations.

References

[Blaha-2001] Michael Blaha. *A Manager's Guide to Database Technology.* Upper Saddle River, New Jersey: Prentice-Hall, 2001.

[Bruce-1992] Thomas A. Bruce. *Designing Quality Databases with IDEF1X Information Models.* New York: Dorset House, 1992.

Appendix C

Glossary

This book defines the following terms.

abstraction the ability to focus on essential aspects of an application while ignoring details.

alternate key a candidate key that is not chosen as a primary key. Thus each candidate key is either a primary key or an alternate key. An entity type can have any number of alternate keys. (See *candidate key* and *primary key*.)

antipattern a characterization of a common software flaw. An antipattern shows what not to do and how to fix it.

archetype a prominent abstraction that cuts across problem domains. This book's archetype models are small and focus on core concepts.

attribute a named property of an entity type that describes a value held by each entity of the entity type.

candidate key a combination of attributes that uniquely identifies each entity of an entity type. The combination must be minimal and not include any columns that are not needed for unique identification. No attribute in a candidate key can be null. (See *alternate key* and *primary key*.)

canonical model a submodel that provides a service for many applications. A canonical model is an abstract service that is not bound to a particular problem domain in contrast to a seed model.

cardinality the count of elements that are in a collection. (Contrast with *multiplicity*.)

Chen model a graphical approach to modeling originated by Peter Chen that shows entities and the relationships between them. The UML class model is based on the Chen model.

class model (of the UML) the data structure model of the UML.

constraint a boolean condition that governs the validity of a model. Entity types, attributes, and relationships can all have constraints.

data warehouse a database that takes the disjointed, functional applications of a business and integrates them, accumulating the history of past data. A data warehouse puts data in one database and stores data in a common format for reporting purposes.

database a permanent, self-descriptive store of data that is contained in one or more files. Self-description is what sets a database apart from ordinary files.

database management system the software for managing access to a database.

DBMS (acronym) *database management system.*

default value the value used to initialize an attribute.

denormalization the violation of normal forms. Developers should violate normal forms only for good cause, such as to increase performance for a bottleneck. (See *normal form.*)

dependent entity type an entity type that can exist only if some other entity type(s) also exist. Accordingly, the primary key of a dependent entity type incorporates one or more foreign keys. Also called a *weak entity type.* (Contrast with *independent entity type.*)

derived element an element that is defined in terms of other elements. Entity types, attributes, and relationships can all be derived.

design identity the ability to find data within a database. (Contrast with *intrinsic identity.*)

dimension (for a data warehouse) a basis for facts. (Contrast with *fact.*)

directed graph a set of nodes and a set of directed edges. Each directed edge originates at a source node and terminates at a target node (which may be the same as the source node). The nodes of a directed graph can have any number of edges.

discriminator an attribute that indicates the appropriate subtype record for each supertype record.

domain the set of possible values for an attribute.

entity a concept, abstraction, or thing that can be individually identified and has meaning for an application.

entity type a description of a group of entities with the same attributes, kinds of relationships, and intent.

entity type icon a reference to an entity type that is defined elsewhere in a model. An entity type icon does not display attributes and shows only the entity type name.

enumeration a data type that has a finite set of values.

existence-based identity the identification of individual entities for an entity type with an artificial field that has no application meaning. (Contrast with *value-based* identity.)

fact (for a data warehouse) a measure of the performance of a business. (Contrast with *dimension*.)

foreign key a reference to a primary key. It is the glue that binds tables. (See *primary key*.)

generalization an organization of entity types by their similarities and differences.

generic diagram a picture for viewing an underlying model.

hardcoded value the direct representation of a value with a row and a column of a database table. (Contrast with *softcoded value*.)

homomorphism a mapping between two *item description* templates that expresses an analogy.

IDEF1X a standard notation for designing databases that specifies tables, keys, and indexes.

identifier one or more attributes that unambiguously differentiate an entity from all others.

identifying relationship a relationship that contributes to the primary key of a dependent entity type. (Contrast with *non-identifying relationship*.)

identity the means for distinguishing individual entities, so that they can be found.

independent entity type an entity type that can exist on its own. The primary key of an independent entity type does not include any foreign keys. Also called a *strong entity type*. (Contrast with *dependent entity type*.)

index a data structure that locates records according to attribute values. Indexes are also used to enforce uniqueness. Most relational DBMSs create indexes as a side effect of declaring primary keys and candidate keys.

inheritance the mechanism that implements generalization.

intrinsic identity the ability to find data with fields that have application meaning. (Contrast with *design identity*.)

item description the template that arises when a model concerns both an item and its description.

logical horizon the set of entity types reachable by one or more paths terminating in a combined multiplicity of one. The purpose of the logical horizon is to compute the entities that can be inferred from a starting entity.

master application an application that enforces the identity of occurrences of a critical concept and unifies its data across an organization's applications.

mathematical template See *template*.

metadata data that describes other data.

model an abstraction of some aspect of a problem. Most software models are expressed as graphical diagrams and by their form appeal to human intuition.

multiple inheritance a generalization for which an entity type inherits information from multiple supertypes. (Contrast with *single inheritance.*)

multiplicity the number of occurrences of one entity type that may connect to an occurrence of a related entity type. Multiplicity is a constraint on the size of a collection. (Contrast with *cardinality.*)

n-ary relationship a relationship involving three or more relationship ends.

non-identifying relationship a relationship that does not contribute to the primary key of an entity type. (Contrast with *identifying relationship.*)

normal form a guideline for relational database design that increases data consistency. (See *denormalization.*)

null a special value denoting that an attribute value is unknown or not applicable.

Object Constraint Language (OCL) a language for defining constraints within the UML. You can also use the OCL to navigate data models.

Object Management Group (OMG) a standards forum that is the owner of the UML.

OMG (acronym) *Object Management Group.*

ordered relationship a relationship that has an ordering imposed on a many end.

path a sequence of traversals of relationships and generalization levels.

pattern a model fragment that is profound and recurring. A pattern is a proven solution to a specified problem that has stood the test of time.

primary key a candidate key that is preferentially used for cross-table references. Normally, an entity type should have a primary key; an entity type can have at most one primary key. (See *alternate key, candidate key,* and *foreign key.*)

qualified relationship a relationship in which one or more attributes (called *qualifiers*) disambiguate the entities for a "many" relationship end.

qualifier an attribute that selects among the entities at a "many" relationship end.

referential integrity a database mechanism that ensures that data references really exist and that there are no dangling foreign keys.

relational database a database in which the data are perceived as tables.

relational DBMS a DBMS that manages tables of data and associated structures that increase the functionality and performance of tables.

relationship a physical or conceptual connection among entities.

relationship end an end of a relationship. A binary relationship has two ends, a ternary has three ends, and so forth.

relationship entity type a relationship that is also an entity type. Like a relationship, the occurrences of a relationship entity type derive identity from the related entity types.

Like an entity type, a relationship entity type can have attributes and participate in relationships.

relationship type a description of a group of relationships with similar structure and meaning.

reverse engineering the process of examining implementation artifacts and inferring the underlying logical intent.

role one end of a relationship.

scenario the execution of a state diagram for an entity of the state diagram's entity type.

schema the structure of the data in a database.

seed model a model that is specific to a problem domain. A seed model provides a starting point for applications from its problem domain.

single inheritance a generalization in which an entity type inherits information from only one supertype. (Contrast with *multiple inheritance*.)

softcoded value a piece of data that is stored in a generic structure that transcends individual entity types. (Contrast with *hardcoded value*.)

SQL the standard language for interacting with a relational database.

star schema represents data as facts that are bound to dimensions. (See *data warehouse*, *dimension*, and *fact*.)

state diagram a diagram that specifies the permissible states for the entities of an entity type and the stimuli that cause changes of state.

strong entity type an entity type that can exist on its own. The primary key of a strong entity type does not include any foreign keys. Also called an *independent entity type*. (Contrast with *weak entity type*.)

structured field a field that is composed from constituent pieces with a specified grammar. Structured fields are synthetic but when parsed the pieces have meaning. Many structured fields are backed by standard protocols.

subject area a group of elements (entity types, relationships, and generalizations) with a common theme that is a portion of a larger model.

subtype an entity type that adds specific attributes and relationships for a generalization. (Contrast with *supertype*.)

supertype the entity type that holds common attribute and relationships for a generalization. (Contrast with *subtype*.)

surrogate identity the identification of an entity via another entity with which it is closely related.

template an abstract model fragment that is useful for a variety of applications and is devoid of application content. Templates are driven by deep data structures that often arise in database models.

ternary relationship a relationship among three relationship ends that cannot be restated as binary relationships.

traversal the navigation of a database via foreign-key-to-primary-key bindings.

tree a set of nodes that connect from child to parent. A node can have many child nodes; each node in a tree has one parent node except for the node at the tree's top. There are no cycles — that means at most one path connects any two nodes.

trigger a database command that executes upon the occurrence of a specified event and satisfaction of a condition.

tuning (of a database) the definition of ancillary database structures for the purpose of speeding performance. These ancillary structures have no effect on the semantics of the database structure and solely are intended for boosting performance. Physical clustering and indexes are common tuning techniques.

UML (acronym, trademark of the OMG) *Unified Modeling Language.*

undirected graph a set of nodes and a set of edges. Each edge connects two nodes (which may be the same). The nodes of an undirected graph can have any number of edges.

Unified Modeling Language (trademark of the OMG) a suite of models that is often used for software development.

universal antipattern an antipattern that should be avoided for all applications.

user-defined field an anonymous field in a table that is used to store miscellaneous data. Vendors often include a few anonymous fields in important application tables.

value-based identity the use of some combination of real-world attributes to identify each record in a table. (Contrast with *existence-based identity.*)

value metadata affiliated data for a value of an entity. For example, a value may have a data source, unit of measure, default value, and time of entry.

view a table that a relational DBMS dynamically computes from a query that is stored in the database.

weak entity type an entity type that can exist only if some other entity type(s) also exist. Accordingly, the primary key of a weak entity type incorporates one or more foreign keys. Also called a *dependent entity type*. (Contrast with *strong entity type.*)

XML (acronym for *eXtensible Markup Language*). XML provides a language that combines data with metadata that defines the data's structure.

Index

241

Summary of Antipatterns

Antipattern name	Observation	Exceptions	Resolution
Symmetric relationship (common)	A self relationship has the same multiplicity and roles on each end.	None.	Promote relationship to an entity type.
Dead elements (common)	A model has unused elements.	Acceptable in small amounts.	Delete them or isolate them.
Disguised fields (common)	Field names do not describe data.	A few user-defined fields.	Use meaningful names.
Artificial hardcoded levels (occasional)	There is a fixed hierarchy of similar entity types.	Use only with great caution.	Consolidate the levels and use a tree pattern.
Excessive generalization (occasional)	There is a deep generalization.	None.	A db taxonomy should be at most four levels deep.
Disconnected entity types (occasional)	A model has free-standing entity types.	A few can be acceptable.	Add the missing relationships.
Modeling errors (occasional)	There is a serious conceptual flaw.	None.	Fix the model.
Multiple inheritance (seldom)	A model has multiple inheritance.	Avoid for data models.	Use a work-around.
Paradigm degradation (seldom)	A relational db is degraded to some other paradigm.	Highly questionable.	Rework the model and architecture.

Summary of universal antipatterns

Antipattern name	Observation	Exceptions	Resolution
Derived data (common)	A model has elements that are not fundamental.	OK for critical elements, bottlenecks, and data warehouses.	Rework the model to eliminate derived data.
Parallel attributes (occasional)	An entity type has groups of similar attributes.	Often used for data warehouses.	Abstract and factor out commonality.
Parallel relationships (occasional)	Two entity types have several similar relationships.	Can be acceptable for a data warehouse.	Abstract and factor out commonality.
Combined entity types (occasional)	An entity type has disparate attributes.	OK for I/O staging and data warehouses.	Make each concept an entity type.

Summary of non-data-warehouse antipatterns

Summary of Archetypes

Archetype	Definition	Sample applications
Account	A label for recording, reporting, and managing a quantity of something	• Financial • Travel
Actor	Someone or something that is notable in terms of data	Widespread use across applications
Address	A means for communicating with an actor	
Asset	Something of value	• Business • Financial
Contract	An agreement for the supply of products	• Business • Financial
Course	A series of lessons about a subject	• Education
Customer	Someone involved in the purchase of products	CRM (customer relationship management)
Document	A physical or electronic representation of a body of information	
Event	An occurrence at some point in time	
Flight	The travel by an airplane between airports	• Aviation • Shipping • Trucking
Item	A part or a service	• Commerce • Manufacturing
Location	A physical place in space	
Opportunity	An inquiry that can result in business	• Marketing • Sales
Part	A specific good that can be described	• Manufacturing • Engineering
Payment	The assignment of money in return for something of value	• Business • Financial
Position	A job held by someone in an organization	• Human resources
Product	The packaging of a physical item for a particular marketplace	• Banking • Parts and service
Role	A function played by someone or something	
Transaction	An exchange that must be completed in its entirety or not at all	• Computing • Financial
Vendor	Someone involved in selling products	

Summary of archetypes

Printed and bound by CPI Group (UK) Ltd, Croydon, CR0 4YY

25/10/2024

01779363-0001